THE GHOSTS OF HOPEWELL

The Ghosts of **Hopewell**

Setting the Record Straight in the Lindbergh Case

JIM FISHER

Southern Illinois University Press

Carbondale and Edwardsville

02 01 00 99 4 3 2 1

Library of Congress Cataloging-in-Publication Data
    Fisher, Jim, 1939–
    The ghosts of Hopewell : setting the record straight in the Lindbergh
    case / Jim Fisher.
        p. cm.
    Includes bibliographical references and index.
    1. Lindbergh, Charles Augustus, 1930–1932—Kidnapping, 1932.
    2. Lindbergh, Charles A. (Charles Augustus), 1902–1974.
    3. Hauptmann, Bruno Richard, 1899–1936. 4. Kidnapping—
    New Jersey—Hopewell. 5. Trials (Kidnapping)—New Jersey. I. Title.
    HV6603.L5F55
    364.15′4′0974965—dc21   99-23945
    ISBN 0-8093-2285-4 (cloth : alk. paper)   CIP

I dedicate this book to

Ross H. Spencer

who died on July 25, 1998.

Spence was a brilliant writer

and a great friend.

He gave me the title to this book.

Nothing is as strong in human beings as the craving to believe in something that is obviously wrong.

—Joel Achenbach

Contents

Illustrations

Preface

When my book *The Lindbergh Case* came out in the fall of 1987, many, if not most of the people familiar with the so-called "crime of the century" believed the man electrocuted for the 1932 murder of the Lindbergh baby was innocent. Of those who still considered Bruno Richard Hauptmann guilty, mostly older folks who remembered the case from the newspapers, only a handful believed he had committed the crime alone.

Following Hauptmann's 1936 execution, a vast majority accepted his guilt in the face of what seemed to be overwhelming, albeit circumstantial, evidence. Few would have guessed that fifty years later a book in support of Hauptmann's guilt would run against the grain and be controversial.

The modern movement dedicated to exonerating Bruno Richard Hauptmann began in 1976 with the publication of a book called *Scapegoat,* in which author Anthony Scaduto argues that the baby was kidnapped by a disbarred lawyer named Paul Wendel. According to Scaduto, every prosecution witness at the Hauptmann trial lied under oath. Besides finding Hauptmann guilty on fabricated or altered physical evidence, the jury, in Scaduto's opinion, sent the defendant to the electric chair for a murder that never occurred. The Lindbergh baby, in Scaduto's view, was kidnapped but not killed and is living today in the person of a man named Harold Olson.

Scapegoat encouraged and lent support to a series of federal lawsuits filed in the 1980s by Hauptmann's widow, Anna. Mrs. Hauptmann's multi-million dollar wrongful death suits attracted national media attention and helped convince even more people that the wrong man had been convicted in the Lindbergh case. The fact that she lost these cases didn't affect public opinion to the contrary. She had lost in the courts but had won the hearts of the American people.

In 1982, a widely viewed television "documentary" called *Who Killed the Lindbergh Baby?* made an unsupported but convincing case for Hauptmann's innocence. The film, narrated and written by a British true-crime writer and TV personality named Ludovic Kennedy, evolved into a 1985 book by Kennedy called *The Airman and the Carpenter.* The book, supporting Scaduto's view of Hauptmann's innocence but ridiculing the idea that the baby was not killed, received favorable reviews on both sides of the Atlantic.

The case for Hauptmann's innocence was advanced in 1994 with the publication of a major, award-winning book on the case by the respected novelist and true-crime writer Noel Behn. In his book, called *Lindbergh, the Crime,* Behn tries to make the case that the baby was murdered in the Lindbergh house by the child's aunt. The kidnapping, therefore, was nothing more than an elaborate hoax to cover up the killing. Hauptmann, having nothing to do with the crime, was framed and executed to save the Lindbergh family name.

The 1996 HBO movie, *Crime of the Century,* starring Stephen Rea and Isabella Rossellini, depicted the Hauptmanns as a romantic, heroic couple fighting a losing but noble battle against a corrupt criminal justice machine out to destroy them. This movie, shown on television several nights, put the revisionists over the top. Bruno Richard Hauptmann was no longer the killer of America's most famous baby. Like his wife, he was a victim.

There are a number of reasons why historic, celebrated crimes are vulnerable to revision by true-crime writers. For one thing, a new angle on an old case, particularly a famous one, comprises an attractive publishing opportunity. Since Americans tend to be more interested in injustice than justice, it's hard for writers to resist turning cold-blooded killers into victims of heavy-handed prosecutors and cops. Since complicated, intrigue-filled mysteries are more fascinating than cases involving more straightforward, obvious explanations, revisionist true-crime writers prefer conspiracies over lone-wolf criminals. Sometimes, in their eagerness to plug a new conspiracy into a historic case, these writers, by ignoring the truth, deprive themselves of the more fascinating, truthful account. This is particularly true in the Lindbergh case.

Making Bruno Richard Hauptmann innocent also works well for writers who do not think much of law enforcement. People strongly opposed to capital punishment also find the execution of an innocent man in a celebrated case quite useful to their cause. The politically motivated pro-Hauptmann revisionists have captured the Lindbergh case and in the process have rewritten history to achieve their ideological goals. They have turned the Lindbergh case into a symbol, a code word for heavy-handed law enforcement and criminal injustice. As a result, taking a position on Hauptmann's guilt or innocence has less to do with evaluating the reliability of the evidence than making a political statement.

The Ghosts of Hopewell is an attempt to set the record straight regarding the issue of Hauptmann's guilt in the crime of the century. The various revisionist theories of the crime are examined, analyzed, and debunked. New evidence is presented that, coupled with the facts of the case not in dispute, proves beyond a reasonable doubt who kidnapped and murdered the infant son of Charles and Anne Lindbergh.

Acknowledgments

I would like to thank the following people who have contributed to this book: Jan Beck, Bill Blakefield, Michael Busichio, Oscar Collier, Dr. David A. Crown, Lt. C. Thomas DeFeo, Donald F. Doud, John Eddowes, Mark W. Falzini, Robert J. Felicito, Dr. Alan Filby, Armen Fisher, James D. Fisher, Susan G. Fisher, Jonathan Goodman, Ray Hagen, Pat Hipko, James J. Horan, John T. Huddleson, Thomas J. Irey, Harry Kazman, Reva Kazman, Dr. John Kelly, Dorris Lessig, Greg Lessig, Thelma Miller, Clinton L. Pagano, Frank Pizzichillo, Cornel D. Plebani, Robert W. Radley, Delores Raisch, Mark Ridge, Stephen Romeo, Chester C. Rose, Patterson Smith, Ross H. Spencer, Raymond Vanden Berghe, Albert L. Weeks, and Robert J. Whelan. Special thanks to professor E. Ernest Wood, Edinboro University of Pennsylvania, who contributed his computer skills to the project. I am also grateful for the outstanding copyediting of Geraldine Hall.

The account of the kidnapping, murder, investigation, and trial of Bruno Richard Hauptmann in chapters 1–3 derives in part from the more detailed account in *The Lindbergh Case* by Jim Fisher. Portions of chapter 5 have appeared in the preface to the paperback edition of *The Lindbergh Case*. Reprinted by permission of Rutgers University Press. Robert W. Radley's letter of September 7, 1992, is reprinted courtesy of Robert W. Radley. Jan Beck's letter of July 13, 1989, is reprinted courtesy of Jan Beck. All photographs are from the author's collection.

Lindbergh Case Chronology

Mar. 1, 1932	Baby taken from his crib near Hopewell, New Jersey, sometime between nine and ten o'clock at night. A ladder, chisel, and fifty-thousand-dollar ransom note are left at the scene.
Mar. 8, 1932	New Jersey State Police (NJSP) officer George G. Wilton photographs rail sixteen of the kidnap ladder. These photographs will be exhibits 5302 and 5303 at the kidnapper's trial.
Mar. 9, 1932	Retired Bronx school teacher John F. Condon receives a message from the kidnapper. Lindbergh makes Condon (a.k.a. JAFSIE) his ransom intermediary. He will communicate with the kidnapper with an ad in the *New York American*.
Mar. 12, 1932	Condon meets with "John" in the Woodlawn Cemetery in the Bronx. No money is exchanged.
Mar. 16, 1932	Condon receives, in the mail, a package containing the baby's sleeping garment. Charles Lindbergh goes to Condon's house to identify it. The garment has been laundered.
Mar. 21, 1932	JAFSIE receives a letter from "Cemetery John."
Mar. 29, 1932	JAFSIE receives a letter from the kidnapper.
Apr. 1, 1932	The baby's nursemaid, Betty Gow, finds the infant's thumb guard on the gravel driveway to the Hopewell estate. JAFSIE receives another ransom letter from "Cemetery John."

Apr. 2, 1932	Condon, with Charles Lindbergh nearby, pays the kidnapper a fifty-thousand-dollar ransom at St. Raymond's Cemetery in the Bronx. In return, Condon receives a note saying that the baby can be found on the "Boad Nelly." The kidnapper slips into the night with the ransom, most of which consists of gold notes. All serial numbers have been recorded.
Apr. 8, 1932	A twenty-dollar gold certificate ransom bill turns up in the Bronx.
May 12, 1932	The Lindbergh baby is found dead by a truck driver a few miles from Lindbergh estate. Betty Gow identifies the baby's clothing and Charles Lindbergh goes to the morgue to confirm the identification. The coroner finds that the baby died from a blow to the head.
May 16, 1932	John Hughes Curtis, a Norfolk, Virginia, business-man who has been telling Colonel Lindbergh that he has been in touch with the kidnappers, confesses that it has all been a hoax.
May 21, 1932	The NJSP circulate a facsimile of portions of two of the ransom notes in an effort to identify the hand-writing.
May 23, 1932	The governor of New Jersey offers a twenty-five thousand-dollar reward for information on the case.
June 6, 1932	Colonel Lindbergh returns to work, leaving the investigation to the police.
June 8, 1932	Gaston Means, a noted swindler and con man, is tried for fraud in Washington, D.C., for bilking Evalyn McLean of $104,000, money she had given him to ransom back the Lindbergh baby. He is found guilty and sent to prison.
June 10, 1932	Violet Sharpe, a domestic employee at the Morrow estate in Englewood, New Jersey, commits suicide following four interview sessions with the police who were trying to eliminate her as a possible inside-job suspect.

June 22, 1932	Congress makes ransom kidnapping a federal offense. The new crime is called the Lindbergh Law.
June 27, 1932	John Curtis, the Lindbergh case hoaxer, is tried and found guilty of obstruction of justice. He is fined.
Aug. 16,1932	Jon Lindbergh, the Lindberghs' second child, is born.
Oct. 10, 1932	New York City psychiatrist Dr. Dudley D. Shoenfeld, after studying the ransom notes, files a report with the New York City Police containing a psychological profile of the kidnapper that turns out to be remarkably accurate.
Mar. 8, 1933	Arthur Koehler, a federal government expert on trees and wood, files with the NJSP a report that contains his detailed analysis of the wooden, homemade kidnap ladder.
Apr. 5, 1933	President Roosevelt orders the switch from gold notes to greenback bills. Gold notes are to be exchanged for the new currency. Suddenly the Lindbergh ransom money will be easier to spot and identify.
Nov. 19, 1933	Arthur Koehler locates a store in the Bronx where five pieces of the kidnap ladder were purchased.
Nov. 26, 1933	Cecile Barr, a cashier at a movie house in Greenwich Village, takes a five-dollar gold note from a man she later identifies as Hauptmann.
Sept. 15, 1934	A gas station attendant, suspicious of a ten-dollar gold note, pencils the customer's license number— 4U-13-41—on the margin of the bill. The car, a 1930 blue Dodge, is registered to Richard Hauptmann at 1279 East 222nd St., the Bronx.
Sept. 18, 1934	The NJSP, the New York City Police, and the FBI set up a surveillance of Hauptmann's house.
Sept. 19, 1934	Bruno Richard Hauptmann is arrested at 9:15 A.M. while he's en route, in his Dodge, from his home to Manhattan. Officers find a twenty-dollar ransom bill on his possession. Officers search his house and

he is taken to the Greenwich Street police station for questioning.

Sept. 20, 1934   Hauptmann provides samples of his handwriting and is identified in a line-up by Cecile Barr, Amandus Hockmuth, Joseph Perrone, Ben Lupica, and the gas station attendants who broke the case with the license number. John Condon angers the police by withholding his line-up identification. Hauptmann refuses to confess and is taken before a magistrate and charged with extortion.

New York, New Jersey and FBI investigators find $13,760 in ransom bills hidden in Hauptmann's garage. When confronted with this evidence, Hauptmann comes up with the "Fisch Story." According to Hauptmann, a business associate named Isidor Fisch on December 2, 1933, left in Hauptmann's care a shoe box, which Hauptmann stored in his kitchen closet. In August 1934, Hauptmann opened the box and, to his surprise, found fifteen thousand dollars in cash, money he subsequently started spending due to the fact Fisch owned him seven thousand dollars. Hauptmann had kept all of this from his wife. Fisch had died of tuberculosis in Leipzig, Germany, on March 29, 1934. He died penniless.

Sept. 24, 1934   Inspector Henry D. Bruckman, New York City Police, finds John Condon's phone number and address penciled on a piece of door trim in a closet in Hauptmann's house. Also on this board are the serial numbers to a five-hundred-dollar and a one-thousand-dollar bill. Hauptmann concedes that this writing is in his hand. He denies, however, any involvement in the kidnapping.

Sept. 26, 1934   Police find more ransom money—$840—hidden in Hauptmann's garage. They also find a .25-caliber handgun. Meanwhile, as Hauptmann is being indicted for extortion in the Bronx, NJSP officer

	Lewis J. Bornmann finds the gap in Hauptmann's attic floor that had once been filled by rail sixteen of the kidnap ladder.
Sept. 27, 1934	In the office of the Bronx District Attorney, Lindbergh identifies Hauptmann's voice as the voice he heard coming from "Cemetery John" at St. Raymond's when the ransom money exchanged hands.
	Police tear down Hauptmann's garage and collect the wood for Arthur Koehler, the federal wood expert, to analyze.
Oct. 8, 1934	Hauptmann indicted for murder by the Hunterdon County Grand Jury.
Oct. 9, 1934	Arthur Koehler matches rail sixteen of the kidnap ladder to the floor board gap in Hauptmann's attic floor.
Oct. 10, 1934	The FBI officially ends its investigation of the Lindbergh kidnapping.
Oct. 16, 1934	Hauptmann is taken to Flemington, New Jersey, and placed into the Hunterdon County jail where he will await his trial.
Nov. 2, 1934	The flamboyant Brooklyn defense attorney, Edward J. Reilly, replaces James M. Fawcett as Hauptmann's lead attorney. Reilly is being paid by the *New York Journal* in return for Mrs. Hauptmann's exclusive story.
Jan. 2, 1935	The Hauptmann murder trial begins in the Hunterdon County Court House in Flemington, New Jersey. David T. Wilentz is the lead prosecutor and Thomas W. Trenchard is the presiding judge. Edward J. Reilly, Hauptmann's defense lawyer, is assisted by C. Lloyd Fisher, Frederick A. Pope and Egbert Rosecrans.
Jan. 9, 1935	John F. Condon begins his two days of dramatic testimony where he identifies Hauptmann as "Cemetery John."
Jan. 11, 1935	The state puts on its handwriting case comprised of

eight documents examiners whose testimony takes four days and five hundred pages of trial transcript.

Jan. 23, 1935   Arthur Koehler takes the stand and impresses the jury with his wood testimony that connects the kidnap ladder to Hauptmann's attic and his carpenter tools.

Jan. 24, 1935   The prosecution rests its case. The defense puts on the stand Hauptmann, who testifies for five days, which includes eleven grueling hours of cross-examination.

Jan. 31, 1935   John Trendley, the sole defense handwriting witness, testifies that Hauptmann was not the writer of the ransom documents.

Feb. 13, 1935   Hauptmann is convicted of murder without the jury's recommendation for mercy, which means, under New Jersey law, that Hauptmann must be executed.

Feb. 14, 1935   Edward J. Reilly, Hauptmann's lawyer, visits Hauptmann in jail and tries to get him to confess in exchange for a life sentence. Hauptmann refuses.

June 20, 1935   Hauptmann's case goes to the New Jersey Court of Errors and Appeals. Fourteen judges will consider 193 points of appeal.

Oct. 15, 1935   Hauptmann is granted a stay of execution while the U.S. Supreme Court considers his appeal.

Oct. 16, 1935   Governor Hoffman shocks the nation by announcing publicly that he does not think the Lindbergh case has been completely solved.

Dec. 9, 1935   The U.S. Supreme Court decides not to hear Hauptmann's appeal.

Dec. 12, 1935   Hauptmann writes the first of two handwritten letters to Governor Hoffman.

Dec. 22, 1935   Hounded by the press and the public, the Lindberghs flee America and sail to England.

Jan. 11, 1936   The New Jersey Court of Pardons refuses Hauptmann's plea for clemency.

Jan. 12, 1936	Governor Hoffman grants Hauptmann a thirty-day reprieve and orders the NJSP to reopen its investigation into the case.
Jan. 14, 1936	The U.S. District Court in Trenton, New Jersey, denies Hauptmann's habeas corpus petition. Hauptmann appeals this decision.
Jan. 16, 1936	The U.S. Supreme Court denies Hauptmann's writ of habeas corpus and a stay of execution.
Feb. 13, 1936	The famed attorney Samuel S. Leibowitz visits Hauptmann and tries to get him to confess and name his accomplices. Hauptmann says he is innocent. Four days later the attorney tries again. He fails.
Feb. 29, 1936	Disbarred attorney Paul H. Wendel, after being kidnapped by Ellis Parker Sr., and others, is released. He repudiates the confession he gave Parker in which he claimed to be the kidnapper of the Lindbergh baby.
Mar. 31, 1936	Hauptmann is granted a forty-eight-hour reprieve while Paul H. Wendel's role in the Lindbergh case is being investigated. The New Jersey Court of Pardons denies Hauptmann's final plea for clemency.
Apr. 3, 1936	Hauptmann dies in the electric chair at the New Jersey State Prison at Trenton. He is electrocuted by the famous executioner, Robert Elliott.
May 2, 1936	Hauptmann's article, "Why Did You Kill Me?" is published in *Liberty* magazine.

Part I The Case

The Crime

The twenty-month-old first-born son of the world's aviation hero, Colonel Charles A. Lindbergh, was snatched from his crib and carried out a second-story window onto a homemade ladder sometime between 9:00 and 9:30 on the leap year night of March 1, 1932. The colonel and his wife, Anne Morrow Lindbergh, had been spending weekends in their newly built estate in the remote Sourland Mountains near Hopewell, in the west central part of New Jersey. Also in the house that cold and rainy Tuesday night were Elsie and Oliver Whately, the cook and butler, and Betty Gow, the baby's twenty-eight-year-old nursemaid.

Colonel Lindbergh and his wife, Anne, the daughter of Dwight Morrow, one of the wealthiest men in America, were residing in Englewood, New Jersey, at the Morrow mansion, a fifty-acre estate called Next Day Hill. The Lindberghs were planning to move into their new home on the other side of the state. On this particular Tuesday, the Lindberghs had not returned to Englewood because the baby was recovering from a cold. Earlier that day a Morrow family chauffeur, Henry Elleson, had driven Betty Gow from Englewood to the four-hundred-acre Hopewell estate so she could help Mrs. Lindbergh care for the child.

At 6:00 that evening, the nursemaid carried the child to the nursery for his supper. Mrs. Lindbergh entered the room to help prepare the baby for bed. Because it was a cold night, Betty Gow decided to make the boy a little flannel shirt to wear next to his skin for warmth. She cut out this sleeveless garment from a piece of flannel cloth she had been saving. The nursemaid placed a second shirt, a store-bought one, over the one she had made. The baby now wore two shirts and a pair of diapers enclosed in a rubber covering. Next came the one-piece sleeping suit with enclosed feet and buttons in the back. The night garment also had a flap in the seat. Betty hooked on the two metal guards that kept the baby from sucking his thumbs by tying the strings securely around the wrists and over the sleeves of the sleeping suit. Finally, she covered him with a blanket and pulled it snugly across his shoulders, then fastened it to the mattress with two large safety pins.

After putting the baby to bed, Mrs. Lindbergh closed the shutters to the three nursery windows. She closed and latched the shutters to the French windows on the south wall, and in the same way secured the shutters on the north side window on the east wall. The shutters on the southeast window were warped and couldn't be brought together tightly enough to be latched. Having attended to the windows, Mrs. Lindbergh returned to the first floor. Betty Gow sat in the nursery until 8:00 then reported that the baby was sleeping peacefully.

At about 8:30, Colonel Lindbergh pulled his Franklin Sedan into the garage at the west end of the house. He had been in New York City where he was scheduled to be the guest of honor at an alumni dinner at New York University. He had gotten his dates mixed up and instead of appearing at the dinner, had driven home.

After supper, the Lindberghs walked into the living room and sat down on the sofa. It was 9:00. While seated there, the colonel heard a noise that made him think that slats from an orange crate had fallen off a chair in the kitchen.

At 10:00 P.M., Betty Gow decided to check on the baby. When she felt for his body in the crib, she couldn't find him and frantically alerted the Lindberghs.

Colonel Lindbergh rushed to the nursery where he saw the right-hand shutter to the southeast window standing open. The window itself had been closed. On top of the steam radiator case that formed the sill to this window, Colonel Lindbergh noticed a white envelope. He did not pick up this envelope for fear of smudging the kidnapper's fingerprints.

The first police to arrive at the scene were two local officers from Hopewell. They arrived at the estate at 10:40 and were taken to the nursery where they noticed clumps of soil on the baby's leather suitcase beneath the southeast window. Outside, the officers found two indentations in the mud beneath this window, impressions made by a ladder. Using a flashlight, they followed sets of footprints that led in a southeasterly direction to the kidnap ladder seventy-five feet from the house.

At 10:55, Corporal Joseph A. Wolf from Troop B in nearby Lambertville was the first member of the New Jersey State Police to arrive at the scene. Trooper Wolf was followed, twenty minutes later, by two troopers from the state police headquarters in West Trenton.

An examination of the three-piece homemade extension ladder revealed that although it extended to a maximum length of eighteen and one half feet, it weighed only thirty-eight pounds. Although crudely made, it was quite functional and ingeniously designed. The rungs were cut into the side rails, and the three sections of the ladder were made to fit on the top of each other, compressing the ladder's overall length to slightly over eighty and one half inches. Three twelve-inch dowel pins, inserted through holes in the side rails of the adjoining sections, kept the ladder in the extended position. When these wooden pins were slipped out and the three sections positioned into each other, the ladder could be easily carried by one man and was short enough to be hauled inside an automobile.

A closer inspection of the ladder revealed that it was broken. The side rails of the middle section had split along the grain at the dowel point where this section and the bottom part of the ladder came together. The officers speculated that the ladder had held the weight of the kidnapper going up, but when he descended with the extra weight of the baby, it had given way.

Corporal Frank A. Kelly, the state trooper responsible for processing the crime scene for latent fingerprints, arrived from the Morristown Barracks. Corporal Kelly was unable to develop any identifiable fingerprints from the nursery note or its envelope. The note itself, handwritten in blue ink, read:

Dear Sir!
have 50,000 $ redy 25 000 $ in
20 $ bills 1,5000 $ in 10$ bills and
10000 $ in 5$ bills. After 2–4 days
we will inform you were to deliver
the Mony.
We warn you for making anyding public
or for notify the Police the chld is in
gute care.
Indication for all leters are
singnature and 3 hold   (SYMBOL)

On the bottom right-hand corner of the note was a symbol consisting of two interlocking circles each slightly larger than a quarter. In the oval formed where these circles overlapped was a solid red mark about the size of a nickel. Three small holes had been punched through this logo—one was in the center of the red mark and the other two were in line with it just outside the two larger circles.

In search of fingerprints, Corporal Kelly dusted the crib, the baby's sun lamp, the walls, both sides of the glass on the southeast window, and the leather suitcase. He brought up dozens of latents (fingerprints left on objects that have been touched), but they were either smudged, smeared, or mere fragments. He also dusted the chisel found in the mud beneath the southeast nursery widow but did not develop any fingerprints. Later in the week, a New York City physician and private fingerprint expert—Dr. Erastus Mead Hudson, using a process of developing fingerprints that involves silver nitrate, found five hundred finger stains on the kidnap ladder. But only 206 of these marks represented complete prints—the rest were merely fragments, too incomplete to identify. Of the 206, only eight were clear enough for identification purposes. The rest of these finger marks were worthless smudges. The kidnap ladder, by this time, had been handled by hundreds of people. The police were able to identify one of the sight prints as belonging to a New Jersey state police detective, the rest have never been identified.

Immediately after the crime, Colonel Lindbergh made it perfectly clear to the police that the first priority in the case was the safe return of his son. At this point Colonel Lindbergh was in firm control of the investigation, and although the police could process the crime scene and follow up leads, they were not to interfere in any way with Lindbergh's attempts to contact the kidnapper or kidnappers. When it came time to negotiate the ransom payoff, the police were not to be anywhere near—and if possible, were to be kept totally in the dark. Once the baby was ransomed back alive, the police could go after their man. Until then, however, Colonel Lindbergh would be in charge. But Lindbergh had a problem—he was worried that with all the publicity and excitement surrounding the case, the kidnappers would be afraid to negotiate. Moreover, with thousands of letters pouring into the Lindbergh estate every day, many of them extortion attempts, how would he know who the real kidnappers were?

Two days after the kidnapping, Colonel Lindbergh and his wife publicly issued the following appeal to the criminals who had their child:

Mrs. Lindbergh and I desire to make personal contact with the kidnappers of our child. Our only interest is in his immediate and safe return. We feel certain that the kidnappers will realize that this interest is strong enough to justify them in having complete confidence and trust in any promise that we may make in connection with his return. We urge those who have the child to send any representatives that they may desire to meet a representative of ours who will be suitable to them at any time and at any place they may designate.

If this is accepted we promise that we will keep whatever arrangements may be made by their representatives and ours strictly confidential and we further pledge ourselves that we will not try to injure in any way those connected with the return of the child.

The following day the Lindberghs received their first authentic communication, since the nursery note, from the kidnapper. The envelope, postmarked Brooklyn, 9 P.M., contained a single sheet of paper with writing on both sides. It read as follows:

Dear Sir: We have warned you note to make
anyding Public also notify the Police
now you have to take the consequences. ths
means we will holt the baby untill everyding
is quiet. We can note make any appointment
just now. We know very well what it
means to us. It is rely necessary to
make a world affair out off this, or to
get yours baby back as sun as possible.
To settle those affair in a quick way
will better for both seits. Dont by
afraid about the baby two ladys
keeping care of its day and night.
She also will fed him
according to the diet.   (SYMBOL)
            Singtuere on
            all letters

On the other side, it read as follows:

We are interested to send him back in
gut health. ouer ransom was made aus
for 50000 $ but now we have to take
another person to it and probable have
to keep the baby for a longer time as we
expected So the amount will by 70,000 $
20,000 in 50$ bills 25,000 $ in 20 $ bills
15000 $ in 10 $ bills and 10,000 $ in 5 $ bills.
dont mark any bills. or tacke them
from one serial nonmer. We will
inform you latter were to deliver hte
mony. but we will note to so
until the Police is out of the case
and the Pappers are quiet.
        The Kidnaping was preparet
        for yeahs. so we are preparet
        for everything.
(THREE HOLES)

On March 7, Colonel Henry Breckinridge, Lindbergh's trusted friend,
attorney, and personal advisor, received at his Manhattan law offices a plain
envelope containing a short note, which read:

Dear Sir.
    Please handel inclosed letter
to Col. Lindbergh. It is in
Mr. Lindberg interest not to
notify the Police.

This enclosure for Colonel Lindbergh, one sheet of the same type of paper
with handwriting on both sides and the unique symbol of circles and holes
found on the nursery note, read:

Dear. Sir: Dit you receive ouer letter form March
4. We sent the mail in one off the letter pox near
Burro Hall—Brooklyn. We know Police interfere
with your privatmail; how can we come to any
arrangements this way. In the future we will send
ouer letters to Mr. Breckenbridge at 25 Broadway.
We belive Polise cupturet our letter and tit note
forwardet to you. We will note accept any go-

between from your seid. We will arrangh thiss
latter. Thers is no worry about the Boy. he is
very well and will be feed according to the diet.
Best dank for Information about it. We are
interested to send your Boy back in gud Health
                                    (SYMBOL)
singnature

On the other side:

Is it nessisery to make a word's affair out off it,
or to gett your Boy back as son as possible: Wy tit
you ingnore ouer letter which we left in the room:
the baby would be back long ago. You would note get
any result from Police, becauce this Kidnaping whas
planet for a year allredy. but we was afraid, the
boy would not bee strong enough.
and ransom was madeout for 50,000 $ but now we have
to but another lady to it and propperly have to hold
the baby longer as we exspectet so it will be 70,000
$.
20000 in 50$ bills 25000 in 25$ bills 15000
in 10$ bills 10000 in 5$ bill. We warn you agin
not to mark any bills or take them from one serial
No. We will inform you latter how to deliver
(THREE HOLES)   the mony, but not befor
the Police is out of this cace and the
pappers are quiet.
Please gett a short notice aboud this letter in the
New-York American.

Colonel Lindbergh had no doubt that the writer of this letter had written the nursery note and the letter received two days earlier. The writer
acknowledged his authorship of the previous documents, the dollar sign
was placed after the numerals, the greeting "Dear Sir" was used, and the
words *our* (ouer), *money* (mony), and *signature* (singtuere and singnature)
were misspelled the same way. The word *redy* in the nursery note became
allredy in the message to Colonel Breckinridge. The writer of these letters
also spelled the word *not* as *note* and *be* as *bee*. Dozens of other words, in
all three letters, were misspelled: *case* (cace), *police* (polise), *necessary*

(nessisery), *sides* (seits), *did* (dit), *captured* (cupturet), *forward* (forwardet), and *prepared* (preparet).

As for the ransom symbol, the three holes lined up so perfectly, it was reasonable to assume that a sharp instrument had punched these holes simultaneously through a stack of sheets to preclude imitation by an impostor.

On March 8, a letter appeared in the *Home News*, a local Bronx, New York newspaper. The letter writer, Dr. John F. Condon, a retired school-teacher and village eccentric, offered his services to the kidnapper as Colonel Lindbergh's ransom intermediary. Condon, who idolized but had never met Colonel Lindbergh, had injected himself into the case on his own initiative.

On the evening of the following day, Dr. Condon found in his mailbox, at 2974 Decatur Avenue, a bulky envelope addressed to him. The envelope enclosed a note and a smaller, sealed envelope. The note, written in ink and unsigned, read:

> Dear Sir: If you are willing to act
> as go-between in Lindbergh cace please follow stricly
> instruction. Handel incloced letter *personaly*
> to Mr. Lindbergh. It will explain
> everyding. Don't tell anyone about
> it. as son we find out the Press
> or Police is notifyd everyding are
> canselt and it wil be a further
> delay. Affter you gett the Mony from
> Mr. Lindbergh but them 3 word's
> in the *New-York american*
>   *mony is redy.*
> Affter that we will give you further
> instruction. Don't be affrait we are
> not out fore your 1000 $ keep it.
> only act stricly. Be at home every
> night between 6–12 by this time
> you will hear from us

The enclosed, smaller envelope was addressed: "Mr. Col. Lindbergh, Hopewell."

Dr. Condon reached Colonel Lindbergh by telephone and was told to open the letter and read it. Dr. Condon complied, and the letter said:

Dear Sir, Mr. Condon may act as go between. You
may give him the 7000 $. make one packet. the size
will bee about . . .

Describing the crude drawing of a box, which appeared in the body of
the letter, he continued:

We have notifyt your allredy in
what kind of bills. We warn you
not to set any trapp in any way. If
you or someone els will notify the
Police ther will be a further delay
after we have the mony in hand we
will tell you where to find your boy
You may have a airplain
redy it is about 150 mil.   (SYMBOL)
awy. But befor telling
you the adr. a delay of 8 houers
will be between.

After Dr. Condon described the symbol of interlocking circles, Colonel
Lindbergh invited him to Hopewell. That night Dr. Condon slept in the
baby's nursery and, the next morning, was officially made the Lindbergh
intermediary. From Dr. Condon's initials—JFC—was devised the pseud-
onym, "Jafsie," the code name Condon would use when signing newspaper communications to the kidnapper or kidnappers.

The ad requested by the kidnapper appeared in the personal columns of
the *New York American* (a morning newspaper that hit the stands the night
before) the morning of March 11 and read:

MONEY IS READY. JAFSIE.

Early the next evening, Saturday, March 12, a taxicab driver brought a
message to Dr. Condon's house from the kidnapper. It read:

Mr. Condon,
We trust you, but we will note come
in your Haus it is to danger. even
you cane note know if Police or
secret servise is watching you
      follow this instrunction.

Take a car and drive to the last
supway station from Jerome Ave
line. 100 feet from the last station
on the left seide is a empty frank-
further-stand with a big open Porch
around, you will find a notise in
senter of the porch underneath a stone.
this notise will tell
you were to find uns.

(SYMBOL)

Act accordingly.
after ³/₄ of a houer be
on the place. bring the mony with you.

The cab driver, Joseph Perrone, had been handed the note by a man who had stopped him on Gun Hill Road in the Bronx.

Dr. Condon, in his friend Al Reich's car, drove to the frankfurter stand described in the letter. There he found an envelope on a table held down by a stone. Condon opened the envelope and read the following directions:

cross the street and follow
the fence from the cemetery.
direction to 233 street
I will meet you.

This note did not contain the signature symbol.

The note referred to the fence enclosing the northern boundary of the Woodlawn Cemetery. Al Reich brought the car to a stop fifty feet south of 233rd Street. Ahead, at the intersection of 233rd and Jerome Avenue, were the gates to the main entrance to the cemetery. Dr. Condon got out of the car and walked along the fence to where he saw the waving of a white handkerchief through the bars of the gate. "Have you gottit the money," asked the man behind the gate.

"No," answered Condon. "I could not bring the money until I saw the baby or heard where the baby is."

At this point, the man in the cemetery climbed over the fence and started to run. Dr. Condon followed and eventually caught up to him in Van Courtlandt Park where the two men sat down on a bench to converse.

The man asked to be called John, and at one point asked, "Would I burn if the baby is dead?"

"Is the baby all right?" asked Condon.

The man assured him that he was, and instructed Condon to put into the Sunday edition of the *Home News* an ad that was to read: "Baby is alive and well; money is ready."

After telling Condon he had several accomplices, and that the kidnapping had been "planned a year already," the two men parted.

The next day, the ad requested by "Cemetery John" appeared in the Home News (an afternoon paper). It read:

BABY ALIVE AND WELL—MONEY IS READY. CALL AND SEE US. JAFSIE.

The next day, a Monday, the following ad appeared:

MONEY IS READY. NO COPS. NO SECRET SERVICE. NO PRESS. I COME ALONE LIKE LAST TIME. CALL JAFSIE.

Dr. Condon got his answer on Wednesday, March 16, in the form of a compactly wrapped package stuffed into his mailbox. Upon receiving the package, Dr. Condon summoned Colonel Breckinridge, and when the two men unwrapped the package, they found a gray, one-piece Dr. Denton sleeping suit that looked like the one the baby had on the night he was kidnapped. The night garment had been laundered. A few hours later Colonel Lindbergh, in Dr. Condon's living room, identified the sleeping suit as his son's. The package from the kidnapper also contained a letter, which read:

Dear Sir: Ouer man faills to collect the
mony. Thre are no more confidential
conference after the meeting from March
12. those arrangements to hazardous
for us. We will note allow ouer man
to confer in a way licke befor.
circumstance will note allow us
to make a transfare licke you wish.
It is imposibly for us. Wy chould we
move the baby and face danger to
take another person to the plase is
entirerly out of question. It seems
you are afraid if we are the rigth
party and if the boy is allright. Well

you have ouer singnature. it is always
the same as the first one
specialy them 3 hohls   (SYMBOL)

It continued on the other side:

Now we will send you the sleepingsuit
from the baby besides it means 3 $ extra
exspenses becauce we have to pay
another one. Pleace tell Mrs. Lindbergh
note to worry the baby is well. we only
have to give him more food as the tied says
    You are willing to pay the 70000
note 50000 $ without seeing the baby first
or note. let us know about that in the
New York-american. We can't to it other ways.
becauce we don't licke to give up
ouer safty plase or to move the baby.
If you are willing to accept this deal
put those in the paper
    I accept mony is redy
            ouer program is:
after 8 houers we have the Mony receivd
we will notify you where to find the
baby. If thers is any trapp. you will be
                        responsible what
                            will follows.
(THREE HOLES)

Three days passed with no word from the kidnapper. Worried that he
had lost contact with the abductor, Lindbergh asked Condon to place the
following ad in the Sunday edition of the *Home News:*

INFORM ME HOW I CAN GET IMPORTANT LETTER TO YOU.
URGENT. JAFSIE.

On Monday morning the kidnapper responded with an ultimatum:

Dear Sir: You and Mr. Lindbergh know
ouer Program. If you don't accept
den we will wait untill you
    agree with ouer Deal, we know

you have to come to us any way
But why shoul'd Mrs. and Mr.
Lindbergh suffer longer as necessary
We will note communicate with
you or Mr. Lindbergh until you write so
     in the appaer.
        We will tell you again; this kid
     naping cace whas prepared for a
     yaer already so the Police would
     have any look to find us or the child
     You only puch everyding further out
dityou send that
little package to
Mr. Lindbergh? it contains
the sleepingsuit from the   (SYMBOL)
the baby is well.Baby.

And, on the other side, but one sentence:

Mr. Lindbergh only wasting
time with hiss search.
(THREE HOLES)

The next day the following ad was placed in the *Home News:*

THANKS. THAT LITTLE PACKAGE YOU SENT
WAS IMMEDIATELY DELIVERED AND ACCEPTED
AS REAL ARTICLE. SEE MY POSITION. OVER
FIFTY YEARS IN BUSINESS AND CAN I PAY
WITHOUT SEEING GOODS? COMMON SENSE
MAKES ME TRUST YOU. PLEASE UNDERSTAND
MY POSITION. JAFSIE.

Receiving no response to this message, Condon, on Saturday, March 26, placed another ad:

MONEY IS READY. FURNISH SIMPLE CODE FOR
US TO USE IN PAPER. JAFSIE.

Colonel Lindbergh had raised the seventy thousand dollars in ransom money, and it was being held in a special vault at the Fordham Bank in New York City. When Elmer Irey of the IRS learned that no one had made a record of the ransom bills' serial numbers, he insisted that this be done and that a new ransom package be assembled. The new bundle of money would contain gold notes, making the bills easier to recognize when passed. The bundles of money would be delivered to the kidnapper in a box built to the specifications outlined by the kidnapper. The construction of this box had been arranged by Dr. Condon himself.

It took eight hours to gather, package, and record the ransom money. The bills were divided into two bundles. The first package contained fifty thousand dollars. All but fourteen thousand dollars of it was in gold certificates. The second, smaller package contained four hundred fifty-dollar gold notes, bills Elmer Irey thought would be the easiest to spot when spent. Together, the packages contained 5,150 bills. No two of the serial number were in sequence.

On Wednesday, March 30, Dr. Condon received word from "Cemetery John":

Dear Sir: It is note necessary to furnish
any code. you and Mr. Lindbergh know
ouer Program very well. We will keep
the child on ouer save plase until we
have the money in hand, but if the deal
is note closed until the 8 of April we
will ask for 30000 more.-also note 70000
-100000.

how can Mr. lindbergh follow
so many false clues he know's we
are the right paety ouer singnature
is still the same as on the ranson
note. But if Mr. Lindbergh likes to
fool around for another month.-
we can help it.
once he hase to come to us anyway
but if he keep's on waiting we will double
ouer amount. there is absolute no fear
aboud the child.
it is well   (SYMBOL)

In response, Dr. Condon promptly placed the following ad:

I ACCEPT. MONEY IS READY. JAFSIE.

Two days later, on the afternoon of April 1, the mail brought the following letter:

Dear Sir: have the money ready by Saturday
evening. we will inform you where
and how to deliver it. have the money
in one bundle we want you to put
it in on a sertain place. Ther is
no fear that somebody els will
tacke it, we watch everything
closely. Pleace lett us know if
you are agree and ready for action
by Saturday evening. — if yes —
put in the paper
    Yes everything O.K.
It is a very simble delivery but we
find out very sun if there is any trapp.
after 8 houers you gett the adr; from
the boy, on the place
you finde two
ladies. the are
    innocence.   (SYMBOL)

And on the other side:

If it is to late to put it in
the New York American for Saturday
evening put it in New York Journal.
(THREE HOLES)

Early the next afternoon, Saturday, April 2, Colonel Lindbergh and Colonel Breckinridge brought the ransom money to Dr. Condon's house. That evening, "Cemetery John" sent another cab driver to Condon's residence with the following message:

Dear Sir: take a car and follow
tremont Ave to the east
until you reach the number
3225 east trement Ave.
    It is a nursery.
    Bergen

> Greenhauses florist
> there is a table standing
> outside right on the door, you
> find a letter undernead the table
> covert with a stone, read and
> follow instruction.
>   (SYMBOL)

And on the other side:

> don't speak to anyone on
> way. If there is a ratio
> alarm for policecar, we
> warn you, we have the same
> equipment. have the money
> in one bundle.
> We give you ³/₄ of a houer to
> reach the place.
> (THREE HOLES)

At 9:00, just ten minutes after receiving the message, Colonel Lindbergh drove Dr. Condon to the Bergen Greenhouse. The nursery was directly across the street from the sprawling St. Raymond's Cemetery. Beneath a table in front of the greenhouse flower shop, Dr. Condon found a white envelope weighted down by a stone. The note inside read:

> cross the street and
> walk to the next corner
> and follow Whittemore Ave
> to the soud
>   take the money with
> you. come alone
>   and walk
> I will meet you
>   (SYMBOL)

Dr. Condon walked along Tremont Avenue, which ran along the northern border of St. Raymond's Cemetery. He stopped under the street light on the corner of Whittemore and Tremont and looked down the dark and deserted road leading into the huge, East Bronx cemetery. Along the eastern side of this lane were bushes, and beyond the shrubbery stood the tombstones. Condon walked a hundred yards along Tremont then turned around and headed back to Colonel Lindbergh, who was waiting in the car. When Condon returned to the car he and Colonel Lindbergh heard a voice coming from the cemetery, "Hey, Doctor!"

"All right," Condon answered back.

"Here, Doctor. Over here. Over here."

Leaving Lindbergh, Dr. Condon walked down Whittemore Avenue to the cemetery. When he got inside the graveyard, Condon saw a figure moving along the tombstones in the direction he was walking. About a hundred feet south of Tremont, the man in the cemetery came to the access road that shot east of Whittemore. A five-foot cement wall ran along this road, cutting across the path of the man who was keeping up with Condon. Dr. Condon watched the figure climb the wall, cross the access road, then scale a low fence that ran along the south side of the little road. After jumping to the ground on the other side of that fence, the man crouched behind a shrub directly to Condon's left.

"Hello," he said from behind the bush.

Dr. Condon walked slowly to the spot where the man was hiding. "How are you?" he said. "What are you doing crouched down there?"

The man stood up and Condon recognized him as John, the man he had conversed with in Van Cortlandt Park across from the Woodlawn Cemetery. This man was wearing the same fedora hat and black suit.

"Have you gotitt the money?" the man asked.

"No, it's in the car."

"Who is up there?"

"Colonel Lindbergh. Where is the baby?"

"You could not get the baby for about six, eight hours."

"You must take me to the baby."

"I have told you before that is impossible. It cannot be done. Give me the money."

"Not until you give me a receipt, a note showing where the baby is."

"I haven't got it with me."

"Then get it," Condon said.

"All right. You will wait."

"Yes," said Condon. "And John—these are bad times. Colonel Lindbergh is not so rich. He had a hard time raising the $50,000. I can go to the car and get that much."

"Since it is so hard it will be all right, I guess. I suppose if we can't get seventy we'll take fifty."

"Now where is the receipt—the note showing where the baby is?"

"I'll be back with the note in ten minutes," John replied. He turned and disappeared beyond the tombstones.

Condon headed back to the car. It was 9:16.

Carrying the box containing the fifty thousand dollars, Condon retraced his steps across Tremont Avenue. He reached the access road and the low fence running beside it. He stopped there and waited. A few minutes later Condon heard footsteps coming from within the cemetery. It was 9:29. John had been gone thirteen minutes.

The moment John reached the bushes along Whittemore Avenue, he asked, "Have you gottit the money?"

"Yes. Have you got the note?"

"Yes."

Dr. Condon handed over the box containing the money as John tendered the note. When the exchange was made, John turned and disappeared into the cemetery with fifty thousand dollars of Colonel Lindbergh's money. Dr. Condon hurried back to the car.

Colonel Lindbergh opened the envelope and read the note inside which said:

> the boy is on Boad Nelly
> it is a small Boad 28 feet
>   long, two person are on the
>   Boad. the are innosent.
>   you will find the Boad between
> Horseneck Beach and gay Head
>   near Elizabeth Island.

The Lindbergh baby had been missing one month, the police had been kept at bay, and now Colonel Lindbergh, having paid the ransom money and fully expecting to get back his child, simply had to find him.

2 The Investigation and Trial

Colonel Lindbergh spent several days frantically flying up and down the east coast in search of the "Boad Nelly." Such a craft was not to be found. John had broken his word.

During the period Colonel Lindbergh was trying to negotiate the safe return of his son, and ex-FBI agent turned con man named Gaston Means bilked Evalyn McLean, a wealthy Washington, D.C., socialite, of $104,000 by leading her to believe he was in touch with the kidnappers and could ransom back the baby. Gaston Means was exposed as a fraud when the infant corpse was found dead in the woods, and several months later he was convicted federally for fraud and sent to prison. The FBI, however, never recovered Mrs. McLean's money.

At a time when it seems the Lindbergh baby was never going to be found, John Hughes Curtis, a Norfolk, Virginia, shipbuilder on the verge of bankruptcy, used his connection in high places to convince Colonel Lindbergh that he had been in contact with a band of seafaring kidnappers who were keeping the baby on a boat in the Atlantic off Cape May, New Jersey. Colonel Lindbergh would spend weeks with Curtis and his associates looking for the baby until it became obvious that Curtis was a fraud and his dealings with the kidnappers had been an elaborate and extremely cruel hoax. Curtis would be convicted of obstructing justice, but, unlike Gaston Means, would not go to prison. The overwrought shipbuilder had gotten carried away by his desire—his fantasy—to help the Lindberghs get their baby back and become a hero.

On May 12, 1932, seventy-two days after the kidnapping, the badly decomposed body of an infant was found in a wooded area two miles (as the crow flies) from the Lindbergh home. The tiny corpse was found in a shallowed-out grave by an African American truck driver named William Allen who had walked fifty feet into the woods along the Princeton-Hopewell Road to relieve himself. The child's skin, wet and shiny from the rain that had been falling, was leatherish and almost black. The left leg was missing from the knee down—probably devoured by wild animals. Both hands were gone, which meant the child could not be identified by fingerprints.

The police tentatively identified the remains as the Lindbergh baby by matching up Betty Gow's homemade undershirt with the cloth remnant from which it had been cut. Colonel Lindbergh and Betty Gow identified the body at the morgue in Trenton. Besides the gravesite clothing, other points of identity included the baby's teeth, his hair, the dimple on his chin, and his overlapping toes.

The baby's autopsy was performed at Walter Swayze's Funeral Home in Trenton. Swayze, a mortician, was the county coroner. The Mercer County physician, Dr. Charles H. Mitchell, was the man who normally would have performed the autopsy, but because the doctor had arthritis in his hands, he had to talk the mortician through the procedure.

Inside the baby's skull, below and to the right of the left ear, Dr. Mitchell noticed four fracture lines radiating from a point of impact. At this spot he found a decomposed blood clot, evidence of a hemorrhage. This meant the baby was alive when the wound was inflicted. The skull fracture and the blood clot led Dr. Mitchell to the conclusion that the baby had been killed by a blow to the head. The doctor, however, had no way of knowing how this injury had been delivered.

Upon further examination of the skull, Dr. Mitchell found a one-quarter-inch hole opposite the fracture. This opening was located below the right ear. This "perforated fracture," as the doctor called it, was the hole made by a gravesite detective who was poking around the site with a stick. The county physician concluded that this wound had been inflicted after death. The doctor was satisfied, he said, that the Lindbergh baby had died from a "fractured skull due to external violence."

The Lindbergh child was cremated at the Roseville Crematory in Linden, New Jersey. Burying the body in a cemetery would have created a problem. The gravesite would have had to be guarded around the clock against souvenir hunters and grave robbers. A newspaper photographer had already photographed the Lindbergh baby's remains in the morgue following the autopsy, pictures that would be sold on the street for five dollars apiece.

Now that the baby was known dead, the police were no longer restrained in their search for the kidnapper or kidnappers. The investigation had entered a new phase, but unfortunately, the trail had grown cold. The investigation spearheaded by Colonel H. Norman Schwarzkopf, the head of the New Jersey State Police, had been plagued from the beginning by dead ends, wild-goose chases, and interagency rivalry between the New Jersey State Police, the New York City Police, and the FBI, headed by the headline hungry J. Edgar Hoover.

During the first months of the investigation, the New Jersey State Police had covered more than two hundred thousand leads. The FBI had run down fifty thousand tips and the New York City Police Department sixteen thousand.

In the beginning, everyone was a suspect in the kidnapping—neighbors, the Lindbergh-Morrow servants, relatives, people who had built the Lindbergh house, local gangsters, and anyone who in any way acted or looked suspicious. Thousands of people all over the country were questioned, and in many cases arrested, as Lindbergh case suspects. But nothing panned out.

The once frantic investigation gradually slowed to a crawl, then floundered for more than two years. The most promising leads in 1933 and the first nine months of 1934 involved the ransom bills that were popping up around New York City.

Lieutenant James Finn of the New York City Police Department had been keeping a large map of the city in which he had stuck pins that showed where the Lindbergh bills had turned up. The man in charge of the FBI's investigation, Special Agent Thomas H. Sisk, was doing the same thing.

On April 5, 1933, President Roosevelt took steps to stop the hoarding of gold, and, by executive order, he directed all persons possessing gold bullion, coins, or gold certificates valued at more than a hundred dollars to deposit them at a Federal Reserve Bank on or before May 1, 1933. Lieutenant Finn hoped that Roosevelt's order would make bank tellers and others more alert to the ransom money. In May of 1933, Lieutenant Finn and Special Agent Sisk visited the offices and cashiers of the Federal Reserve Bank of New York City and asked them to check the serial numbers on all incoming gold certificates against a fifty-seven-page ransom booklet that listed all of the bills John Condon had handed over to the man in St. Raymond's Cemetery on April 2, 1932.

On May 1, 1933, the last day of President Roosevelt's deadline, a man walked into the Federal Reserve Bank in New York City and exchanged $2,980 in gold notes for the equivalent amount in greenbacks. Every gold note in the pack was a ransom bill. The only clue to this man's identity was a deposit slip bearing the name J. J. Faulkner and the address 537 West 149th Street, New York. Lieutenant Finn's detectives checked out the address and found no such person living there. The follow-up investigation failed to identify this man and no one at the bank could provide a description of the depositor.

So far, most of the ransom bills that had been recovered were in the same condition. Each note had been folded in half along its full length, then doubled over twice along its length so that, when it was unfolded and laid flat, the bill had creases dividing it into eight sections. Lieutenant Finn had also discovered a pattern in the way the bill passer tendered the money. He would take a small, folded bill from his watch or vest pocket and toss it onto the counter for the bank or store clerk to unfold. Those who remembered the bill passer described him as a white male of average height with blue eyes, high cheekbones, flat cheeks, and a pointed chin. This man spoke with a German accent and wore a soft felt hat that pulled down over his forehead. This composite portrait tallied with Dr. Condon's description of the man in the cemetery as well as the one given by Joseph Perrone, the cab driver who had delivered one of the ransom notes to John Condon's house. The accent also fit with the opinions of several handwriting experts who believe the writer of the ransom notes was German.

By the fall of 1933, about a year and a half after Lieutenant Finn started sticking pins into his map, a pattern had emerged. Originally, the bill passer had made an effort not to spend the money in the same area. But as time went on the bill passer had become careless. The increasing number of red (ten-dollar) and black (five-dollar) pins were now clustered in the same places. They were along Lexington and Third Avenues in Upper Manhattan and were also grouped in the German-speaking section of Yorkville.

In January 1934, the ransom money was turning up at the rate of forty dollars a week. Although the bill passer was spending more of it, he was still being cautious. There were no more five-dollar bills turning up. So far, four hundred of the fives had been pulled out of circulation. In all probability the kidnapper had spent them all and was now dipping into his tens.

On Tuesday, September 18, 1934, the head teller of the Corn Exchange Bank in the Bronx came across two ten-dollar gold certificates. The teller checked the ransom list and found one of the bills on it. The bank teller called the FBI and within minutes Special Agent Sisk, Lieutenant Finn, and New Jersey State Police detective Arthur T. Keaten were at the bank where they found, penciled on the margin of this bill, the New York license number 4U-13-41. This license was registered to Richard Hauptmann, 1279 East 222nd Street, the Bronx. Hauptmann's car was 1930 Dodge sedan, dark blue in color. The automobile registration card indicated that Hauptmann was almost thirty-five, German-born, and a carpenter by trade. Physically, he met the descriptions of the ransom bill passer. Moreover, he lived in the Williams Bridge section of the Bronx, not far from the two cemeteries, John F. Condon, and the store where pieces of the kidnap ladder had been purchased.

The next morning, three detectives from New York City, three with the New Jersey State Police, and three FBI agents arrested Hauptmann as he traveled south on Park Avenue. Hauptmann's car was stopped a half block north of East Tremont Avenue in the South Bronx. He had in his possession a twenty-dollar ransom bill, one that had been folded into eight sections like many of the bills passed in 1933 and 1934.

Bruno Richard Hauptmann, an illegal alien who had come to America after three tries as a stowaway, lived in a rented second-story apartment with his wife Anna and his eleven-month-old son, Manfred. Hauptmann denied any knowledge of the kidnapping and told the police he did not have a police record in Germany—a statement that later turned out to be a lie. Hauptmann also lied when he told the officers he didn't have any more gold certificates hidden away. The prisoner said he hadn't worked as a carpenter since quitting a construction job in the spring of 1932. Since that time Hauptmann had been living off money he said he had earned by playing the stock market.

Hauptmann was taken to the 2nd Precinct Police Station on the Lower West Side of Manhattan where he was roughed up, interrogated for hours on end, and made to write carefully constructed paragraphs dictated to him by the police. These paragraphs contained key words and phrases linked to the ransom notes. Although exhausted and under extreme pressure, Hauptmann maintained his innocence through it all. His known handwriting samples were sent to a pair of private New York City document examiners, the internationally recognized pioneer in the field, Albert S. Osborn, and his son, Albert D., who reported that Hauptmann had written all of the ransom documents. These experts would later be joined by several other document examiners who would share their opinion. The police also learned that Hauptmann had a serious felony record in Germany, including the second-story burglary of a small-town mayor's house, where entry was gained through the use of a ladder.

In a quickly arranged line-up, Hauptmann was identified by Joseph Perrone, the cab driver, and several others who had seen him near the Lindbergh estate on the day of the kidnapping. John Condon, the most important eyewitness the police had, infuriated detectives by failing to come through with a positive identification.

On Thursday, September 20, the police decided to focus on Hauptmann's 15-by-11 foot garage, located on the other side of Needham Avenue, a block-long dirt road that ran along the east side of Hauptmann's house. A New York City detective, when checking the area around Hauptmann's work bench, noticed that a board had been nailed across two wall joists above the bench. The detectives pried the board off and uncovered a shelf that held packages wrapped in newspaper. The detective took one the bundles off the shelf and unwrapped it. When he did, he realized he had discovered a stack of ten-dollar gold notes—one hundred of them. The police officer unwrapped the other package and found more ten-dollar gold certificates, eighty-three in all. All of this money were Lindbergh bills—a total of $1,830. About an hour later another detective found a board nailed between two joists. When this plank was removed, the officer found a one-gallon shellac can sitting in the recess of the garage window. In the shellac can, beneath a couple of rags, the officer found twelve packages of gold notes. These bills had been wrapped in newspapers—the June 25 and September 6, 1934 editions of the *New York Daily News*. The shellac can contained, in ten-dollar and twenty-dollar denominations, $11,930 of Colonel Lindbergh's money. There were 390 tens and 493 twenties.

When confronted with the ransom money, Hauptmann said he had obtained the cash from a friend and partner in the fur trading business named Isidor Fisch. In December 1933, Fisch, in poor health, had sailed to his home in Leipzig, Germany, where he died on March 29, 1934. Before sailing for Germany, Fisch had left some of his belongings with Hauptmann for safekeeping. There was a trunk, some suitcases, and a shoe box tied up with a string. Hauptmann said he placed this shoe box on the top shelf of the broom closet in his kitchen. About a month before his arrest, water from a heavy rain had leaked through the kitchen ceiling and into the closet. When Hauptmann removed the wet items, he came upon Fisch's forgotten shoe box. Fisch, according to Hauptmann, had left him fifteen thousand dollars in gold certificates.

Without telling his wife, Anna, Hauptmann stashed the bundles of money in his garage where nobody could find them. Sometime in August 1934, Hauptmann started spending the money. He said he felt privileged to do so because Isidor Fisch had owed him seven thousand dollars.

On Monday, September 24, a New York City detective found John Condon's phone number and address penciled on a trim board inside the nursery closet in Hauptmann's house. When confronted with this evidence, Hauptmann conceded it was his handwriting. He explained, "I must have read it in the paper about the story. I was little bit interest, and keep a little bit record of it and maybe I was just in the closet and was reading the paper and put down the address."

On Wednesday, the 26th, police, in Hauptmann's attic, noticed that a floor plank in the southwest corner of the room was shorter than the rest. About eight feet of this board had been sawed off and removed from the attic. In each of the four joists exposed because this board was missing, a detective found a nail hole where the absent plank had been secured to the floor. It would be determined later, by a federal wood expert named Arthur Koehler, that a side rail from the kidnap ladder, the so-called rail sixteen — had been cut from this place in Hauptmann's attic.

While the detectives were searching Hauptmann's attic, a group of officers and police carpenters were in the process of dismantling Hauptmann's garage. One of the carpenters knocked down a short two-by-four that was wedged between two wall joists. When he examined this eight-inch piece of wood, he found that it contained five wads of ten-dollar gold notes. The bills were rolled up and stuffed into five holes that had been drilled into the board. All of the bills were listed as Lindbergh money. The ransom cache totaled $840, bringing the total amount of Lindbergh money in Hauptmann's possession to $14,600.

That wasn't all. There was a sixth drilled-out area, larger than the others, in this piece of wood. This hole contained a tiny silver-colored pistol with a white plastic grip. The three-and-one-half inch gun, a German Liliput KAL 4.25 (.25 caliber), model 1926, was loaded with five rounds.

The police had tied Hauptmann to the kidnapping through the ransom money, the kidnap ladder, and the extortion notes. Hauptmann met the description of the man in the cemeteries, had a criminal record, and had written John F. Condon's address and phone number in his closest. What the prosecution didn't have was a confession, and they would have liked, but did not have, Hauptmann's fingerprints on the ransom notes, on the ladder, or in the nursery. They also didn't have an eyewitness to the kidnapping or the murder. The police, so far, had gathered plenty of evidence but, at this point, all of it was circumstantial.

Four months after his arrest, Bruno Richard Hauptmann was tried for murder in Flemington, New Jersey. The sensational trial lasted six weeks and produced front-page headlines all over the world. The prosecution offered the jury two theories of how the baby had died. The kidnapper had either murdered the baby in his crib, or had dropped him while climbing down the homemade ladder. According to one theory, the ladder had split when the kidnapper descended with the added weight of the thirty-pound child.

Eight prominent handwriting experts, led by the world renowned Albert S. Osborn, testified that Hauptmann had written the fifteen extortion letters, including the one in the nursery. Four more document examiners had been in the wings, ready to testify on rebuttal, but they were not needed because the Hauptmann defense did not bring to the stand a battery of experts to say that he had not written the ransom notes. The only handwriting witness who testified for Hauptmann was a man from St. Louis named John Trendley who was exposed on cross-examination as an "expert" who had testified for the side that had paid him the most.

The federal wood expert, Arthur Koehler, testified that the carpenter tools in Hauptmann's garage had their unique marks on the kidnap ladder. He also testified that one of the boards used to make the ladder, rail sixteen, had once been a floor plank in Hauptmann's attic. Koehler had also traced pieces of the kidnap ladder to a builder's supply store not far from Hauptmann's residence.

Dr. Condon took the stand and identified Hauptmann as "Cemetery John." This was interesting and a bit surprising because when Condon first encountered Hauptmann at the line-up shortly after his arrest, the doctor had refused to positively identify him as "Cemetery John." At the trial however, Condon was quite positive. Colonel Lindbergh testified that it was Hauptmann's voice he had heard say, "Hey, Doctor," at St. Raymond's Cemetery on the night the ransom money exchanged hands. Three other witnesses testified they had seen Hauptmann near Hopewell on the day of the crime. For a variety of reasons, these witnesses were not reliable and turned out to be an embarrassment for the prosecution.

Cecile Barr, a cashier who worked at the Greenwich Village movie house, testified that Hauptmann had passed a five-dollar ransom bill at her theater on November 26, 1933, weeks before Hauptmann said he had discovered Isidor Fisch's shoe box.

Hauptmann's chief defense attorney, a noted trial lawyer from Brooklyn, New York, named Edward J. Reilly, tried to prove the kidnapping was an inside job by implicating the Lindbergh-Morrow servants, John Condon, and others. Reilly infuriated the other four defense attorneys by conceding that the remains found on Mount Rose Heights were the Lindbergh baby's.

Hauptmann took the stand and made an unsympathetic witness who got caught in several lies. Hauptmann said he had been with his wife at her place of employment on the night of the kidnapping, said he was at home celebrating his birthday on the night the five-dollar ransom bill was passed at the theater in Greenwich Village, and offered his "Fisch story" to explain the ransom money found hidden in his garage. The defendant denied any connection to the kidnap ladder and accused the police of trying to beat a confession out of him. Hauptmann also denied writing the ransom notes, explaining the misspelling in his request writings that matched up to the misspellings in the ransom notes by claiming that the police had made him write these words that way.

Unable to match the prosecution's handwriting case, or counter the State's wood expert who had hung the kidnap around Hauptmann's neck, and failing to satisfactorily explain his possession of all that money, Reilly's defense, damaged by a series of crackpot witnesses, degenerated into tragic burlesque then collapsed. At one point, Hauptmann leaned over to Reilly and said, "Where are you getting these witnesses? They are killing me."

On February 13, 1935, after thirty-two days of testimony, the jury, consisting of four women and eight men, found Hauptmann guilty of first-degree murder. Since the jurors did not recommend mercy, the judge had no choice under the law but to sentence Hauptmann to death in the electric chair. Hauptmann's attorneys immediately appealed, but the New Jersey Appellate Court unanimously affirmed the conviction.

3 Bruno and the Governor

Two days after the Appeals Court handed down its decision, Bruno Richard Hauptmann announced that he wanted to talk to Harold G. Hoffman, the governor of New Jersey. Hoffman had been elected governor six weeks after Hauptmann's arrest. As a politician on his way up, Hoffman had his eye on the 1936 Republican vice presidential nomination. His original interest in the Lindbergh case was based on his long-time personal and political association with Ellis Parker Sr., the flamboyant Burlington County detective who, because he had been on the outs with former governor A. Harry Moore, had been denied access to the inner circles of the Lindbergh investigation.

Parker Sr., the "small-town detective with a world-wide reputation," had been trying to make life difficult for H. Norman Schwarzkopf from the beginning. Fuming with jealousy and rage over his role as an outcast, and desperately trying to get into the Lindbergh limelight, Parker had tried to get attention by claiming that the corpse found on Mount Rose Heights was not the Lindbergh baby. Believing that the New Jersey State Police and the prosecutors had railroaded Hauptmann, Parker had been conducting his own investigation.

Influenced by Detective Parker's views on the case, Governor Hoffman thought that Hauptmann may have been the ransom note writer, but not the one who had actually kidnapped and murdered the baby. Hoffman figured he might be able to get Hauptmann to confess his true role in the crime in exchange for a life sentence, so he called the warden at the state prison in Trenton and arranged a meeting with Hauptmann.

A few days later, the governor went to Hauptmann's cell where Hauptmann told him he was innocent and that he hadn't been properly represented by his chief defense attorney, Edward J. Reilly. Reilly had since been fired from the case by Mrs. Hauptmann.

C. Lloyd Fisher, the Flemington, New Jersey, lawyer in charge of Hauptmann's case now that Reilly was out of the picture, was elated over Governor Hoffman's personal interest in Hauptmann. Fisher rejoiced over the fact that the governor had taken the trouble to hear Hauptmann's side of the story. The attorney had not spoken directly to Hoffman, but had learned through Ellis Parker Sr. that the governor had been very impressed, indeed moved, by the prisoner.

In early December 1935, the press learned of Hoffman's meeting with Hauptmann, and the story of his visit to the prison and his doubts about Hauptmann's guilt was on the front page of every newspaper in the country.

When New Jersey attorney general and the prosecutor of the Hauptmann trial, David T. Wilentz, found out about Hoffman's meeting with Hauptmann, he met with the governor to express his shock and outrage.

On December 9, 1935, the United States Supreme Court, in a terse, twelve-word statement, announced that it had decided not to review the constitutionality of the Hauptmann trial, thus moving the prisoner one step closer to the death chamber. On December 13, Judge Trenchard, the trial judge, set the execution for Friday, January 17, 1936.

After Governor Hoffman's views on the Lindbergh case had become public, Lindbergh case outsiders and dissenters, like Ellis Parker Sr., came forward to assist the governor in his investigation. One such person was Dr. Erastus M. Hudson, the physician and fingerprint expert who had processed the kidnap ladder and the Lindbergh baby's toys with silver nitrate to bring out the latent fingerprints. Dr. Hudson believed that Hauptmann was innocent because his fingerprints were not found on the kidnap ladder, the ransom notes, or in the nursery. Governor Hoffman shared Hudson's thesis and was somewhat receptive to Ellis Parker Sr.'s notion that the baby found at the Mount Rose Heights gravesite was not baby Lindbergh. For that reason, Governor Hoffman was interested in the fingerprints Dr. Hudson had developed off the child's playthings. In the event the Lindbergh child turned up someday, the boy could be identified by those latents.

On January 3, 1936, Governor Hoffman wrote a letter to state police superintendent Schwarzkopf requesting numerous documents, trial exhibits, and articles of evidence connected with the case.

Among the items the governor wanted were "A set of the fingerprints of Charles Augustus Lindbergh, Jr., made by Dr. Erastus M. Hudson, or any other fingerprints taken from the child's toys."

Three days before Hauptmann's scheduled execution, Governor Hoffman met again with Attorney General Wilentz to tell him that he was meeting with Mrs. Hauptmann in the morning. The governor wanted to offer Hauptmann this deal: If he confessed to his true role in the case, the governor and attorney general would ask the Court of Pardons to commute Hauptmann's sentence to life. Would the attorney general go along with this—even if Hauptmann admitted killing the baby in cold-blood? Yes, Wilentz said, he would join the governor in asking for a life sentence— even if Hauptmann confessed to that. Governor Hoffman said he would ask Mrs. Hauptmann to convey the deal to Bruno Richard, and if necessary, talk him into it.

Governor Hoffman met with Mrs. Hauptmann and asked her to go to her husband and talk him into confessing in order to save his life. Anna Hauptmann was appalled by the idea and said she wouldn't even consider it. When Hauptmann himself got wind of the proposition, he too rejected it without further discussion.

On January 14, 1936, Governor Hoffman called a press conference and announced that he was granting Hauptmann a thirty-day reprieve. Hoffman had asked David T. Wilentz and Anthony Hauck, another member of the prosecution team, to come to the executive suite and stand with him when he made his announcement. The prosecutors' grim faces made it clear that although they were standing next to the governor, they weren't standing with him.

Governor Hoffman declared that he had his doubts that "complete justice" had been done in the Hauptmann case. "A shocking crime was committed," he said, "and in the interest of society, it must be completely solved. A human life is at stake. As governor of New Jersey I have a duty to perform. It is my heart, my conscience, my job—and this is my decision."

The response to Governor Hoffman's action was immediate, broad-based, and intense. People were stunned, confused, and infuriated. The governor of the state, a public servant, a politician, was second-guessing the police, the prosecution, the judge, the jury, three appeals courts and his own Court of Pardons. *The Trenton Times* carried a front-page editorial under the heading "IMPEACH HOFFMAN." The writer of the editorial declared the governor had "dishonored himself, disgraced the state and converted New Jersey into international laughing stock."

If Governor Hoffman had wanted headlines, he had certainly gotten them. He had also incurred the wrath of millions, something he apparently had not counted on. The governor was genuinely shocked and angered by the severe criticism being leveled against him.

On Thursday, January 17, Governor Hoffman issued a statement that offended many journalists, insulted the state police, and enraged David T. Wilentz. The governor seemed to be declaring war on his own state:

> I have never expressed an opinion upon the guilt or innocence of Hauptmann. I do, however, share with hundreds of thousands of our people the doubt as to the value of the evidence that placed him in the Lindbergh nursery on the night of the crime; I do wonder what part passion and prejudice played in the conviction of a man who was previously tried and convicted in the columns of our newspapers; I do, on the basis of evidence that is in my hands, question the truthfulness and mental competency of some of the chief witnesses for the state; I do doubt that this crime could have been committed by any one man, and I am worried about the eagerness of some of our law enforcement agencies to bring about the death of this one man so that the books can be closed in the thought that another great crime mystery has been successfully solved.
>
> I make no apology for granting a reprieve in this case. During the period we may calmly consider some of the baffling phases of the crime and the subsequent trial of Hauptmann.[1]

Politically, Governor Hoffman was in a fix. If he couldn't justify his reprieve by proving that Hauptmann was just an extortionist, or by identifying more kidnappers, or by showing that the condemned man had been railroaded by the police and the prosecution, he would look like a busybody, headline grabbing fool. Hoffman needed to uncover something earthshaking — something really big. If he did not, his political career would be sitting on Hauptmann's lap when they threw the switch.

Frustrated by what he called foot-dragging by his own state police, Governor Hoffman called New York City Police commissioner Lewis J. Valentine and asked him to reopen New York's case and to re-assign his men to the investigation. The commissioner applauded the governor's eagerness to get at the truth and promised to give the matter some thought, but he was just being polite. Commissioner Valentine had no intention of reopening the Lindbergh investigation.

Governor Hoffman next got in touch with J. Edgar Hoover of the FBI. Although Hoover was convinced of Hauptmann's guilt, he still considered Schwarzkopf a rival and therefore took delight in the colonel's problems with his governor. Because Hoover was still smarting over what he considered Schwarzkopf's uncooperative attitude toward the FBI and was jealous of Schwarzkopf's success in the Lindbergh investigation, he could not help discrediting Schwarzkopf by indicating that he had not been impressed by many of the eyewitnesses in the case. Hoover then added fuel to the governor's suspicions by saying that he questioned the authority of the rail sixteen evidence. However, that was as far as Hoover would go. He said he was not interested in reopening the Bureau's Lindbergh investigation.

Colonel Schwarzkopf, in a weekly progress report, submitted to the governor on February 28, 1936, one day shy of the fourth anniversary of the kidnapping, charged that officials from Hoffman's office had tried to get some of his men to say they had helped frame Hauptmann by fabricating the rail-sixteen evidence to make it appear that part of the ladder had once been a plank in Hauptmann' s attic. State detectives Lewis J. Bornmann, John B. Wallace, and William F. Horn were told that if they cooperated with the governor by telling him how they had helped fabricate this evidence, they would keep their positions on the state police force after Colonel Schwarzkopf had been replaced at the end of the superintendent's term. If they did not come clean, these officers would be demoted and transferred. Corporal Frank A. Kelly, the state fingerprint man, was also approached and told that if he did not tell how the latent fingerprints had disappeared from the nursery, he would lose his job. In the meantime, Colonel Schwarzkopf had submitted his report to Governor Hoffman, but it contained nothing in the way of new developments or leads relative to the reopened Lindbergh case investigation.

Frustrated by the lack of progress in the investigation, and angered by Schwarzkopf's sandbagging, Governor Hoffman wrote a letter telling the colonel not to bother sending him any more of his so-called progress reports. In this letter, Governor Hoffman offered his views on the case:

My opinion, which is shared by thousands of people, is that the Lindbergh kidnapping, murder, and the extortion of $50,000 was not a one-man job. Had sound and ordinary police methods been used following the commission of the crime, many doubts entertained today might have been eliminated. The Lindbergh matter is quite generally referred to as the most bungled case in police history, and it is in your interest and to the interest of all members of your organization as well as the public interest, to work sincerely and effectively to bring about its complete solution.[2]

In March, with the new execution date fast approaching, Governor Hoffman's investigation centered on rail sixteen in Hauptmann's attic. If the governor could prove that the wood evidence had been planted, that the police had taken a plank of southern pine, cut it in two, put one section into the attic and the other onto the ladder as rail sixteen, he would in one bold stroke break Schwarzkopf's back and save Hauptmann's life. The governor would also be a hero and that much closer to the vice president's office in the White House.

To get the proof he needed, the governor was counting on Robert W. Hicks, a Washington, D.C., lawyer and criminalist. Hicks had rented Hauptmann's old apartment and was working with a so-called wood expert named Arch W. Loney, an employee of the Public Works Administration.

In mid-March 1936, Loney reported to Governor Hoffman that he could prove that rail sixteen and the board from which it had been cut had been planted in Hauptmann's attic. The governor immediately called Wilentz to arrange a confrontation between Loney and Arthur Koehler, the Department of Agriculture wood expert who had been one of the prosecution's star witnesses, the man who said part of the ladder had come from Hauptmann's attic.

On March 26, six men were gathered in Hauptmann's attic: Governor Hoffman, Arch W. Loney, Attorney General Wilentz, Koehler, the assistant prosecutor Anthony Hauck, and Detective Lewis J. Bornmann, the state trooper who had discovered the gap in the flooring where rail sixteen had supposedly been. The governor had brought along rail sixteen, he had carried it into the attic himself. Governor Hoffman picked up rail sixteen and laid it into the gap, carefully lining up its four nail holes with the holes in the four crossbeams. Taking four nails from Loney, the governor tapped each one through rail sixteen into the joist, and when he did, they did not go in all the way flush to rail sixteen.

When Arthur Koehler and Detective Bornmann had tapped the four nails into these exact holes, the nails had supposedly sunk flush to the surface of the plank. Both men had testified to this at Hauptmann's trial. Anthony Hauck, the Hunterdon County prosecutor and Wilentz's chief assistant at the trial, responded by charging that someone working for Hauptmann had recently tampered with the nail holes. Hauck suggested they take the four sections of the joist containing the nail holes to Columbia University where Dr. Lincoln T. Work, a physics professor, could examine the wood to determine if the holes had in fact been altered in some way. They did just that, and when Dr. Work took the four pieces of wood into his laboratory, he found wooden plugs on the bottom of each nail hole. When the plugs, consisting of sawdust, were removed, the nails sunk through rail sixteen into the joist the way they had gone in when tested by Koehler, Detective Bornmann, and Prosecutor Hauck.

That evening, Attorney General Wilentz and Anthony Hauck confronted Governor Hoffman with Professor Work's findings. The governor, obviously unhappy with this development, promised to look into the matter. The next morning, however, Governor Hoffman held a press conference in his office and declared that he still had doubts about the authenticity of the rail sixteen evidence. The governor failed to mention Dr. Work or his findings. Attorney General Wilentz called the attic confrontation "nonsensical and ridiculous."

Governor Hoffman had gambled his political career on the chance he could prove that the Lindbergh case had not been completely solved. He had lost this gamble when the investigation he had launched failed to shed anything earthshaking about the case.

Immediately after Governor Hoffman's death in 1954, it was discovered that during his governorship, Hoffman had embezzled over three hundred thousand dollars from the state of New Jersey. This led to speculation that the fuss Hoffman had created over the Lindbergh case was an effort to distract attention from his thefts and to cover his tracks.

Just before Hauptmann was to be executed, the governor's friend, Burlington County detective Ellis Parker Sr., kidnapped a disbarred lawyer named Paul H. Wendel and forced him to confess to the Lindbergh kidnapping. As soon as Wendel was free, he repudiated his confession, and within a year Parker and his accomplices were tried, convicted, and sent to federal prison. Ironically, they were the first to be convicted under the new Lindbergh Law, a statute, thanks to the Lindbergh case, that made kidnapping a federal offense.

On April 3, 1936, at 8:47 in the evening, Bruno Richard Hauptmann died in the electric chair at the New Jersey State Prison in Trenton. He went to his grave proclaiming his innocence. Only a handful of people stood outside the death house that night, and when told of Hauptmann's death, quietly went home.

4 The Aftermath

There was not a person involved in the Lindbergh case who was not in some way permanently affected by the experience. Many were ruined by the case, others used it to their advantage, and the rest simply survived it. Some who used the Lindbergh case to their advantage were writers. Sixteen books and hundreds of newspaper, journal, and magazine articles have been published about the case, making it one of the most written about crimes in the world.

The Lindbergh case attracted skeptics from the start. Shortly after the story broke in 1932, Laura Vitray, a Hearst reporter, rushed into print a little-known book called *The Great Lindbergh Hullaballo: An Unorthodox Account*. Vitray, sensing a hoax, wrote derisively of the Lindbergh family, referring to the Lindbergh baby as the "golden-haired Eaglet," and accused certain vaguely defined "powers" of having "deliberately arranged the Lindbergh 'kidnapping,' not for ransom, but as a story, to divert public attention from the grave disaster that threatens this nation at their own hands today." No one but the author was sure what all that meant. One month after Vitray signed the preface, the baby's body was found in the woods, two miles from the Lindbergh estate. The Hearst Corporation fired Vitray.

Laura Vitray had a sister-skeptic in Mary Belle Spencer, a Chicago lawyer who seems to have had a problem with the massive law enforcement effort that was thrown into the hunt for the Lindbergh child and its kidnapper. In 1933, after the discovery of the infant corpse, but before Hauptmann's arrest, Spencer published a pamphlet bearing the cover title: *No. 2310, Criminal File Exposed! Aviator's Baby Was Never Kidnapped or Murdered*.

Spencer argued that no crime had been committed, that the child had merely wandered off into the woods where he had met his death by animals. The pamphlet also includes a mock trial in which the author defends a vagrant "John Doe" who has been indicted for kidnapping and murder. In her burlesque, Spencer makes thinly veiled substitutions for names prominent in the case such as "Limbergh" for Lindbergh and "Elizabeth Gah" for Betty Gow, the baby's nursemaid.

Spencer's odd little book was mailed to every member of the Hauptmann jury panel, causing the judge to consider granting a change of venue.

On the magazine front, a popular and prolific pulp crime writer named Alan Hynd glorified the law enforcement effort in the Lindbergh case in twenty or so articles for *True Detective Mysteries* between November 1932 and May 1937. The following year Hynd changed sides to help Governor Harold G. Hoffman write a sixteen-part article for *Liberty* magazine called, "What Was Wrong with the Lindbergh Case? The Crime, The Case, The Challenge."

In 1938 Evalyn McLean, the wealthy socialite from Washington, D.C., who had been bilked by Gaston Means, with Alan Hynd wrote a ten-piece article for *Liberty* called "Why I Am Still Investigating the Lindbergh Case." Eleven years later, Alan Hynd would write a long, pro-Hauptmann article in *True Magazine* called, "Everyone Wanted to Get into the Act" that in 1956 was reprinted in a book as, "Why the Lindbergh Case Was Never Solved." In this article, written in Hynd's casual, breezy style, he echoed Ellis Parker Sr.'s earlier questioning of the infant corpse's identity, accused the police of lying and fabricating evidence, and argued that Hauptmann had not received a fair trial. Hynd's defection from the pro-law-enforcement side to Hauptmann's cause made it obvious that he wrote for the people who paid him, regardless of their or even his, point of view.

Two of the early books on the Lindbergh case, *The Lindbergh Crime and The Trial of Bruno Richard Hauptmann: Edited with a History of the Case,* were written or edited by Sidney B. Whipple, a newspaper reporter who had covered the case.[1] Many of the books and magazine articles on the crime would be written by journalists such as Samuel G. Blackman, Sid Boehn, David D. Davidson, Al Dunlap, Leigh Matteson, George Waller, and Tom Zito. The case would also draw the attention of true-crime book writers Edmund Pearson, Edward D. Radin, Francis X. Busch, Charles Still, and Theon Wright. More recently, a pair of British true-crime writers, Ludovic

Kennedy and Jonathan Goodman have joined the club along with mystery writer Max Allan Collins and novelist and true-crime writer Noel Behn.

Two books by Lindbergh case principals, Dr. John F. Condon and Dr. Dudley D. Shoenfeld, came out in 1936. Condon's book *Jafsie Tells All*, although corny and self-serving, is the only account of what took place between Condon and "John" in the two Bronx cemeteries. Condon tries, in his book, to explain why he had vacillated Hauptmann's line-up (he did not want to prematurely ID the suspect). Prior to coming out in a hardback book, *Jafsie Tells All* was serialized in *Liberty* magazine.[2]

Dr. Shoenfeld, a New York City psychiatrist. had profiled the kidnapper for the New York City police by studying all of the ransom letters. In his book, *The Crime and the Criminal: A Psychiatric Study of the Lindbergh Case,* Dr. Shoenfeld compared his profile of the ransom note writer with what the police later found out about Hauptmann, and concluded that Hauptmann was the ransom note writer, the kidnapper, and the man Condon had met twice in the two cemeteries.[3] Having sat in the courtroom every day of Hauptmann's trial, Dr. Shoenfeld carefully explained, in psychological and psychiatric terms, Hauptmann's reaction to the prosecution's evidence and the witnesses against him.

In 1937, a private handwriting expert from Newark, New Jersey, named J. Vreeland Haring, published a book called *The Hand of Hauptmann: The Handwriting Expert Tells the Story of the Lindbergh Case.*[4] Haring was first brought into the case by the Hauptmann's defense, who asked him to study the ransom notes and testify that Hauptmann was not the writer of these documents. Haring compared Hauptmann's known handwriting with the ransom notes and concluded that Hauptmann was the one who had written them all. That opinion led him, and his son, who was also in the questioned-document business, to the prosecution's side of the case. The Harings, rebuttal witnesses at Hauptmann's trial, were not called to the stand because Hauptmann's sole handwriting witness was thoroughly discredited, therefore rendering the prosecution's rebuttal witnesses unnecessary.

The Harings also analyzed Isidor Fisch's handwriting and had compared it to the J. J. Faulkner signature on the mysterious bank slip used to exchange the $2,980 in ransom gold notes in May of 1933. The Harings concluded that Fisch had not written any of the ransom notes nor had he signed the Faulkner bank deposit slip.

The Harings had also made a detailed handwriting study of the two lengthy, handwritten "mercy letters" Hauptmann had written to Governor Hoffman following his conviction. In so doing, they called special attention to the similarities in Hauptmann's letters to the ransom notes. They also made a point of comparing this known writing to the writing in the note left in the baby's nursery. The Harings did this in response to critics of the prosecution who were asserting that none of the handwriting experts at the trial had established that Hauptmann had written this particular note. This was an important point because the nursery note was evidence that linked Hauptmann to the kidnapping site, making him more than just an extortionist.

Anyone who believes the field of questioned documents is a solid, forensic science, and that J. Vreeland Haring was a competent practitioner in that field, would have no doubt, after plowing through this heavily illustrated text, that Hauptmann, if nothing more, was the one who had written all of the ransom notes. This book, obviously, was Haring's way of capitalizing professionally on the Lindbergh case. During his long career, he had been involved in many celebrated cases, but when he died in 1954 at age eighty-six, he was remembered mainly for his work in the Lindbergh case, and his book.

In 1961, a newspaper reporter named George Waller published *Kidnap: The Story of the Lindbergh Case*. The 597-page book, twenty-five years in the writing, was the most comprehensive work on the case to date. Waller's book became a Book-of-the-Month Club selection, and, in 1962, was published by Dell in paperback. The book was also published and widely read in England.[5] Waller's account of the crime, the investigation, and the trial leaves little doubt in the reader's mind that Hauptmann had kidnapped and murdered the Lindbergh baby. Waller did not have access to any of the police documents or the full trial transcripts. His account was based principally on newspaper and other published accounts. As a result, the book contains some major errors. It also suffers from not having an index.

In 1976, two years after Colonel Lindbergh's death, a man from Biddleford, Maine, named Kenneth Kerwin, claiming to be Charles A. Lindbergh Jr., the kidnapped child, sued Colonel Lindbergh's estate as a rightful heir entitled to the Lindbergh inheritance. Although Kerwin's suit was eventually dismissed, it delayed, for two years, the administration of Colonel Lindbergh's will.

Kenneth Kerwin's story has a familiar ring—the baby identified by Colonel Lindbergh, Betty Gow, and the police, had been a plant. Kerwin said that the people who had raised him, Mildred and Manser Kerwin, had been involved in the kidnapping and had ended up with the Lindbergh baby, whom they had brought up as their own child.

One day, in the early 1960s, when he was about thirty years old, Kerwin showed up in Darien, Connecticut, where he confronted Colonel Lindbergh with the news that he was his son. Someone in the house called the police who came and hauled Kerwin away. No charges were filed, but Kerwin was told to stay away from the Lindberghs.

The idea that the Lindbergh baby was kidnapped but not murdered goes all the way back to Detective Ellis Parker Sr. and his theory (later altered when he got Paul H. Wendel to confess to killing the child) that the corpse on Mount Rose Heights had been dead for more than seventy-two days, which meant the child in the woods had been murdered before the kidnapping. The remains in the woods, therefore, could not be the Lindbergh baby's. Ellis Parker Sr. said he had consulted a physician who had looked at the gravesite photographs of the baby and concluded the child, based on it's postmortem condition, had been dead before the kidnapping took place.

Ellis Parker Sr.'s theory was further enhanced by the fact that the body in the woods measured 33 1/2 inches long. On the Lindbergh baby's wanted poster, the child was described as being 29 inches tall, a discrepancy of 1 1/2 inches. Moreover, because the fontanelle (the so-called soft spot at the top of a newborn's head, which normally closes within a year) was still open on the corpse in the woods, Parker believed this baby was too young to be the Lindbergh child. Detective Parker also questioned the reliability of Colonel Lindbergh's and the nursemaid's, Betty Gow's, visual identification of the corpse at the morgue, and Dr. Philip Van Ingen, the prominent New York City pediatrician who had attended the Lindbergh baby shortly before the kidnapping, did not positively identify the infant corpse in the Trenton morgue as the Lindbergh baby.

In fact, there is no doubt that the Lindbergh baby was killed, and that his remains were found in the woods by the truck driver, William Allen. The length of the corpse discrepancy can be explained: the 29 inches on the wanted poster was supposed to read "2 feet, 9 inches," the baby's true height, which comes to 33 inches. This so-called discrepancy was nothing more than a printing error. Also, by measuring the baby's one-piece sleeping suit, it becomes obvious that the child was taller than the poster's 29 inches.

It can also be proven, with scientific certainty, that the homemade undershirt and the store-bought T-shirt on the corpse were the garments worn by the Lindbergh baby on the night he was kidnapped. In 1977, Dr. Alan T. Lane, the senior forensic chemist at the New Jersey Crime Laboratory in West Trenton, reexamined the gravesite garments and concluded these were the Lindbergh baby's clothing. For one thing, a remnant of the cloth from which Betty Gow had cut the homemade undershirt matched the gravesite shirt perfectly. They came together like two interlocking pieces of a jigsaw puzzle. Moreover, the blue thread Betty Gow had used to fashion the shirt was at the gravesite. Dr. Lane examined the gravesite thread with the thread that had been on Betty Gow's spool. They matched.

Although the gravesite corpse was badly decomposed generally, the face, having been buried in the cold mud, was remarkably preserved to the point where the resemblance to the Lindbergh baby—the high forehead, chin dimple, and so forth—was obvious. Those who question the identity of the remains note that the body was so badly decomposed one could not tell if it was a boy or a girl. That may be true, but since bodies are not identified by their genitals, this fact is not relevant to the issue of the child's identity.

The corpse in the woods was also identified by its hair, teeth, and over-lapped toes. Moreover, the gravesite body and the Lindbergh child had the same number, location, and kinds of teeth a twenty-month-old baby would have. In 1977, Alan T. Lane compared samples of the Lindbergh baby's hair with follicles found at the gravesite and concluded they had come from the same head.

If one assumes, for the sake of argument, that the corpse in the woods was not Charles A. Lindbergh Jr.—then who was it? And how did it get there? A few writers have argued that the dead baby found in the woods had been stolen from a nearby orphanage, murdered, then abandoned along the Princeton-Hopewell Road. The reason: to clear the area of Lindbergh case searchers who were interfering with the illegal liquor traffic along this highway. But if this were true, the baby in the woods would have been killed after the kidnapping.

If the Mount Rose Heights corpse was someone else, and the Lindbergh baby was not murdered and dumped elsewhere, what became of him? Over the years, fourteen people in addition to Kenneth Kerwin have come forward claiming to be the kidnapped son of Charles and Anne Lindbergh. In addition to Kerwin, one of the most persistent and publicized claimants is a man named Harold Olson. Olson's story is as follows: In 1952, Harold Olson's adopted parents told him that Al Capone and his mob were behind the Lindbergh kidnapping, and that he was the Lindbergh child. The bootleggers who had kidnapped him took him to Escanaba, Michigan, where he was found in a sack in the bow of a fishing boat by Roy and Sarah Olson, the people who raised him as their own. Harold Olson, a computer supply salesman living in Hartford, Connecticut, says he has "twenty-one body identifications" that match baby Lindbergh and prove his true identity. Olson's prolonged effort to determine his identity is motivated, he says, not for money, but for peace of mind.[6]

In 1977, Olson and a fingerprint expert traveled to the New Jersey State Police Headquarters in West Trenton to examine the latent fingerprints taken off the Lindbergh baby's toys in 1932 by Dr. Erastus M. Hudson, the physician and private fingerprint expert. Dr. Hudson had processed the toys with a solution of silver nitrate to bring out the finger marks. His efforts resulted in thirteen latents, which were photographed. When Olson and his fingerprint man asked to look at these prints, they were told the latents could not be found. In 1985, after these prints were found among Governor Hoffman's papers, Harold Olson was invited back to New Jersey for a fingerprint examination. He did go back, and it turned out that the ink impressions of his fingerprints did not match any of the thirteen latents. Instead of accepting that he was not Charles A. Lindbergh Jr., Harold Olson insisted that the latents against which his prints had been compared were not the prints from the baby's toys.[7]

In 1988, Olson, appearing on a nationally syndicated television show, asked Mrs. Lindbergh to submit to a DNA test in order that he might establish, through DNA imprinting, that he is her son. Mrs. Lindbergh, then in her late eighties, and long reconciled to her son's death at the hands of Bruno Richard Hauptmann, did not, and, to this day, has not, subjected herself to such a test.[8] Olson agrees that his story is speculative and convoluted, and that the media has pretty much ignored him. "To me, for practical purposes, you could say the press is brain-dead about the Lindbergh case."[9]

There are many other theories about the facts of the Lindbergh baby. For example, Wayne Jones, a retired constable, and long-time Lindbergh buff and believer that Hauptmann was innocent and that the baby did not die, claims the Lindbergh baby was seen in Colombia, South America, by a detective and a priest who were subsequently assassinated. Jones has written a manuscript on the case *and* his theories about the crime but was unable to find a royalty-paying publisher willing to print it because, according to him, the book was just too hot to handle. (In 1998, Jones's 1,168-page book, *Murder of Justice — New Jersey's Greatest Shame,* was published by Vantage Press, a subsidy publisher.)

Beginning in 1976, following a period of thirty years in which the Lindbergh case was relatively dormant, the case exploded back into the public's consciousness with the publication of several books, six in all, that argue Bruno Richard Hauptmann's innocence. The historic case was made even more newsworthy by a series of lawsuits filed in the 1980s by Hauptmann's widow against the state of New Jersey and others. As a result of Mrs. Hauptmann's legal action against New Jersey, the Lindbergh case archives, under the supervision of New Jersey trooper Cornel D. Plebani, was opened on November 23, 1981. The Lindbergh data, consisting of more than 200,000 documents, 518 pieces of physical evidence, 300 court exhibits, and hundreds of photographs, all catalogued and indexed by thirty-five thousand name and subject cards (now all on computer), were housed in a large room on the lower level of the main administration building on the grounds of the New Jersey State Police Headquarters in West Trenton. It had taken the New Jersey State Police five years to sort through, arrange, and catalog this mountain of information. The New Jersey archives also contained material from the FBI and the New York City files on the case.

In February 1983, the prestigious American Academy of Forensic Sciences, at its Thirty-Fifth Annual Convention held that year in Cincinnati, Ohio, sponsored a plenary session entitled, "The Lindbergh Kidnapping Revisited: Forensic Science Then and Now." Presenting papers at this special session were seven experts in the fields of forensic pathology, law, questioned documents, forensic chemistry, criminal investigation, and criminal psychiatry. These experts had studied the Lindbergh case, and except for the quality of Dr. Mitchell's autopsy of the baby, they agreed that the Lindbergh investigation was a high watermark in the history of criminal investigation and forensic science.[10]

In the 1990s, people interested in the Lindbergh case could examine the documents and see the exhibits—the kidnap ladder, the ransom notes, the baby's sleeping suit, and so on—at the newly built New Jersey State Police Museum and Learning Center on the grounds of the State Police Headquarters in West Trenton. In addition to the Lindbergh case archives, visitors could view memorabilia depicting the history of the New Jersey State Police since its inception in 1921 under the leadership of H. Norman Schwarzkopf, the man who headed the investigation of the Lindbergh case.

Interest in the Lindbergh case remained high in the 1990s. The case was featured as an off-Broadway play, the trial was regularly reenacted in the Flemington Courthouse, interested groups sponsored Lindbergh case symposiums, professors offered college courses featuring the crime, a fan of the case started a newsletter and a Web site, and HBO, a cable TV broadcaster, produced a movie depicting the Hauptmanns as a romantic couple caught up in a web of perjury and fabricated evidence that resulted in the execution of an innocent man.

Anna Hauptmann died in 1994 at the age of ninety-five. The only Lindbergh case principal to outlive her was Mrs. Lindbergh. Mrs. Hauptmann had failed to officially exonerate her husband through her lawsuits but had played a major role in turning public opinion in favor of the notion that her husband, innocent of the crime, had been framed and wrongfully executed.

The Lindbergh case, then and now, has affected people in bizarre and tragic ways. It has attracted its share of oddballs, crackpots, and cranks, has caused otherwise normal people to do strange things, and continues to have a hold on millions. The crime itself, and its immediate aftermath, destroyed or shortened many lives. It put some people into prison, and others into mental institutions. Careers were made and lost, and some sixty-plus years after the most famous abduction in history, some people still suffer while others seek to exploit the crime of the century.

Part 2 The Theories

5 New Age Revisions

In 1976, *New York Newsday* reporter Anthony Scaduto published a book called *Scapegoat* in which he alleged that every piece of physical evidence against Hauptmann was fabricated or distorted and that all of the key prosecution witnesses took the stand and lied. Scaduto also recycled Burlington County detective Ellis Parker Sr.'s old claim that the Lindbergh baby hadn't been killed. Parker had pointed to the discrepancy in the length of the corpse found in the woods — 33 1/2 inches — "and the Lindbergh baby's height — 29" " — as published on his wanted poster. Scaduto took Detective Parker's idea one step further by suggesting that Harold Olson, the businessman from Hartford, Connecticut, might be the living Lindbergh son.[1]

On October 14, 1981, five years following the publication of Scaduto's book, San Francisco attorney Robert S. Bryan filed, on Mrs. Hauptmann's behalf, a $100 million lawsuit in which he asked the federal court to vacate Bruno Richard Hauptmann's 1935 murder conviction.

In deciding who to sue for this travesty of justice, Bryan left no stone unturned. He sued David T. Wilentz, the Lindbergh case prosecutor; former New Jersey State Police officers Lewis J. Bornmann, John B. Wallace, Joseph A. Wolf, and Hugo Stockburger; former New Jersey governor Brendan T. Byrne; New Jersey State Police superintendent Clinton J. Pagano; ex-FBI agent Thomas H. Sisk; and the Hearst Corporation, the money behind the defense attorney Edward J. Reilly. After filing the initial suit, Bryan followed up with four amended complaints, the last being filed on March 7, 1983.

Attorney Bryan was not new to the Lindbergh case. In the mid-1970s he was the lawyer who had brought the suit against Colonel Lindbergh's estate on behalf of Kenneth Kerwin, one of the men claiming to be the kidnapped but not murdered Lindbergh heir.

In the winter of 1982, public television aired a one-hour BBC film called *Who Killed the Lindbergh Baby?* Written and narrated by the British television personality and true-crime writer Ludovic Kennedy, this shameless piece of propaganda, cleverly disguised as a documentary, made a moving, if not factual, case for Hauptmann. This program, *Scapegoat* set to pictures and music, turned Mrs. Hauptmann into a made-for-TV victim, transformed her husband into a dead hero, and painted the men who had solved the Lindbergh crime and brought a murderer to justice as a bunch of malicious, headline-grabbing persecutors.

Attorney Bryan's lawsuit was dismissed in 1983. In throwing out the case, Federal judge Frederick B. Lacey wrote the following: "Plaintiff's allegations of conspiracy are deficient as conclusory and nonspecific." Bryan appealed Judge Lacey's decision and lost. He lost again when the United States Supreme Court denied his petition for further review.[2]

Ludovic Kennedy, in 1985, came out with his own vindication of Hauptmann in a book called *The Airman and the Carpenter.* Although Kennedy ridiculed the idea the Lindbergh baby had not been killed, he repeated Scaduto's general thesis of manufactured evidence and perjured testimony.[3] Like Scaduto, Kennedy had his way with the critics. The reviewer for the *New York Times Book Review* wrote, "One puts down 'The Airman and the Carpenter' troubled, and certain that what was billed as the trial of the century was an awful miscarriage of justice."[4] Even the conservative book critic for the *National Review* was taken in: "The jury convicted him, and he went expeditiously to the chair. But was he guilty? The answer seems to be almost certainly not."[5]

In 1985, shortly after Ludovic Kennedy's book came out, 23,000 Lindbergh case documents were discovered in a South Amboy, New Jersey, garage. These papers had been gathered by Governor Harold G. Hoffman, the politician who had gambled his political career on Hauptmann and had lost. The so-called Hoffman Papers consist of hundreds of documents from the investigative files of the New Jersey State Police and the reports, memos, and letters generated by a dozen or so of the private investigators who had worked on the case for the governor.

One of these investigators, George H. Foster, had volunteered his services in the hopes of getting a job with the New Jersey State Police after the governor fired H. Norman Schwarzkopf.[6] Although Governor Hoffman did fire Schwarzkopf, his own career was ruined, which meant that George H. Foster did not get on the force. Hoffman's reinvestigation of the Lindbergh case was a bust, but that didn't stop attorney Robert S. Bryan, fifty years later, from using the historically interesting but generally irrelevant and redundant Hoffman Papers to justify another lawsuit. This suit was dismissed in 1986 by federal judge Garrett E. Brown Jr., who wrote, "Mrs. Hauptmann's suit is based upon broad and conclusory allegations . . . with no attempt to tie those allegations to the 'evidence' contained in the recently discovered documents."[7]

In November 1987, Bryan appealed Judge Garrett E. Brown's dismissal of is federal suit, and the following month, in a newspaper interview, promised to reveal the identity of the real Lindbergh kidnapper. The Third Circuit Court of Appeals on July 7, 1988, turned down Bryan's appeal, thus ending eight years of legal grandstanding and repetitive suing. Just hours after the Federal Court of Appeals court in Philadelphia rejected Bryan's case, David T. Wilentz died in his sleep at his summer home in Long Branch, New Jersey. Although the ninety-three-year-old former attorney general had been a dominant figure in New Jersey's Democratic party for thirty years, he would be remembered as the man who had sent Bruno Richard Hauptmann to the electric chair.

Having exhausted his legal remedies, Robert S. Bryan turned to the New Jersey legislature, sending letters to the forty state senators and eighty assembly members, asking them for permission to appear before the legislature or its appropriate committee to plead Hauptmann's case. "I am prepared," he wrote, "to present credible evidence pertaining to the massive fraud spanning the entire spectrum of the case perpetrated by the New Jersey officials, which proves the unfairness of the trial and Mr. Hauptmann's lack of culpability." Bryan added that "newly discovered evidence unequivocally demonstrates Mr. Hauptmann was not involved in the crime and that a mistake of outrageous proportions occurred."[8] John F. Russo, the president of the New Jersey Senate, replied: "We're not a court of last resort. We will not get involved."[9]

Mrs. Hauptmann had lost in the courts, but she had won the hearts of the American people. She had won by staying alive into the 1980s, a time when ordinary citizens found it reasonable to believe that the New Jersey State Police, the FBI, and the New York City Police had joined forces to orchestrate a massive conspiracy of lies and fake evidence. Perhaps her less-zealous supporters would have been a bit skeptical had they known that to accomplish this frame-up, forty prosecution witnesses would have had to have committed perjury with the knowledge of at least two hundred others. As for the physical evidence, the prosecution had presented more than three hundred exhibits. If the police had tampered with or fabricated a large number of these items, someone would have spilled the beans. Moreover, it is a fact that faking physical evidence is easier said than done.

In May of 1990, Mrs. Hauptmann, in a letter to New Jersey governor Jim Florio, asked if they could meet to discuss some kind of formal recognition of her husband's innocence. The governor, with enough problems of his own, was not interested in hers. Refusing to take no for an answer, Bryan flew to New Jersey to hold another press conference in Trenton, across the street from the State Capitol. Mrs. Hauptmann, ninety-one and still fighting for her husband, was there with him. "She shouldn't have to beg like this," Bryan told reporters. Mrs. Hauptmann said she could not understand why Governor Florio was ignoring her. After all, Anthony Hopkins, the actor who had played Hauptmann in a made-for-TV docudrama, had written a letter to the governor. Having portrayed Hauptmann in the 1976 movie, the British actor was convinced of his innocence, and was adding his voice to the multitudes of concerned people who demanded a review of the case.[10]

Later that day, Governor Florio announced that he would talk to his attorney general about legal options in the case. He suggested that Mrs. Hauptmann write him another, more detailed letter, setting out exactly what she wanted from the state.[11]

Bryan, in October 1991, was back in New Jersey, this time in Flemington where a local theater group was reenacting the Hauptmann trial in the original courtroom. Although Mrs. Hauptmann was not up to seeing the performance, she did meet with reporters afterward at the Union Hotel, across the street from the Hunterdon County Courthouse.[12] Governor Florio had said that his attorney general was reviewing the material Bryan had sent him, but he could see no reason to meet with Mrs. Hauptmann. Mrs. Hauptmann, however, wanted to see the governor, and once again she begged for a meeting. The governor did not respond.

The following spring, Governor Florio announced through a spokesperson that the material Robert S. Bryan had sent failed to justify a reopening of the case.[13] It seemed that Florio was in no mood to follow in the footsteps of Massachusetts's governor Michael S. Dukakis who, on August 23, 1977, on "Sacco and Vanzetti Memorial Day," had issued a proclamation that the 1921 murder trial of Nicola Sacco and Bartolomeo Vanzetti had been "permeated with unfairness."

Robert S. Bryan was still telling reports he knew the identity of the real kidnapper, but, when pressed, said only that he believed the culprit was no longer alive.[14] Regarding his promise to unmask the true kidnapper, Bryan had a problem. He could name, for example, Isidor Fisch, everybody's favorite patsy. He could also finger John Condon, Betty Gow, Violet Sharpe, Paul Wendel—or even Al Capone. His problem was this: these people have all been fingerprinted, and their prints do not match the latents, identified by Bryan as the kidnapper's, on the ransom note. Bryan has painted himself into a corner.

Rebuffed by the governor's office (Bryan says "stonewalled") the so-called "F. Lee Bailey of the South" petitioned the New Jersey Parole Board in March of 1992 for a posthumous pardon. Bryan's request was denied.

After ten years of lawsuits, newspaper interviews, TV appearances, and press conferences with Mrs. Hauptmann at his side, people were starting to catch on to Robert S. Bryan. In September 1991, two of Mrs. Hauptmann's closest friends publicly criticized Bryan for using Mrs. Hauptmann to generate publicity for himself and his anti-death penalty coalition.[15] They also accused him of holding back the identity of the true kidnapper, saving that bombshell for a book, or lucrative movie deal.[16] Bryan said he was not writing a book, and reminded his critics that he had not charged Mrs. Hauptmann a dime for his services, and has incurred, on her behalf, expenses that have come out of his own pocket.

The second major television documentary on the Lindbergh case, produced by New Jersey Network and featuring narrator Edwin Newman, old film clips, and just about everybody who has ever had the slightest brush with the case, was aired in New Jersey in March of 1989. The producers of *Reliving the Lindbergh Case* had the opportunity, and perhaps the obligation, to make an honest attempt to present an accurate historical account of the crime, but they just could not resist Mrs. Hauptmann and her tale of woe, which resulted in one of those "you be the judge" programs.

The one-hour show was telecast nationally over PBS on October 17, 1989, just as the big earthquake hit San Francisco. A few months later it aired again in America and for the first time in Britain.

Fiction writers occasionally use celebrated crimes as a basis for their novels. Agatha Christie, for example, used the Lindbergh kidnapping as a plot device in her 1934 mystery, *Murder on the Orient Express*. In 1991, Max Allan Collins published a book called *Stolen Away: A Novel of the Lindbergh Kidnapping*.[17] Collins mixes historical happenings and real people with characters, dialogue, and events he has made up. His narrator-protagonist, a salty private eye named Nate Heller, has an affair with Evalyn McLean, the Washington, D.C. socialite who was bilked out of thousands by Gaston Means, the con man who said he was in a position to ransom back the Lindbergh baby. Heller gets his pal Colonel Lindbergh to admit privately that he lied under oath when he identified Hauptmann's voice as the one he had heard in the cemetery, repeatedly makes a fool out of Colonel Schwarzkopf, ridicules Hoover's FBI agents as a bunch of law school flunkies, and proves that Al Capone was the brains behind the kidnapping.

Perhaps an even worse problem are nonfiction books so unbelievable they ought to be classified as fiction. Such a book came out in 1993. Written by a small-town police chief from Goffstown, New Hampshire, and a lawyer from the same area, *Crime of the Century: The Lindbergh Kidnapping Hoax* advances the authors' belief that Colonel Lindbergh accidentally killed his son while carrying the baby down the homemade ladder as a practical joke on his wife.[18] Lindbergh buried his son in a shallow grave along the Princeton-Hopewell Road, where it was found ten weeks later. To cover his tracks, Lindbergh reported the baby as kidnapped. He then sat by quietly as Bruno Richard Hauptmann, a mere extortionist in the case, was tried, convicted, and executed for his son's murder.

The authors, Gregory Ahlgren and Stephen Monier, became interested in the case after Ahlgren had read the 1949 article by the well-known pulp writer of the time, Alan Hynd. The article, "Everyone Wanted to Get into the Act," a heavy-handed rehabilitation of Hauptmann and his dismal defense, coupled with Ellis Parker Sr.'s absurd theory that the Lindbergh baby was not dead, caused Ahlgren "concern," and "raised his suspicions."[19] Apparently Ahlgren did not know that in the 1930s Alan Hynd had written twenty or so articles for *True Detective Mysteries* in which he glorified the investigative work of the Lindbergh case crime busters. Hynd's entertaining, tongue-in-cheek piece convinced Ahlgren and Monier that something was terribly wrong in the Lindbergh case.[20] The irony becomes obvious: Alan Hynd, when he wrote "Everyone Wanted to Get into the Act," had clearly in mind people like the New Hampshire men.

In *American Heritage* magazine, journalist and historian Geoffrey C. Ward, referring to true-crime authors who come up with provocative new theories about old crimes, writes: "The presumption of innocence is carried a very long way by the reading public, at least when it comes to celebrated crimes. Despite the weight of the evidence against them, Lee Harvey Oswald, Sirhan Sirhan, and James Earl Ray all have their dogged defenders in print." According to Ward, the theory of the Lindbergh case presented by Ahlgren and Monier, a preposterous take on the case that ignores the most basic questions of the Lindberghs' character and motivation in order to titillate a new generation of uniformed readers, goes beyond the righting of an old purported wrong. Ward believes that Ahlgren and Monier, who are without one shred of evidence to support the notion that Colonel Lindbergh actually killed his own baby, have dishonored the dead and maligned the living. Ward reveals his contempt for *Crime of the Century* by noting that the authors cite the television shows *Geraldo* and *Hard Copy* in their bibliography.[21]

Pulp writer Alan Hynd would have admired a 1994 book called *Lindbergh, the Crime* by Noel Behn, a New York City novelist who retells the case, then, at the end of the book, suggests that the baby was murdered by Elisabeth Morrow, Anne Lindbergh's oldest sister. Behn, admitting that he has no evidence to prove or even sustain his theory, asserts that Elisabeth threw the child out the nursery window on Saturday, February 27, three days before Colonel Lindbergh and his lawyer Henry Breckinridge staged the kidnapping to cover up the murder. According to Behn, Elisabeth, insanely in love with Colonel Lindbergh, killed the child out of jealousy.[22] If this were true, then Colonel Lindbergh; his wife, Anne; Henry Breckinridge; and the three servants in the house at the time committed perjury at the Hauptmann trial.

Elisabeth Morrow, of course, never confessed to this crime, no one saw her commit it, and there is no physical evidence linking her in any way to the murder. The source of Behn's preposterous theory is a ninety-three-year-old man named Harry Green who had a brush with the case through Governor Harold G. Hoffman. Just before Green died, he told Behn that a chauffeur for the Morrows told him he suspected that Elisabeth may have had something to do with the baby's death. From this scrap of third- or fourth-hand information comes a 464-page book on the Lindbergh case.

Geoffrey C. Ward calls Behn's book ludicrous—and because it is well-written, published by a well-known New York publisher, and comes with blurbs from four highly regarded journalists—insidious. To illustrate the absurdity and irresponsibility of Behn's accusation, Ward writes:

> So far as anyone knows, Elisabeth Morrow was not even present at the Lindberghs' estate on the day in question. Nor, though both sisters were smitten by Lindbergh when they first met him, is there any indication that Elisabeth was seriously envious when her younger sister won his heart or bore his child. Meanwhile, scattered through the first three volumes of Anne Morrow Lindbergh's published letters and diaries, there is ample documentation of the sisters' deep affection for each other: when Elisabeth Morrow died of pneumonia at the age of thirty after a long series of crippling heart attacks, her grieving sister wrote that "life wasn't going to be worth much without her, as the world would be without sun or fire"—hardly the sentiments of a mother writing about someone who she knew had slaughtered her child. Nor, I think, could any reasonable person reading Mrs. Lindbergh's heartbreaking letters and diary excerpts after her child's disappearance and death entertain for a moment Behn's bizarre suggestion that they represent merely an after-the-fact attempt to "keep the fib intact," to make sure the record supports her husband's scenario and there are no slip-ups that could point to her sister.[23]

Mrs. Hauptmann made her final television appeal on January 10, 1992. She was featured, along with her attorney Robert S. Bryan, in a *Current Affair* segment called, "A Half-Century of Heartache."[24] Old, frail, and pathetic, she appeared on national television one last time as the victim-widow who had spent nearly sixty years trying to convince the world her husband was not a baby killer. Now she was making, out of sheer desperation, an incredible request. She wanted Mrs. Lindbergh, herself very old and frail, to set the record straight before it was too late. How Mrs. Lindbergh was to do this was not made clear, but the mere asking carried an unsavory, and unfounded, implication, the kind of thing that has been plaguing the Lindbergh family—the true victims of the crime—since the baby's murder. First it had been rumors that the Lindberghs had disposed of the child because he was somehow defective, then the crackpots claiming to be the Lindbergh baby could not understand why Mrs. Lindbergh would not submit to a DNA test so they could prove they were her sons, and now, sixty years after the crime, two guys from New Hampshire were saying that the Lindbergh baby had been killed by his father. If that was not bizarre enough, the wife of the real killer now wanted the dead baby's mother to help clear her husband's name.

"A Half-Century of Heartache" also featured scenes from a two-act play called *Hauptmann* that appeared at the Victory Gardens Theater in Chicago and was moving to New York. Written by John Logan, and starring Dennis O'Hare as Hauptmann, the play begins in prison just before Hauptmann's execution, flashes back to the crime, then moves to the trial in Flemington.[25] The trial is depicted as a circus, and the play is really about capital punishment and how innocent souls—like Hauptmann—can be executed.

In 1993, Mrs. Hauptmann continued her effort to clear her husband's name by asking New Jersey governor Christie Whitman to re-open the case. While waiting for the governor to respond, Mrs. Hauptmann, on October 10, 1994, died at the age of ninety-five. She had been living in an apartment in New Holland, Pennsylvania, a village in the center of Amish country, forty miles west of Philadelphia. She had moved to New Holland a few years earlier from Yeadon, Pennsylvania, in Delaware County in order to be closer to her son, Manfred, and his wife.

In 1941, five years after her husband's execution, Mrs. Hauptmann and Manfred moved from the Bronx to south Philadelphia, where Mrs. Hauptmann lived and worked until moving to Yeadon in 1959. Mrs. Hauptmann never remarried or changed her name. Her son, going by the name Fred Hauptmann, a former employee of the state, lived in Churchtown, Pennsylvania.[26] Fred Hauptmann, if he had an opinion regarding the guilt or innocence of his father, has kept it to himself or between himself and his mother. A private man, he has refused to comment publicly on this matter.

Mrs. Hauptmann did not live to see herself and her husband lovingly portrayed in a HBO movie called, *Crime of the Century: When Innocence Was Murdered Twice*. Aired for the first time on September 14, 1996, the film, based on Ludovic Kennedy's book, *The Airman and the Carpenter: The Lindbergh Kidnapping and the Framing of Richard Hauptmann*, and starring Isabella Rossellini as Anna Hauptmann and Stephen Rea as Bruno, is a portrait of marital love and devotion in the face of tribulation. The *Wall Street Journal* reported that shortly before the film aired, Isabella Rossellini told a *TV Guide* reporter that at first she had been tortured by the possibility that Hauptmann had actually been guilty of the kidnapping and murder of the Lindbergh baby. She felt she could only play Mrs. Hauptmann if she were totally convinced that Hauptmann was innocent. She changed her mind, however, when a fellow actor soothed her conscience by reminding her that her role as an actor was that of a storyteller, not a juror.[27] In other words, why let a little history get in the way of a good movie?

Over the years Mrs. Hauptmann did not have much luck with judges, criminal justice practitioners, criminalists, and forensic scientists who had given the case serious study. She did a lot better with TV hosts, book reviewers, and anti-capital punishment crusaders.

Alan M. Dershowitz, the celebrated defense attorney, recognizes how a celebrated case can be put to good purpose by campaigners against capital punishment. In his introduction to a 1989 reprint of Sidney B. Whipple's 1937 book, *The Trial of Bruno Richard Hauptmann*, Dershowitz writes:

> Indeed, one of the most powerful arguments offered by opponents of the death penalty is the assertion that innocent defendants—some say a few, others claim many—have been executed for crimes committed by others.
>
> The execution of Bruno Richard Hauptmann on April 3, 1936, is frequently cited as an instance of the capital punishment of an innocent defendant.[28]

It is probably not a coincidence that people opposed to capital punishment believe a lot of innocent defendants—including famous ones like Hauptmann—have been executed. Of course there is no way to disprove this proposition, but that does not make it true. The evidence presented in this book, however, clearly shows that the guilty man in this case was justly convicted. It comes down to what one wants to believe.

6 How Many Conspirators Does It Take to Steal a Baby?

Presidential assassinations and ransom kidnappings, where the victims are famous and powerful, are usually committed by one man, acting on his own behalf, for reasons no rational person can understand.[1] Geoffrey C. Ward, in writing about the John F. Kennedy assassination, makes the following point: "The country had been traumatized by the assassination, then robbed of the emotional catharsis the accused assassin's trial could have provided. Such profoundly unsettling events demanded a more sweeping explanation, a criminal conspiracy equal to the enormity of the crime."[2]

Gerald Posner, the author of *Case Closed: Lee Harvey Oswald and the Assassination of John F. Kennedy,* a book that re-establishes Oswald as the lone Kennedy killer acting on his own, observed that, "The notion that a misguided sociopath had wreaked such havoc made the crime seem senseless and devoid of political significance. By concluding that JFK was killed as the result of an elaborate plot, there is the relief he died for a purpose, that a powerful group eliminated him for some critical issue."[3] Likewise, in the Lindbergh case, people find it difficult to believe that an illegal alien with a homemade ladder and a crudely written ransom note could snatch and murder America's most famous baby then extort fifty thousand dollars from his father. Geoffrey C. Ward, although referring to the Kennedy assassination, makes a point that also applies to the Lindbergh case when he writes: "The truly frightening thing about what happened . . . is not the notion that vast murky forces somehow rule our lives, but that not even the greatest among us is safe when madness and sheer chance happen to converge."[4]

A lone-wolf kidnapping of the Lindbergh baby is perhaps a more frightening scenario than one man shooting President Kennedy. When a politician is elected president of the United States, he knowingly becomes a target for the likes of Oswald. Moreover, President Kennedy was not murdered in the White House, but in public, where the risk of death at the hands of an assassin is significantly greater. In the Lindbergh crime, the baby was snatched from his crib under the noses of his parents, the butler, cook, and his nursemaid. If the son of the most beloved hero in the world can be taken from his nursery by a stranger who got into the house by climbing up a ladder, then no one is safe anywhere. That does not go down easy.

The Kennedy assassination is the subject of some five hundred books, of which all but a few take exception to the theory that one man could fire a bolt-action rifle three times, hitting the president twice, as he rode past the Texas Book Depository in the back seat of a convertible. If the idea of a lone wolf does not seem right in the Kennedy assassination, it seems even less probable in the Lindbergh case. Could one man, a complete stranger who had never been in the Lindbergh house, have climbed into the nursery without alerting the dog, grab the baby who did not cry out, leave a ransom note, shut the window, climb down the ladder, then carry the baby and the ladder seventy-five feet to a waiting car? Could this same man have killed the baby, written the ransom letters that followed the nursery note, mailed Colonel Lindbergh the child's sleeping suit, met face to face with John F. Condon, and walked off with the ransom money after handing Condon the "Boad Nelly" note in St. Raymond's Cemetery? And could such a daring, clever criminal turn out to be an obscure, unemployed carpenter who had come to America as a penniless stowaway? Most people who have an opinion on the Lindbergh case say "no" to both questions. Almost everyone, regardless of their views on Hauptmann, believe the Lindbergh kidnapping and murder was not the work of one man.

If there is physical evidence in support of the theory that more than one person kidnapped the Lindbergh baby, it is the footprints mentioned in the initial crime scene report by New Jersey state trooper Joseph A. Wolf. In his report, dated March 1, 1932, Corporal Wolf wrote, "The ground on the east side of the house was muddy and showed the imprints of the base of the ladder when placed against the wall also apparently two sets of fresh footprints leading off in a southeast direction."[5]

Trooper Wolf was the third police officer to arrive at the Lindbergh estate that night. He had been preceded by two local officers from the village of Hopewell. It is interesting to note that Corporal Wolf does not describe seeing any footwear impressions leading to the house from the southeast, begging the question as to how the kidnappers walked to the house without leaving any prints. When Wolf testified at Hauptmann's trial, he spoke of only two prints—a man's shoe impression under the nursery window and a smaller impression, believed to have been made by a woman's shoe, a few feet back from the house, pointing toward the structure. In his trial testimony, Corporal Wolf does not mention the two sets of prints he had referred to in his initial report.[6] This apparent contradiction was not brought to his attention on cross-examination by Edward J. Reilly. According to a 407-page FBI report dated February 16, 1934, Colonel Lindbergh, on the morning after the crime, asked a local hunter and tracker named Oscar Bush to examine the crime scene foot impressions. According to this report, Bush identified the woman's footprint as being made by Mrs. Lindbergh, who had walked about the house on the afternoon of the crime. He concluded that the larger footprints had been left by two different people, both wearing burlap bags tied over their shoes.[7] According to true-crime writer Alan Hynd, however, in a December 1932 article in *True Detective Mysteries,* Oscar Bush was helped by tracker Jim Wyckoff. Both men, according to Hynd, concluded that four sets of prints—two leading to the house and two leading away—were made by the same man who had made two round trips to the house from his car, on Featherbed Lane.[8]

Alan Hynd, of course, had not been to the crime scene, and he did not have access to Corporal Wolf's initial report. The FBI Summary Report was not based on direct knowledge of the crime scene, and neither Oscar Bush nor Jim Wyckoff testified at a preliminary hearing or the trial. In a report filed on March 13, 1932, by New Jersey trooper Lewis J. Bornmann, the officer noted that he had questioned Oscar Bush. Trooper Bornmann wrote the following:

> Found him living in an old hotel bordering on the Raritan Canal in a section known as Princeton Basin, Windsor Township, with a woman named Mrs. Mildred Kugler who, he stated, worked for him. Living conditions were found to be very bad. Questioned him as to his whereabouts on the night of March 1st. . . . He had known nothing of the kidnapping until he had been informed of it early the next morning by his uncle, Jim Wyckoff, who lives with him, that he was wanted as a guide to assist in searching the vicinity surrounding

the Lindbergh estate. He had immediately proceeded to Lindbergh's home with his uncle and had aided in searching the surrounding mountains.[9]

When Trooper Bornmann wrote this report, it was assumed by the police that the Lindbergh baby had been kidnapped by some kind of gang; therefore, the absence of any reference to Bush's identification of crime scene footprints is noteworthy.

In an article written eight months before Hauptmann's arrest, a writer for the *North American Review* outlined his theory of the crime, a view that simply assumed the existence of two sets of footprints:

> The foot-prints outside showed that there were two kidnappers and that one of them was either a boy or a woman. There were two reasons for employing a person of less size than a fully grown man. First, the ladder, in three pieces, was not too sturdy. Secondly, the window was narrow. Of the child's fate, (a bashed head from being dropped) it is not difficult, therefore, to suggest an explanation. Standing on an insecure ladder, in close proximity to Lindbergh's study window, a boy or woman—losing nerve—might have easily dropped the infant. . . .
>
> [T]he foot-prints were traced in a kind of horseshoe trail around the dwelling—always in full view of the windows, had there been light—and across a dirt road into the woods. Apparently one kidnapper went ahead, finding a path, possibly with a flashlight. The other whose steps were better aligned, followed.[10]

There is no crime scene document, photograph, plaster cast, or courtroom testimony in support of this writer's or Alan Hynd's theory of the crime. Aside from Corporal Wolf's observation of "apparently two sets of fresh footprints leading off in a southeast direction," impressions that may, or may not, have had any connection to the abduction, there is no documented physical proof that more than one kidnapper had walked up to the Lindbergh house that night.

Anthony Scaduto, the author of *Scapegoat: The Lonesome Death of Bruno Richard Hauptmann*, interprets this absence of physical clues as further proof that the Hauptmann prosecution destroyed or suppressed evidence. He writes as follows:

> Although I have been unable to find any report about casts of all these footprints leading away from the nursery window, it seems highly unlikely that

Wolf would have assigned several troopers to guard the footprints so that they "could not be destroyed," and then destroy them without taking impressions. One might assume casts were made, or at least careful measurements taken. That was never introduced at Hauptmann's trial. The only inference to be drawn is that it was not produced because it was detrimental to Wilentz's case.[11]

That, of course, is not the only inference to be drawn from this circumstance, and it seems more than a little ingenuous of Scaduto, a bitter critic of the Lindbergh case investigators, to selectively assume that when it came to preserving the footprint evidence, the crime scene troopers had performed up to par.

Although it has become generally accepted that crime scene footprint evidence clearly establishes the participation of two or more kidnappers, it is more accurate to say that there may have been footprints, prints belonging to one or two men, but there is no solid evidence suggesting that these impressions had anything to do with the crime. The shoe print evidence, if you can call it evidence, is therefore inconclusive.

Conspiracy buffs point to other facts suggesting multiple kidnappers, but this evidence is even less probative than the crime scene footwear impressions. For example, John F. Condon, the loose-talking ransom intermediary who became a Lindbergh case celebrity, public speaker, best-selling author, and, eventually, a kidnapping suspect, has been the mother lode for conspiracy theorists. This is not surprising because Condon himself believed, at least initially, that "Cemetery John" was a member of a kidnap gang. He told the FBI, and anyone who would listen, of a shadowy second man he had seen at Woodlawn Cemetery the first night he negotiated with "Cemetery John." Later, the night Condon handed over the ransom money at St. Raymond's Cemetery, there was again talk of another mysterious man who might have been a lookout.[12] Nothing developed from this, no cemetery accomplice was ever identified. Today, Condon's so-called cemetery sightings are what they were in 1932—the fanciful conjecture of a man with an active imagination and an addiction to the limelight.

In the midst of the ransom negotiations, Condon said he received a telephone call from the kidnapper who was responding to one of Colonel Lindbergh's ads in the *New York American*. The man, speaking with a German accent, asked, "Did you gottit my letter with the sing-nature?"

Condon replied that he had then asked, "Where are you calling from?"

"Westchester," the caller replied. "Doctor Condon, do you write sometimes for the papers?"

Condon said that he then heard the caller speaking to someone else: "He says sometimes he writes pieces for the papers," the caller said in a muffled voice. Now, speaking directly into the phone, the caller instructed Condon to be at home every night for the next week. "Stay at home from six to twelve. You will receive a note with instructions. Act accordingly or all will be off."

Condon promised the caller he would stay home and wait for the note with the instructions. Before he hung up, he heard a voice that was not the caller's. "*Statti citto!*" a woman's voice shouted. Condon understood this as Italian for shut up. "All right," the caller said, "You will hear from us." He then hung up.[13] Assuming that Condon, the only witness to this conversation, was not making all of this up, the question remains: Was the woman in the background and the person or persons she was telling to shut up, a gang of Lindbergh kidnappers? Is it not more reasonable to assume that the kidnapper—"Cemetery John"—was calling from a public place such as an Italian restaurant and the voice in the background was a waitress, or perhaps the owner? (Hauptmann did not own a telephone.)

It also seems logical to assume that the kidnapper was attempting to make Condon believe there were others involved—an impression also given by the writer of the ransom notes. To characterize Condon's account of this telephone call as proof of a conspiracy is stretching the evidence.

According to Condon, he had a second encounter with an Italian woman, this one more direct. On Saturday, March 19, eight days after the phone call, a lady approached him at a Harts Island charity bazaar. "Cemetery John" had not responded to Colonel Lindbergh's most recent newspaper ads, and there was concern that contact with the kidnappers had been lost. The woman came up to Condon and said, "Nothing can be done until the excitement is over. There is too much publicity. Meet me at the depot at Tuckahoe, Wednesday at five in the afternoon. I will have a message for you."[14]

As Condon tells the story, he watched this woman walk away—across Webster Avenue toward the Third Avenue elevated line. She climbed the stairs and disappeared into the station. Condon did not ask this woman to identify herself and he did not try to follow her. The following Saturday he showed up at the Tuckahoe depot at the appointed time, but the woman did not.[15] One more mystery in the Lindbergh case, another loose-end the police were unable to tie-up—one more scrap of evidence for the conspiracy buffs.

John F. Condon, reportedly a pompous, self-righteous ex-school teacher with an oversized ego, was a great teller of stories, mostly about himself. Lindbergh conspiracy theorists point out, quite correctly, that Dr. Condon was not a credible person. They claim he lied to the police, lied to Colonel Lindbergh, and lied in court under oath. How convenient then, that amid all this lying, the old man was telling the truth about his mysterious, and quite dramatic, encounter with the Italian woman at the charity bazaar.

If it could be proven that more than one person had written the ransom notes, the conspiracy buffs would have the physical evidence they so desperately need. The fact that the world's best handwriting experts opined that one person had written all of the ransom notes is a hurdle that is difficult to clear.

Author Noel Behn, in search of a handwriting expert to support his theory that Elisabeth Morrow murdered the Lindbergh baby, found a private investigator named Jesse William Pelletreau. It was Pelletreau who determined that the person who had written the nursery note had not written the ransom letters that followed. It obviously does not matter to Behn that Pelletreau, one of Governor Hoffman's private eyes, was not a forensic documents examiner and, therefore, unqualified to make such a judgment. Writer Anthony Scaduto found the notorious courtroom charlatan, Albert Hamilton to bolster his theory that Hauptmann was innocent. Hamilton asserted that a man named Manning Strawl (actually, his name was Strewl) had written the ransom notes. It apparently did not bother Scaduto that the idea of Strewl writing the notes does not fit with his thesis that Paul H. Wendel, the lawyer who had confessed to Ellis Parker Sr., had kidnapped the baby.

Perhaps Scaduto and Behn would have been better served by a man named W. W. Williams, a teacher of penmanship from Portland, Oregon. Three weeks before Hauptmann's arrest, Williams wrote to John F. Tyrrell, the well-known documents examiner from Milwaukee. Williams told Tyrrell that he was in possession of samples of the handwriting of the woman who had written all of the ransom notes. Without identifying this person by name, Williams sent samples of her handwriting to Tyrrell. After comparing these samples against the ransom note writings, Tyrrell informed Williams that his suspect was not the writer of the extortion notes. In June 1935, four months following Hauptmann's conviction, Williams paid Tyrrell a visit at his office in Milwaukee, at which time Tyrrell, using his Hauptmann trial handwriting exhibits, showed Williams why he believed Hauptmann had written the notes. Two weeks later, Tyrrell received word that Williams was lecturing on the Lindbergh case, telling his audiences that the prosecution's handwriting experts were wrong about Hauptmann and that the true ransom note writer was a woman he still refused to identify.

Although Williams laid claim to a thirty-year career as a handwriting expert who had testified hundreds of time in court, Tyrrell had never heard of the man prior to Williams's letter to him.[16] When asked if he knew of Williams, Albert S. Osborn, the most famous documents examiner in the world, said that he did not.

Following Hauptmann's execution in 1936, Williams published a sixty-six-page booklet called, *The Lindbergh Case.* In this strange, self-published work laced with word charts, bizarre-looking diagrams, and accounts of other handwriting cases going all the way back to the turn-of-the-century Dreyfus Affair, Williams states that the ransom letters were not written by Hauptmann, or even a German. He also argues that more than one person, including a female, had drafted the ransom notes as well as the address on the sleeping-suit package sent by the kidnapper to John F. Condon. In his booklet, Williams devotes one sentence to his mystery female ransom note writer: "The reader could not fail to see the shadow of a woman in the ransom notes as well as in all documents presented." He is quite specific, however, about John F. Condon, whom he accuses of writing the J. J. Faulkner deposit slip and, along with the woman, the ransom notes.

Who is this female kidnap accomplice? According to Williams, it is the Italian woman who spoke to Condon at the charity bazaar.[17]

During the thirty months between the kidnapping and Hauptmann's arrest, dozens of conspiracy theories took root and became a permanent part of the Lindbergh legacy. Denied a credible suspect for so long, the public criticized the police, read fiction passed off as news, and let their imaginations explore the possibilities. Most of these homegrown theories, conspiracies that reflect tastes in fiction more than reality, are still alive in the minds of people who remember where they were and what they were doing when they heard the baby was snatched from his crib.

On the morning of September 19, 1934, the New York City Police, accompanied by FBI agents and detectives from the New Jersey State Police, arrested Hauptmann as he drove his 1930 Dodge toward Manhattan from his home in the Bronx. The following day, when the world learned of the unemployed German carpenter, arrested in possession of a twenty-dollar ransom bill, the case suddenly came into sharper focus. A reporter for *News-Week Magazine*, ten days after Hauptmann's arrest, described all the guessing that had gone on before Hauptmann:

> Over breakfast tables and bootleg liquor, the United States speculated and gossiped. Everyone had his own fantastic theory. Betty Gow, his nurse, stole him. The child was a deaf-mute, and the Lindberghs got rid of him themselves. Elizabeth [*sic*] Morrow, jealous of her sister's marriage to Lindbergh, was the murderer. An insane relative of the Morrows was guilty. Violet Sharpe, the Morrow's maid who committed suicide did it. Japanese killed the child to distract attention from their invasion of China.[18]

The possibility of a Japanese connection was the subject of a long, detailed article about the case in *Astrological Forecast*. The piece begins this way:

> If you ever happen into a newspaper morgue and you chance to glance at the front pages of February 1932, you will find screaming headlines telling of the more than brutal attack of the Japanese on the city of Shanghai. We didn't have so many wars to think about in those days, and the American people were aroused. On March 2nd, and the days thereafter, however, you couldn't find anything about the Sino-Japanese war even on the inside of a newspaper. This writer was particularly interested in the Japanese affair at the time, but had to give up that interest and accept the Lindbergh mystery. . . . If a foreign nation or any other great power wanted to take attention off what it was doing, why not pull a crime that would be so great a news story that it would take everything else off the front page? And what bigger news story could there possibly be than the kidnapping of Charles Lindbergh's baby? That was before Lindbergh's fame had begun to wane. That was before *Time Magazine* had branded him an ex-hero. He was still the idolized dream boy of the American public.[19]

At first the Lindberghs feared, and in one sense hoped, that organized criminals had kidnapped their baby. Their thinking was this: professional kidnappers—racketeers—had taken the child for the money and would return the baby when the ransom was paid. Professionals would not harm the child because they were smart enough to know the consequences of such an act. It would be worse than killing a cop. If, on the other hand, a one amateur had slipped into the house and taken the child, a sociopath driven by anger, revenge, and, perhaps, sex, the chances of the baby's survival were slim.

A careful, objective reading of the ransom letters reveals that the baby was not in the hands of professional extortionists. The letters themselves revealed the awful truth from the beginning. Take, for example, the letter received by the Lindberghs on March 5, 1932, their first communication from the kidnapper since the note left in the nursery:

> Dear Sir: We have warned you note to make
> andying Public also notify the Police
> now you have to take the consequences. ths
> means we will holt the baby untill everyding
> is quiet. We can note make any appointment
> just now. We know very well what it
> means to us. It is rely necessary to
> make a world affair out off this, or to
> get yours baby back as sun as possible.
> To settle those affair in a quick way
> will better for both seits. Dont by
> afraid about the baby two ladys
> keeping car it its day and night.
> She also will fed him
> according to the diet.   (SYMBOL)
>   Singtuere on
>   all letters

On the reverse side:

> We are interested to send him back in
> gut health. ouer ransom was made aus
> for 50000 $ but now we have to take
> another person to it and probable have
> to keep the baby for a longer time as we

expected So the amount will by 70,000 $
20,000 in 50 $ bills 25,000 $ in 20 $ bills
15000 $ in 10 $ bills and 10,000 $ in 5 $ bills.
dont mark any bills. or tacke them
from one serial nonmer. We will
inform you latter were to deliver hte
mony. but we will note to so
until the Police is out of the case
and the Pappers are quiet.

    The Kidnaping was preparet
    for yeahs. so we are preparet
    for everyding

(THREE HOLES)

This letter, obviously intended to convince the Lindberghs that a gang
of professionals had carefully orchestrated the abduction, people who were,
in fact, caring for the child, reflects a naiveté that reveals just the opposite.
No experienced extortionist would expect Colonel Lindbergh not to notify the police, not to make a "world affair" out of the abduction of his child,
and not to record the serial numbers of the ransom bills. Only an amateur
would apologize for raising the ransom demand twenty thousand dollars,
use such a silly excuse for doing it, then expect the money to be raised and
paid within two to four days. Even more ominous were the repeated as-
surances that the baby was alive and well, a sure sign that the baby was
dead, and that the kidnapper was worried the Lindberghs would figure this
out and not pay the ransom. Had the Lindbergh baby been taken by professionals, the ransom letters would have been filled with threats to kill the
child if the ransom was not paid.

Perhaps the ransom letters themselves comprise the most solid and convincing evidence that the child had been abducted and murdered by a lone,
desperate man, a sociopath with limited intelligence, imagination and
perspective—a man like Bruno Richard Hauptmann.

Up until the baby was found dead in the woods, the Lindberghs, and even
the police, allowed themselves the luxury of suspecting mobsters rather than
a monster. Colonel Lindbergh, over the objections of Colonel H. Norman
Schwarzkopf of the New Jersey State Police, went so far as to hire three
low-level New York City hoods—Mickey Rosner, Irving Bitz, and Salvatore

Spitale, to make contact with the kidnappers. Bringing these characters into the inner circle of the investigation was a terrible mistake, and turned out be a major embarrassment. (Bitz went to jail in 1934 for jumping bail, and in 1939 Spitale was convicted of grand larceny.) It was a mistake allowing these racketeers access to the nursery note. This access gave rise to speculation that copies of the note were taken to New York City and circulated among criminals. This in turn has opened the possibility that someone other than the nursery note writer, having forged the kidnapper's handwriting and copied the ransom symbol, wrote the subsequent extortion letters. Anthony Scaduto found this theory quite useful, but when he looked around for evidence to support it, had to settle for the concurring opinion of pulp writer Alan Hynd.[20] Al Capone and his operatives came under suspicion (Capone, in jail at the time, asked to be let out so he could get the baby back for the Lindberghs), as did members of the Purple Gang in Detroit, and several hoodlums in New Jersey.

Not all of the gang theories involved racketeers. There was speculation that a gang of escaped mental patients had grabbed the baby. No one could come up with a motive, but when dealing with nuts, who needs one? Another theory: a group of local farmers had kidnapped the child hoping that this would encourage the Lindberghs to move out of the area. According to an early New Jersey State Police report: "They [the local farmers] are not gifted with what is regarded as normal intellect. But, they have the type of mind which would assume that, if the Lindbergh baby was kidnapped, the Lindberghs would move away from the Sourland district."[21] If this had been the farmers' plan, it certainly worked because the Lindberghs did not return to Hopewell after the kidnapping. Of course it is hard to imagine a group of farmers getting together to plot the kidnapping and murder of the Lindbergh baby, simply as a means of getting an unwanted neighbor to move. It may be true that some of the local residents had reason not to want the Lindberghs in the area, but that is hardly a motive for conspiracy, kidnapping and murder. At least not in the real world.

Gerald Posner, in *Case Closed,* the book on the John F. Kennedy assassination, notes that "as in every famous case, people have come out of the woodwork for their fifteen minutes of fame."[22] In the Lindbergh case, the publicity seekers can be placed into several categories. There were politicians,[23] people wanting to help the Lindberghs,[24] hoaxers who wanted to be heroes,[25] false confessors,[26] cops and private investigators seeking advancements,[27] false eyewitnesses,[28] phony experts,[29] and people offering fantastic stories to the police.[30] These folks were either crazy, dishonest, greedy, professionally ambitious, phony, unemployed, or bored, and many of them, including John F. Condon, Gaston Means, and John H. Curtis, are considered suspects by many Hauptmann defenders and conspiracy buffs.[31]

In September of 1933, a year before Hauptmann's arrest, an inmate of the Ohio State Penitentiary at Columbus named George Michael Paulin, a.k.a. George Paul, told warden Preston E. Thomas that four months prior to the Lindbergh kidnapping he had received an encoded message on a postcard telling of the kidnapper's intent to steal the Lindbergh baby. Paulin was taken to New Jersey and questioned by Colonel Schwarzkopf's detectives. Paulin also led New Jersey troopers on a wild-goose chase around New Brunswick and Perth Amboy, where he hoped to find and identify the writer of the postcard that he no longer possessed.[32] The fact the New Jersey State Police expended this much time and effort on Paulin and his story reveals how desperate they were for solid leads in 1933.

A few days following Hauptmann's arrest, George Michael Paulin was still behind bars and still trying to get a piece of the Lindbergh limelight. This time he was telling reporters that the communication he had received back in September of 1933 was signed "B. H." Later he amended that to "Bruno."[33] Paulin's new information, obviously tailored to fit the arrest of Hauptmann, would have been ignored but for the fact that J. Edgar Hoover, having heard of it for the first time, complained to the press that the New Jersey State Police had kept Paulin's story from the FBI, further proof that they had not been cooperating with his agents. Hoover told reporters he had ordered the agent in charge of his Cincinnati office to look into the matter.[34] Hoover's field agents, in fact, had known of George Paulin, but to say so would have contradicted the director, something never done in Hoover's FBI. George Paulin, of course, meant nothing to Hoover other than an opportunity to take a crack at his rival, Colonel H. Norman Schwarzkopf, and to get a little publicity along the way.

George Paulin's name does not appear in any of the books on the Lindbergh case. That is not because his story is phony and full of holes, but because the only person he implicates in the kidnapping is Bruno Richard Hauptmann. Had George Paulin said that the kidnapper's message had been signed, "Jafsie," Isidor Fisch, J. J. Faulkner, Paul H. Wendel, or Betty Gow,

Hauptmann's defenders and the conspiracy people would have cited J. Edgar Hoover 's criticism of Schwarzkopf as further proof of a New Jersey State Police cover-up. In the world of bogus revisionism, that is how it is done.

Joyce Milton, the author of *Loss of Eden,* a dual biography of Anne and Charles Lindbergh, devotes six chapters of her book to the Lindbergh kidnapping.[35] Although she does not question Hauptmann's guilt, she is open to the possibility that he did not commit the crime alone. "Still it is difficult," she writes, "to imagine that Hauptmann, who even had Albert Deibisch along on his honeymoon, undertook to kidnap the Lindbergh baby alone."[36] (Albert Deibisch had known Hauptmann in Germany and ran a coffee shop on Lexington Avenue. He and Hauptmann were friends.) The fact that Hauptmann had taken a friend along on his honeymoon, if proof of anything, says more about his relationship with his wife than his criminal method of operation. Milton shies away from the standard inside-job conspiracies but does believe that Isidor Fisch helped Hauptmann launder some of the ransom money. She also theorizes that Fisch, knowing that Hauptmann was in the country illegally, was trying to blackmail him.[37]

Relying on a twelve-page statement given to the FBI by a Massachusetts prison inmate, Milton theorizes that Hauptmann tried to have Isidor Fisch murdered.[38] This statement, by a criminal named J. R. Russell, was taken three weeks after Hauptmann's arrest and in summary goes as follows:

> In the summer of 1926, Hauptmann, while working on a construction project in Buffalo, New York, met J. R. Russell in a local restaurant. After they had become friends, Hauptmann tried to talk Russell into kidnapping a wealthy Buffalo jeweler then robbing a bank in Batavia, New York. Three years later Russell ran into Hauptmann at a construction site in Vermont. Hauptmann gave Russell a revolver as collateral for a ten dollar loan. Russell was later caught with the gun and was packed off to jail. About a year later Hauptmann showed up driving a blue Nash or Buick and drove Russell to Maine. Along the way they picked up Isidor Fisch. At some point during this trip Hauptmann offered Russell $500 and a handgun in return for the killing of Fisch. Russell resisted, but Hauptmann persisted. In the end, Hauptmann, unable to talk Russell into the murder, gave up.[39]

The Russell statement makes interesting reading and puts Hauptmann in a very bad light. It is therefore no surprise that Russell's name does not appear in the writings of Scaduto and Ludovic Kennedy. But is it true? Probably not. Russell, given his background and the fact he was in jail at the time of his statement, is a questionable source at best. More important, his story does not check out. There is no evidence, for example, that Hauptmann and Fisch were ever in Maine together. There is no record of Hauptmann having worked in Buffalo, New York, or in Vermont. Moreover, Hauptmann never owned a Nash or a Buick. Had the FBI been able to check out Russell's statement, he would have been a government witness at Hauptmann's trial. And finally, if Hauptmann wanted Isidor Fisch dead, why didn't he do it himself? Anyone who can kill a twenty-month-old baby in cold blood for the money could knock off a guy like Isidor Fisch.

Conspiracy theories are fun, and, for some writers, profitable. But are they true? Without solid evidence to support them, they are nothing more than fiction passed off as history. How many kidnappers does it take to steal and murder a baby? Just one.

7 Father Kallok: The Forgotten Story

Putting together a phony conspiracy theory requires a certain kind of tunnel vision. The author must carefully avoid the evidence that does not fit, and the more outrageous the theory, the more there is to ignore. Hauptmann's defenders, by denying his guilt, have limited themselves to conspiracies that do not involve him. This is a shame because there are several good ones that have not been harvested. One such conspiracy features a Slovak-Catholic priest named Michael J. Kallok. Normally, one would take the word of a priest quite seriously, but in the Lindbergh case, there have been men of the cloth who made fools of themselves, got sent to prison, and were defrocked.[1] Not even men of God have been able to resist the mind-bending pull of the Lindbergh case. Father Kallok, however, whether he is to be believed or not, was not crazy, was not a fool, and was not motivated by publicity.

Three months before Hauptmann died in the New Jersey electric chair, Governor Harold G. Hoffman received a letter signed "Just Another Republican. J D." Dated January 2, 1936, the letter, from Milwaukee, Wisconsin, read:

> My dear Governor:
>
> In your anxiety to have persons interview Bruno Richard Hauptmann in the Death House you have overlooked one very important one, the Rev. Michael J. Kallok of St. Jos. Church of Cudahy, Wis. [a suburb of Milwaukee] who gave his statement to the proper authorities and to the press and his statements were largely published.
>
> Have you never hear of him? There is sensational evidence if you want it!
>
> Rev. Kallok lived in the East and knew Hauptmann well enough to call him

"Bruno." Rev. Kallok can tell you how familiar Bruno Hauptmann was with the Lindbergh estate in Hopewell. You should by all means hear his story.

Later Rev. Kallok came to Cudahy to live. For reasons we can all understand the Rev. said nothing until Mrs. Hauptmann came here to extort money from the German people in Milwaukee and to stir up the "Nazi" spirit of revenge. However, our German people of Milwaukee are not that type and they gave Mrs. Hauptmann a very cold shoulder and nothing but riffraff attended her talks.

After that Rev. Kallok told his story. Mrs. Hauptmann's consummate gall was too much for the Father. I an [sic] not Catholic but I believe what he said.

The Rev. Kallok should have the privilege of facing Bruno Hauptmann in the Death House.[2]

Three weeks after the letter to Governor Hoffman, the writer sent letters to J. Edgar Hoover, New Jersey attorney general David T. Wilentz, and Colonel H. Norman Schwarzkopf, head of the New Jersey State Police. The sender enclosed, in each submission, the letter he had written to the governor. Signing his letters "J D," the writer wrote the following to Attorney General Wilentz: "To date I've heard nothing of Governor Hoffman using the information sent him regarding Rev. Kallok. Had Gov. Hoffman not interfered with justice there would have been no need for me to pass this information along."

In J. Edgar Hoover's letter, the writer, signing it "A layman, J D," said:

Surely in the name of justice and for the protection of women and children and future observance of law in these United States, Gov. Hoffman should be willing to make every effort to secure evidence for conviction as well as proof of Hauptmann's innocence. . . .

The Lindbergh kidnapping was one of the most heinous crimes ever committed and the American people are getting fed up to the neck with the manner in which the case is being handled. No one can honestly say Bruno Hauptmann did not have a fair trial. He was caught red handed with evidence enough to convict any man and has never given any sane explanation. Any man who would commit such a heinous crime naturally would be afraid to die, hence the loud protestations of innocence. Hauptmann's story, likewise his wife's, is too thin to believe.

Colonel Schwarzkopf's letter, signed, "From one deeply interested in justice. J D," the longest and most interesting of the three, begins: "So it's *your* hide the Dear Gov. is after. Well, well!"

After praising Colonel Schwarzkopf for his work on the case and paying tribute to John F. Tyrrell, the handwriting expert from Milwaukee, and Arthur Koehler, the Madison, Wisconsin, wood expert whose testimony hung the kidnap ladder around Hauptmann's neck, J D writes:

I read in the paper that Mrs. Bruno Hauptmann had threatened the Gov. that if he did not grant a reprieve she would take her own life and the life of her son.[3] Well that's up to her! The sooner America is rid of alien convicts, their wives and their children, the better Americans will like it. If Bruno Hauptmann goes to the chair and Mrs. Hauptmann did not carry out her threat, then she and her son should be deported immediately. I am for it and millions more Americans are, too. Many are of the opinion the truth was never told by Mrs. Hauptmann, many believe her an accomplice. Surely she told a dumb story about the money. . . . If I can remember correctly a blonde woman passed out one of the first bills of the Lindbergh ransom money. Isn't Mrs. Hauptmann blonde?

Regarding Father Kallok, J D writes:

Every one was deeply impressed with Rev. Kallok's entire story, no one at that time thought it would be needed, but when Gov. Hoffman interfered that put a different light on Rev. Kallok's story. I, too, was greatly impressed with the straight forward manner in which Rev. Kallok told his story. I am not a Catholic, I do not know Rev. Kallok, never saw him but I do believe his story and understand he is a man of high regard.

Having never heard of Father Michael J. Kallok, Schwarzkopf, on January 23, 1936, wrote a letter to the Milwaukee Police Department in which he asked Chief J. G. Laubenheimer to "Kindly contact the Reverend Kallok [sic] and send us a report of your findings."

A week later, Chief Laubenheimer sent Schwarzkopf a three-page statement Father Kallok had given to an editor of the *Milwaukee Sentinel* on April 8, 1935. Father Michael J. Kallok's affidavit reads as follows:

MICHAEL J. KALLOK, being first duly sworn, deposes and says that he is pastor of St. Joseph's Roman Catholic Church in the city of Cudahy, Milwaukee County, Wisconsin, and lives at 1410 Swift Avenue in said City of Cudahy; that he has been such pastor since the twenty-fourth day of December, 1931; that from November 1926, until October, 1931, he was pastor of St. Michael's Church in Trenton, New Jersey.

Deponent further states that while pastor of the church in Trenton, he made the acquaintance of a man named L. C. Thompson, who was the owner of a tract of property about four miles north-east of Trenton where a riding stable was operated under the name "The Willows"; that he also made the acquaintance of a man named Robert A. Schumann, who was a friend of the said Thompson, and who was an architect.

Deponent further states that during the years of 1929, 1930 and the early part of 1931 he frequently visited "The Willows," came to know Thompson and Schumann well; that in 1930, as he remembers, a fire destroyed the stables, and thereafter Thompson transferred his activities to a farm about a mile away, which, as this deponent is informed and believes, had been the home of the father of the said Thompson; that his acquaintance with these men grew out of the fact that Schumann was engaged to build the new rectory for St. Michael's Church which was completed in 1930 and that Schumann brought Thompson to him in connection with insurance on the new building.

Deponent further states that during 1930 he visited "The Willows" frequently, some weeks as often as once or twice, although for other periods he might not go to the place for two or more weeks.

Deponent further states that during 1930 he met a man who was a patron of "The Willows" and who appeared to have a business connection with Thompson and who was introduced to him as Bruno Hauptmann; that during 1930 he saw this man at "The Willows" on at least twelve occasions and on at least three occasions he held conversation with him; that he has studied photographs of the Bruno Hauptmann who has been convicted of the Lindbergh baby kidnapping and he is certain that the man he saw on these occasions at "The Willows" and who was known to him as Bruno Hauptmann is the same Bruno Hauptmann who has been so convicted.

Deponent further states that a man known to him as Carlstrom, who appeared to have business dealings with Thompson was seen by him at the "The Willows" on five or six occasions; that this said Carlstrom was seen by him on a few occasions in the company of Bruno Hauptmann; that he knows of his own knowledge that Hauptmann and Carlstrom were acquainted with each other, that it is his opinion Carlstrom was at that time engaged in illegal liquor traffic; that he has carefully examined photographs of the Elvert Carlstrom who testified as a defense witness at the Hauptmann trial and is convinced that the man he knew at "The Willows" under the name Carlstrom is the same man who testified at this trial.

Deponent further states that he on several occasions saw a woman at "The Willows" who was pointed out to him by Thompson as a Miss Henckel [sic];

that this woman was frequently in the company of Hauptmann, although he recalls seeing her on a few occasions when he did not see Hauptmann; that he recalls seeing Hauptmann and this woman riding horseback together; that it was his impression Hauptmann and this woman often came together from New York City; that he has examined photographs of the Mrs. Greta Henckel [*sic*] who testified for the defense at the Hauptmann trial and believes that the woman he saw at "The Willows" and whom he know as Miss Henckel is the same Mrs. Henckel who testified at the trial.

Deponent further states that in the spring of 1931, after Thompson had transferred his activities to the house of his father about a mile from where "The Willows" was located prior to the fire he walked into the house one day and saw Schumann and Hauptmann standing in front of a bench on which were spread several blueprints; that he stepped between the two men in order to talk to Schumann and as he did so noticed that the top blueprint showed the name Lindbergh printed on the bottom margin of this blueprint; that Hauptmann immediately grasped this blueprint and folded it over; that Schumann thereupon said to Hauptmann, "He's all right," that both men thereupon drew away from the table; that a case of whiskey was on the floor of this room which this deponent gathered Hauptmann had brought there to deliver to Thompson; that at the time he entered the home he saw Carlstrom and another man outside; that it was his impression all three had come together to deliver the whiskey; that this other man was a person he saw frequently in the company of either Hauptmann or Carlstrom or both; that he was a skinny man, slightly bald and apparently from thirty to thirty-three years of age; that as this deponent recollects he was known by a name which sounded like "kisch." That this deponent has examined photographs of Louis Kiss and Isidore [*sic*] Fisch and does not recognize them as being photographs of this person.

Deponent further states that from his many conversations with Schumann during their acquaintanceship, he gained the impression that Schumann hated the Lindbergh family; that after the birth of the Lindbergh baby, Schumann on several occasions told him the baby was destined to be kidnapped; that it was to be raised in ignorance of its parentage by a German family; that this deponent regarded these remarks as being made solely because of Schumann's professed psychological interest in the handicap such a child might be under because of the fame of his parents.

Deponent further states that at the time of the arrest of Hauptmann and the recovery of part of the ransom money, he recognized him from newspaper photographs as the man he had seen at "The Willows," and at that time he recalled seeing Hauptmann with the plans for the Lindbergh home; that he read accounts of the trial and recognized Carlstrom and Mrs. Henckel; that he felt he ought to tell his story to the proper authorities and was deterred only by not knowing how to go about it; that when Mrs. Anna Hauptmann came to Milwaukee with the last week and made appeals for funds for the defense of her husband, this deponent sought the advice of Floyd J. Gonyea, police judge of the City of Cudahy, and was advised to tell his story to the *Milwaukee Sentinel;* that he did so in the hope that the *Sentinel* would place the information in the hands of the proper officials.

In his letter to Colonel Schwarzkopf, Chief Laubenheimer noted that he had sent a detective to question Father Kallok, and as a result of that interview, learned that five months after Kallok gave his statement to the *Milwaukee Sentinel,* he made a vacation trip to New Jersey and spent several days in Passaic and Trenton. Although Hauptmann was in custody at the Trenton prison, Kallok made no effort to see him. When asked by the detective why he had not attempted to identify Hauptmann in person, Father Kallok, according to Chief Laubenheimer, said that "he (Kallok) was absolutely convinced that he was right, that his identification of the newspaper picture was correct, and that he did not want to disappoint himself."[4]

On the 12th of February, less than two weeks after being questioned by the Milwaukee detective, Reverend Kallok checked into the Lincoln Hotel in Passaic, New Jersey, and from there called the New Jersey State Police and asked to speak to Colonel Schwarzkopf. Schwarzkopf wasn't available, so Capt. John J. Lamb sent Det. William F. Horn to the hotel. Reverend Kallok asked to be interviewed in his room at one o'clock sharp but due to bad weather Detective Horn arrived late and found Father Kallok absent. Detective Horn was able, however, to catch up with Reverend Kallok at the Slovak Catholic Church on Madison Avenue in Passaic and interviewed him there.

In his report, Detective Horn recorded the results of Father Kallok's interview as follows:

That during 1931 one L. C. Thompson who was connected with The Willows Riding Academy in Lawrence Township, New Jersey came to him and said, Schumann and Hauptmann are trying to do something behind my back." Then Father Kallok asked him (Thompson) what it meant, and Thompson told him that they were going to kidnap the Lindbergh baby. Then Father Kallok told Schumann what Thompson had told him and Schumann said, "I will fix Thompson," and 10 days later Thompson died. Shortly afterward The Willows Riding Academy burned down, and according to Father Kallok,

Hauptmann built a temporary stable. Father Kallok claimed that a man by the name of Otto informed him of Thompson's death, although he does not know what Otto's last name is, he informs that Otto was known by Chief Stonacker of the Lawrence Township Police. The Reverend Kallok also advised that Schumann had been attacked by Hauptmann in Newark, N. J., and that this information was given to the reverend by Schumann's housekeeper, whose name and whereabouts he does not know.

The Reverend Kallok also informed that one Michael Fedorko, 644 North Clinton Ave., Trenton, New Jersey, also saw Hauptmann on several occasions at the Willow Riding Academy.

In his report, Detective Horn comments on Father Kallok's demeanor during the interview:

> It was noticed by this investigator, during the above interview with the Reverend Kallok, that he seemed to be in great fear, stating that at the time he first divulged information concerning Hauptmann and the Lindbergh case he was interviewed by Det. Louis Dreden of the Milwaukee Police, whom he requested to keep everything very confidential, in spite of which everything appeared in the newspapers throughout the country the following day. The Reverend claims he has received numerous threats from unknown persons who have visited him personally, but he was unable to state the identify of these persons.[5]

Could any of this Kallok business be true? Did Hauptmann and an architect named Robert A. Schumann kidnap the Lindbergh baby? Did Schumann have the blueprints to the Lindbergh house? Did Schumann murder L. C. Thompson because Thompson knew of the plan? Did he burn down Thompson's riding academy? Were Hauptmann's friends Gerta Henkel, Hans Kloppenburg, and Elvert Carlstrom with him at the stables? Did they know of the kidnap plan, did they help pull off the job? Is that why they testified on Hauptmann's behalf at his trial? (Kloppenburg and Carlstrom were alibi witnesses, Henkel was a character witness who confirmed Hauptmann's friendship with Isidor Fisch. There were also rumors that Hauptmann had had an affair with Henkel in the summer of 1932 when Mrs. Hauptmann was visiting relatives in Germany.)

At first blush, Father Kallok's story rings true because it comes, in great detail, from a Catholic priest who had no apparent reason to invent such a tale. Moreover, it seems that Father Kallok, after his accusations were made public, was truly afraid for his life. On closer inspection, however, there are problems with this whole account.

Eleven months after Father Kallok's initial statement, he told Detective Horn of Schumann's threat to "fix" Thompson, after which Thompson died and his riding stable burned down. Why weren't these important facts included in his first statement? The fire, according to Kallok's initial statement, occurred in 1930, but in Detective Horn's report it happened in 1931.

Other questions come to mind. One would assume that a priest, knowing that the Lindbergh baby might be in danger, would notify the police, or at least the Lindberghs. It could have been done anonymously, causing the priest no risk to his safety. Perhaps Father Kallok, afraid that Schumann would figure out who had snitched, would kill him, too. And maybe he did not think anyone would believe him. But the baby *was* kidnapped, and murdered, yet Father Kallok, knowing what he knew, kept silent while the police struggled, the nation suffered, and the kidnappers enjoyed the fruits of their crime. Apparently Father Kallok could live with all of that, but could not stand the idea of Mrs. Hauptmann coming to Milwaukee with her Nazi supporters to raise money for her condemned husband. (As a matter of fact, Mrs. Hauptmann did travel around the country with Nazi groups raising money, and did, in fact, travel to Milwaukee.) And why didn't Father Kallok, when he was in New Jersey in 1935, take the opportunity to come face to face with Hauptmann?

LeRoy C. Thompson, a real estate man and insurance broker did, in fact, die at a relatively young age — fifty-three — in September 1931. But according to his death certificate, Thompson died in a Trenton hospital. The cause of death: "Myocardial failure, hypertension and acute glomerular nephritis" (heart failure and kidney disease).[6]

The Lindbergh house architect was not Robert A. Schumann but a man named Chester Aldrich. Of course that does not mean that Schumann could not have gotten his hands on the blueprints.

Although Hauptmann had been friends with Hans Kloppenburg, a fellow carpenter, he first met Gerta Henkel at Hunters Island in July of 1932. There is no evidence that Hauptmann knew Elvert Carlstrom prior to the trial.

In Hauptmann's personal notebooks and ledgers, there are no references to Schumann, Thompson, Father Kallok, or The Willows Riding Academy.

If the New Jersey State Police questioned Schumann, or Michael Fedorko, Father Kallok's corroborating witness, there is no record of their investigation at the Lindbergh case archives in New Jersey. It is doubtful they gave much credence to Father Kallok's story.

Nearly two years after Father Kallok's fantastic tale appeared in the *Milwaukee Sentinel*, John F. Tyrrell, the Milwaukee questioned-documents examiner who had testified for the prosecution at Hauptmann's trial, kept the Kallok story—albeit a bit twisted—alive in a letter to a friend:

> There are some things in that case that did not develop publicly but should have. For instance, a priest located in Cudahy, just south of Milwaukee, was in charge of the Trenton district the year preceding the kidnapping. He saw Hauptmann down there and saw him poring over the plans of the Lindbergh house. He also saw his carpenter friend who declared he had seen Hauptmann in a coffee house the night of the kidnapping, and Mrs. Henkel who entertained him at her home the night of the payment of the ransom. He, the priest, would have made a good witness for the state but claimed he was afraid to appear in the matter for the reason the architect who drew the Lindbergh plans was murdered over in the Bronx or Brooklyn in October 1932, and he had connected the architect's death with Hauptmann in some way. There are other numerous incidents that have developed since. Some day a real story of this crime will be written.[7]

Father Kallok, and his forgotten story, like so many other subplots, sideshows, and characters on the fringes of the Lindbergh case, could have become the basis of another conspiracy book. One of the intriguing aspects of the Lindbergh case is why otherwise sane and respectable people like Father Kallok allow their Lindbergh-related fantasies get the best of them.

The Lindbergh estate near Hopewell, New Jersey

Charles A. Lindbergh at the
Hauptmann trial

Anne Lindbergh arriving at the
Hauptmann trial on the day of her
testimony

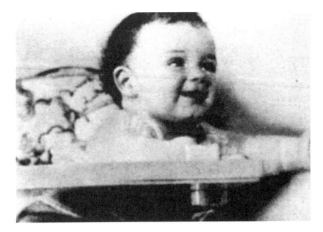

The Lindbergh baby shortly before the kidnapping

The Lindbergh baby as found on May 12, 1932, a few miles from the Lindbergh estate

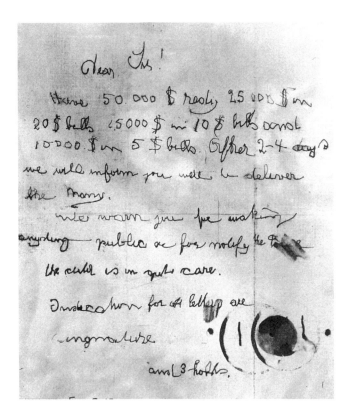

The ransom note left by
the kidnapper in the
Lindbergh baby's room on
March 1, 1932, in
Hopewell, New Jersey

H. Norman Schwarzkopf, head
of the New Jersey State Police,
and Charles A. Lindbergh

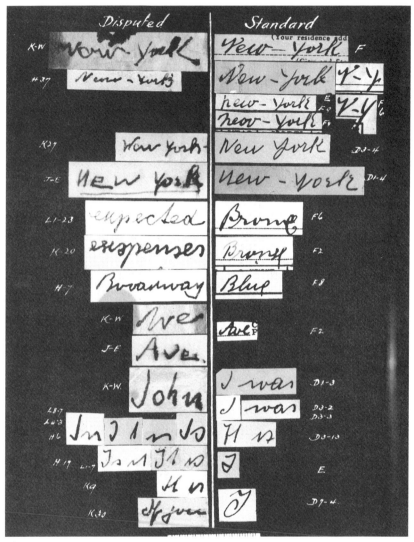

Handwriting exhibit comparing Hauptmann's known (standard) handwriting to that of the ransom (disputed) writings

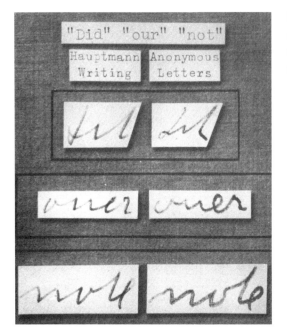

Handwriting exhibit highlighting the similarities between Hauptmann's writing and that of the ransom note writer

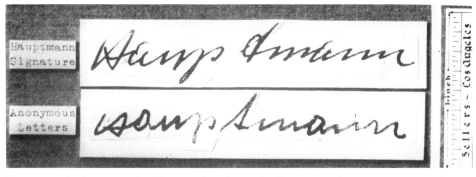

Hauptmann's signature taken from various letters in the ransom documents compared to his known handwriting

Five of the eight prosecution document examiners who testified that Hauptmann was the ransom note writer. *Top, left to right:* John F. Tyrrell, Milwaukee; Dr. Wilmer Souder, Washington, D.C.; Herbert J. Walter, Chicago. *Bottom, left to right:* Albert D. Osborn, New York; James Clark Sellers, Los Angeles

The part of the kidnap ladder that had been a plank in Hauptmann's attic floor

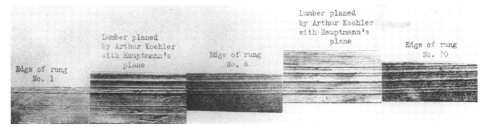

Tool mark evidence connecting Hauptmann's plane with parts of the homemade kidnap ladder

The ransom bill on Hauptmann's person when he was arrested in New York City

Hauptmann's arrest photograph

Anna Hauptmann following her husband's execution, April 3, 1936

8 Other Voices, Other Stories

John F. Tyrrell was correct; many stories of the Lindbergh crime have been written, but no two are alike, and they all claim to tell the real story, including Anthony Scaduto's book, *Scapegoat: The Lonesome Death of Bruno Richard Hauptmann.* Scaduto's book, a treatise designed to exonerate Hauptmann, did not sit well with a man named Delmar C. Merritt Jr., who lived in Hamilton Township, New Jersey, not far from the site of the kidnapping. In 1976, shortly after Scaduto's book came out, Merritt Jr. came forward with his own story, one that did not fit in with Scaduto's thesis that Hauptmann, a completely innocent man, was intentionally framed by police and prosecutors. Merritt Jr.'s story went like this:

On March 1, 1932, fourteen-year-old Delmar C. Merritt Jr. and his father were working on a farm owned by the Sheffield Dairy Company. As they walked out of the milking barn after checking on the cows, a driver in a blue Buick with three passengers — all men — pulled up and asked directions to Hopewell. Merritt Sr. told the driver to turn around and head back on the dirt lane they were on (now called the Dublin Road) to the Pennington-Washington Crossing Road. The driver of the Buick was wearing a gray cap, a white shirt and dark tie, and a top coat. The encounter took place seven miles from the Lindbergh estate.

Two and a half years later, following Hauptmann's arrest, Merritt Sr. and his son realized that Bruno Richard Hauptmann was the man behind the wheel that day, in a car that bore New York license plates. The driver of the car had a German accent and so did one of the men in the back seat, a man they later identified as Isidor Fisch. Merritt Sr., having been only eighteen inches from the back window on the driver's side of the car, got a good look at both men.

Merritt Jr.'s father swore his son to secrecy because he didn't want to get involved and risk having to lose work over the case. There was no need to come forward since the authorities had plenty of evidence to convict Hauptmann The boy was told, by his father, never to tell anyone about what they had seen on that famous day in March 1932.

But in 1976, following the death of Merritt Sr., the son, now fifty-eight and the chief engineer at the Young's Rubber Company in Trenton, decided to break his silence. It was Scaduto's book that prompted his disclosure. "I figure, if they can stand there and shoot the baloney like that inside books, then it's about time I supplied a few facts."[1] Stating that he has never felt guilty about not coming forward with his information, Merritt Jr. said, "They're trying to prove he's [Hauptmann's] innocent. Now that makes other people look dumb. . . . I just want to let them know they've got cock-eyed theories. These guys should get their facts straight."[2]

Delmar C. Merritt Jr.'s Lindbergh case disclosure, reported in a couple of central New Jersey newspapers, did not make much of a splash. Scaduto's book, however, caught the attention of the national media and rode the wave of cynicism engulfing the country. Critics were so enthralled with Scaduto's thesis, his book was swallowed whole. Those who know better were simply ignored.

Following the kidnapping, hundreds of police officers from dozens of law enforcement agencies poured into west central New Jersey to question local residents. Those who were not questioned in the investigative canvas called the police with tips and leads. It seemed that everyone in Hunterdon and Mercer Counties had seen a strange car or a suspicious person or persons on the day of the kidnapping—and none of these suspects or automobiles were the same. The police were running themselves ragged and getting nowhere.

Two elderly widows, for example, had reported hearing a conversation in which the words "Lindbergh," "kidnap," and "baby," had been spoken. The old women led several state troopers through the woods, pointing out places the baby might have been hidden. Several Lindbergh neighbors and residents of nearby towns recalled incidents involving strangers in cars asking directions to the Lindbergh estate. The butler, Oliver Whately, remembered that while talking to a shrub salesman, he saw a man and woman in a green automobile drive up and take photographs of the Lindbergh house. Whately had sent the couple packing, but the salesman said he later saw the woman behind a bush focusing her camera on the nursery windows.

The police at Princeton received a tip that two men in a black or blue sedan with New York plates had asked directions to the Lindbergh estate. The description of the car was sent to police departments in New Jersey and New York. The car was subsequently identified by a resident of Brooklyn who reported that it had been stolen from him earlier that day.

A man named George Jennings, who lived on one of the roads between Hopewell and the Lindbergh estate, reported that, on the night of the kidnapping, a man and a woman in a dark-colored car had asked him directions to the Lindbergh place. A team of detectives were sent out to locate and identify these people.

A postcard sent from Newark, New Jersey, contained the following hand-printed message: "Baby safe. Wait instruction later. Act accordingly." The card was addressed to "Col. Linberg [sic], Princeton, N.J." The Newark police located the store where the postcard had been purchased. The store clerk described the buyer and, after visiting two hundred homes, the police identified the sender, a mentally disturbed boy. Two hundred Newark policemen had been assigned to this lead, an inquiry that turned out to be an investigative dead end.

Hundreds of such messages were sent to the Lindberghs during the weeks following the kidnapping. Another postcard writer told Colonel Lindbergh to "obey instructions or suffer consequences." The seventeen-year-old boy who had sent this message wanted to see if it would get reported in the newspapers.

In Trenton, the police were told that at midnight on the night of the kidnapping, a Pennsylvania Railroad brakeman had seen two men and a woman with a child in her arms on the train platform on Clinton Street. One of the men had nervously asked the brakeman when the next train to New York City was due. The railroad man described the suspects in great detail and the New York City Police Department sent out a general alarm based upon these descriptions. For the next few days, thousands of New York City policemen looked for these people. They were never found.[3]

A week after the kidnapping, Newark police detective Frank Carr and

Corporal Thomas J. Ritchie of the New Jersey State Police questioned Alfred Hammond, a watchman for the Reading Railroad at the Hollow Roads Crossing near Skillman, New Jersey, five miles from the Lindbergh house. The rough, unpaved lane that crossed the tracks at this location led to the village of Zion, where another back road could be taken into Hopewell and onto the Lindbergh estate. According to Hammond, a resident of Woodsbourne, Pennsylvania, the only people who traveled this road were locals, people he knew.

On the morning of the crime, and the four mornings before that, Hammond observed a car, carrying three men, rolling down the lane away from the Lindbergh estate. The 1926 vehicle, make unknown, bore New York plates and crossed the tracks at the Skillman Crossing each of those mornings between 8:00 and 9:00. Hammond said he did not see the car after the kidnapping. The railroad employee told the detectives he got a good look at the man in the back seat, a man he could positively identify if he saw him again. Hammond described this man as an Italian, twenty-five to twenty-eight years old, with a medium build, a dark complexion, and a smooth, cleanly shaven face. The man was wearing a dark suit and a dark-colored cap.

The driver of the car was an American about thirty-five years old, had a medium build, and a dark hat. Hammond could only describe the front-seat passenger as a white male who also wore a dark cap.

The next day, Hammond was driven to police headquarters in New York City where he viewed hundreds of Rogues Gallery photographs without making an identification. It was on this occasion that the witness advised that the questioned New York license plate read 24-Y8-18. (Hauptmann's car, in 1932, bore the license 3U-36-24.) According to the report filed by Detectives Carr and Ritchie:

> We learned that there is no such number and then worked out a combination of numbers with the prefix 24 and 4Y and thoroughly investigated all of these numbers which have been issued by the Motor Vehicle Department. While we were engaged in this we sent Hammond back to his home by train, paying his passage and supplying him with supper money. The investigation of these autos continued until the afternoon of March 10th when we returned to Hopewell. None of the autos could be linked in any way with the auto seen by Hammond.[4]

The detectives also questioned residents along the Skillman-Zion road without finding anyone who had seen the car or the people Hammond had described.

On December 18, 1932, Detective Nuncio DeGaetano of the New Jersey State Police drove Alfred Hammond to a garage on East 9th Street in Manhattan to identify a green Chrysler sedan that had been left for repairs by a local hood named John Gorch Hammond took one look at the car and said it was not the one he had seen at the crossing. Alfred Hammond, who had since lost his job at the railroad, informed Detective DeGaetano that he expected to be paid for his troubles. His request for money was denied.[5]

On several occasions in 1933, detectives from various law enforcement agencies showed Alfred Hammond photographs of possible suspects and people placed in the area of the kidnapping around the time of the crime. Once such person was an African American man who was caught one afternoon prior to the kidnapping sitting in a tree looking in the direction of the Lindbergh estate.

A month before Hauptmann's execution, at a time when Governor Hoffman and his private detectives were trying to uncover new evidence to exonerate Hauptmann or to prove a conspiracy, Alfred Hammond signed a statement taken by Raymond Lyons, a former assemblyman from Middlesex County who worked for the governor from time to time. The statement was taken at the Reading Railroad station in West Trenton. Hammond, on this occasion, described the strange car and the three men he had seen at the Skillman Crossing prior to the kidnapping. The questioning, by Lyons, continued as follows:

Q. In your opinion was Isidor Fisch the man you saw in the back of the machine (car)?
A. Yes
Q. Did you make this known to anybody?
A. To the detective.
Q. Now, after Hauptmann was arrested you made a statement to the state police?
A. Yes.
Q. They showed you Fisch's picture?
A. Yes.
Q. What did you say to the members of the police there present?

A. Now that was the fellow sitting in the back of the machine.

Q. What did he say when you said that?

A. He said it couldn't be because he died broke in Germany, he couldn't have been implicated in the case.

Q. Did the officer of the state police question you in detail as to seeing Fisch?

A. No, he did not.

Q. Did he act as if he wanted you to drop the question?

A. Yes, he didn't want that case brought up.[6]

In response to the accusation that Hammond's implication of Fisch had been suppressed, a spokesman for the New Jersey State Police stated that following Hauptmann's arrest, his photographs were not shown to Hammond. Because Hammond did not identify Hauptmann as one of the men in the car, the matter was dropped. As far as this spokesman was aware, no law enforcement official had shown photographs of Isidor Fisch to Hammond. (The files of the New Jersey State Police show no contact with Hammond after May 1933.)

If Isidor Fisch was the man in the back seat of the car, who were the other people? Who owned the car? Hammond said he had seen that vehicle on five consecutive mornings. (He said ten when questioned by Lyons.) Why was Hammond the only one who had seen this car? Detectives had questioned the other watchmen who worked at that crossing and none of them had seen it.

Hammond would have fit in nicely with some of Edward J. Reilly's defense witnesses—particularly with Benjamin Heier, who testified he had seen Isidor Fisch at St. Raymond's Cemetery on the night of the ransom payoff. (Heier was later indicted for perjury.) Hammond was certainly not shy about coming forward with information. He had offered to help the police in March after the kidnapping and four years later, when Governor Hoffman, notwithstanding Hauptmann's conviction, was reinvestigating the crime. But where was he in 1935 when Reilly needed him as a defense witness at Hauptmann's trial?

In March of 1932, New Jersey governor A. Harry Moore publicly offered a twenty-five thousand dollar reward for information leading to the identification and conviction of the Lindbergh kidnappers. In March of 1936, when Hammond come forward again, the newspapers were carrying stories about this reward money and how it might be distributed by Governor Hoffman following Hauptmann's execution.[7] It therefore seems likely that Hammond's willingness to get involved in the Lindbergh kidnapping had more to do with financial need and the pursuit of money than it did with civic duty and the pursuit of truth.

Finding the truth in the Lindbergh case has never been easy and may be impossible. The more one searches, the more one finds, and the more one finds, the more complicated and confused the case becomes. However, one fact seems certain: most people familiar with the case, and almost all who are not, believe there was some kind of conspiracy. And if there was a conspiracy, with or without Hauptmann, it probably included either the Lindberghs themselves, their household servants, or both.

For the story teller, kidnapping is good; kidnapping and murder are better; but kidnapping, murder, and betrayal are as good as it gets.

9 The Lindberghs: Victims or Suspects?

Writers who accuse Charles and Anne Lindbergh of wrongdoing send a reassuring message that happens to be true: children are rarely abducted out of their homes by strangers. This, of course, is not the accusers' intention, but it helps sell their case. Even among hard-core conspiracy buffs, the vision of Colonel Lindbergh killing his baby, covering his tracks, then helping the police railroad an innocent man into the electric chair is a hard sell.

Soon after the baby was found dead, rumors started flying that the child had been killed by the Lindberghs because the baby was mentally or physically defective. The American public had conferred upon the Lindberghs the unwanted, and perhaps undeserved title of perfect couple. That meant the Lindberghs, as a sort of American royalty, had to produce the perfect child. If the Lindberghs had killed their baby because he was less than perfect, they did it for America as much as for themselves. Of course they did not kill their child, but rumors that they had were inevitable.

One of the principal FBI investigators assigned to the Lindbergh kidnapping, Leon G. Turrou, published a book in 1949 that contained a chapter on the case. Regarding early rumors about the Lindberghs, he wrote:

> After several days of frenzied waiting, during which time the kidnapper had still not revealed his terms of payment, an ugly rumor began to be whispered in newspaper columns that the Lindbergh child had been the victim of a mercy slaying. The child, the gossip mongers had it, had been so hopelessly deformed that its parents had resorted to euthanasia. One semi-official investigator holding a high position in the Department of Labor brought Anne Morrow Lindbergh down into the basement of her home, pointed to the large furnace, and insinuated that she had cremated her son. This official was later severely

reprimanded for his action by the President and forced to halt his investigations. This was a portent of what was to come. It was apparent from the beginning that the case, if not solved quickly, would soon assume grotesque proportions.[1]

Unfortunately for the Lindberghs, the New Jersey State Police, and dozens of Lindbergh case principals who have become kidnappers, murderers, and conspirators between the covers of revisionist's books, the crime remained unsolved until Hauptmann's arrest in September 1934, two and a half years after the commission of the crime.

Forty years later, Anne Morrow Lindbergh, in her published letters and diaries, made reference to the overzealous Department of Labor bureaucrat and his off-the-wall theory regarding the baby's home cremation: "There was one official, acting as self-appointed investigator, who woke me up in the middle of the night and asked me to re-enact his theory of the crime, which ended with the imaginary throwing of a baby into the furnace."[2]

This kind of abuse, at the hands of charlatans, opportunists, nut cases, and hack writers, would continue, in one form or another, throughout Mrs. Lindbergh's long life. Although the Lindbergh case had turned her husband into a quasi-recluse whose hatred of the media was so intense it was debilitating, Mrs. Lindbergh was able to rise above it and continue on.

In 1933, a Chicago lawyer named Mary Belle Spencer, in a forty-eight-page pamphlet entitled, *No. 2310, Criminal File: Exposed! Aviator's Baby Was Never Kidnapped or Murdered,* publicly accused the Lindberghs of parental wrongdoing. It was Spencer's thesis that through negligent parenting, the baby had wandered off into the woods and died. Spencer did not explain how the twenty-month-old child had managed to hike three miles to the spot he was found along the Hopewell-Princeton Road. Spencer called the Lindbergh kidnapping "a stupendous hoax perpetrated upon the state of New Jersey and the public at large by the fears of the panic stricken parent, a sensation seeking press and monstrous ignorance of logic."[3] A year after Spencer published her little expose, the police arrested Hauptmann.

New Jersey governor Harold G. Hoffman's postconviction reopening of the Lindbergh investigation on Hauptmann's behalf unloosed an army of out-of-work private investigators who unearthed many of the old and absurd theories buried after the police caught Bruno Richard Hauptmann with the ransom money hidden in his garage. In a memo to the governor dated February 28, 1936, about a month before Hauptmann's execution, one of these private investigators, a man named William Lewis from Red Bank, New Jersey, recycled the silly but comforting and persistent idea that the Lindberghs, not Hauptmann, had killed the baby because he was defective:

> It is rumored that the Morrow family have [sic] suffered from epilepsy through several generations; and that this may be an explanation for the son John Morrow, the alleged premature retirement of General Morrow from the United States Army, the death of Elisabeth Morrow Morgan, and might have some bearing on the kidnapping of the Lindbergh baby. It is possible that Colonel Lindbergh and Mrs. Lindbergh were finally convinced that their child inherited epilepsy, and that, with a knowledge of the effect it had on other members of the Morrow family, they arrived at the conclusion that it was better to lose the child than to have it grow up to become an imbecile or a degenerate of some type.[4]

There is no biographical evidence that any member of the Morrow family, including Anne Morrow Lindbergh, had ever suffered from epilepsy. Elisabeth, Anne's sister, died in December, 1934, at age thirty. Although sickly most of her life, she was not epileptic. Who John and General Morrow are is a mystery.

In 1976, thirteen days before he died of a cerebral hemorrhage, Arthur Jones, an inmate of Draper Prison near Montgomery, Alabama, informed a reporter from the *National Enquirer* that in 1935 when he was on death row with Bruno Richard Hauptmann, the convicted kidnapper told him a big secret. According to Jones, Hauptmann had told him that he hated Colonel Lindbergh. Hauptmann said the baby was physically deformed, and, as a result, the Lindberghs did not want the child. The sixty-five-year-old prisoner told the tabloid reporter that Hauptmann had confided in him that the baby had soft bones and was deaf.[5] Colonel Lindbergh, as the story goes, planned to have the child taken to a special home in France without his wife's knowledge. Lindbergh and Dr. John F. Condon, the retired school teacher who became Lindbergh's ransom intermediary, planned the caper. Hauptmann also told Jones that Lindbergh had hired him and three other men to take the baby away in an unheated car. The baby, wrapped in a thin blanket, caught pneumonia and died two days later. According to Jones,

"Betty Gow had carried the child downstairs and handed him out the front door to Bruno. It was on a day when Mrs. Lindbergh was not home, but Dr. Condon was there."[6]

Assuming Arthur Jones was on death row when Hauptmann was there (there were seven men on death row, three of whom died in the electric chair before Hauptmann), and assuming Jones and Hauptmann had in fact spoken to each other, what would have compelled Hauptmann to confide in Jones? Hauptmann had not confessed to the police, his lawyers, or even his wife. A confession would have saved his life. Why would he have wasted it on a fellow prisoner? And why did Jones keep Hauptmann's revelation a secret for so long? Surely he did not open up to clear his conscience, or for some similar reason. Governor Harold G. Hoffman would have been interested in this story, but Jones would have actually had to have been in prison with Hauptmann, an easy fact to verify in 1936.

The prisoner's dramatic deathbed statement, coming in 1976, shortly after the publication of Scaduto's book, *Scapegoat,* was simply a timely contribution to the new era of Lindbergh case revisionism. Scaduto had opened the door, and people like Jones were walking in.

Arthur Jones and his so-called deathbed revelation reminds one of Scaduto's Murray Bleefeld and Noel Behn's Harry Green, two old men peddling a pair of theories that had been thoroughly discredited decades earlier—but are so far in the past and forgotten that they can be recycled as new and exciting. To say that Jones, Bleefeld, and Green were on the fringes of the Lindbergh case would be to exaggerate the degree of their involvement.[7]

The idea that the Lindberghs were in some way responsible for their baby's death, and that the kidnapping was nothing more than a cover-up hoax, is the principal theory behind two recent books on the case. In *Crime of the Century,* authors Gregory Ahlgren and Stephen Monier say that Lindbergh probably killed the child accidentally while playing a practical joke on his wife. Noel Behn, the author of *Lindbergh, the Crime,* believes the baby was killed by Elisabeth Morrow, who was jealous of her sister, Anne Morrow Lindbergh.

Given the seriousness of these accusations, their historical significance, the heavy presumption of Lindbergh innocence, and the fact that a man was convicted and executed for the murder, one would expect a mountain of hard evidence supporting these charges—proof more convincing than the evidence that convicted Bruno Richard Hauptmann. Anthony Scaduto had nothing but a phony confession to make his case, but, as a former tabloid reporter, he is good at weaving maybe's, could-have-been's, and what-if's into a plausible theory. Writers Ahlgren and Monier are also good with smoke and mirrors, but because they are pushing such an incredible theory, do not even pretend they are working with real evidence. In their book, they write:

> There is no smoking gun here. In presenting and writing this book we have generated no death bed statement by a witness who now admits to having seen Lindbergh climb the ladder that night; we have uncovered no long lost confessional letter in the Colonel's own handwriting; we have found no Zapruder-like videotape of him disposing of the body in Mount Rose.
>
> But that does not mean that the case against Charles Augustus Lindbergh is weak.[8]

Noel Behn, with a better publisher, but a thesis as silly as the Ahlgren-Monier idea, makes a similar disclaimer at the beginning of his book: "No smoking gun will be offered regarding the Lindbergh case."[9] Later on, he confesses fully: "There is no single, irrefutable item of evidence that links Elisabeth Morrow to the death of her nephew, Charles Lindbergh, Jr. Even the affidavits Harry Green swore to have had in his possession were at best hearsay and, if true, related to an incident to which there were no witnesses other than Elisabeth herself."[10]

These disclaimers should have been printed on the books' covers to warn readers up front they were buying fiction passed off as reality.

Writing a true-crime book that is phony involves making up a theory, selecting and cleverly presenting anything that can be passed off as supporting evidence, then challenging disbelievers to disprove your thesis. For example, who can prove that Elisabeth Morrow *did not* kill the Lindbergh baby? In the bizarre world of phony true-crime writing, everyone is presumed guilty, therefore if some one like Elisabeth Morrow does not have a solid, sixty-year-old alibi, she is fair game and up for grabs. Rather than attempt to prove a negative, the best way to debunk a particular theory is to question why the writer's suspects—or conspirators—would do what he says they did. It involves analyzing their motives then applying a little common sense. This is the Achilles heel of bogus true crime—the motives.

Anthony Scaduto, the author of *Scapegoat,* has invented for his kidnapper, Paul H. Wendel, some interesting motives. Wendel was the disbarred lawyer who was abducted and severely beaten by Ellis Parker Sr. and his gang. Wendel confessed to kidnapping the Lindbergh baby, but took back his confession the moment he was free. Wendel's abductors went to prison for the kidnapping. These facts are not in dispute. The question is—did Wendel, rather than Hauptmann, kidnap and murder the baby? Scaduto says yes. Regarding motive, if you believe Hauptmann committed the crime, you could say quite reasonably that he did it for the money. Why did Paul H. Wendel do it? According to Scaduto, Wendel kidnapped the baby, "because he was going to do something that the world would take notice of. He decided that Lindbergh was an international hero and he waited and waited, until the baby was born, until such time he felt he would have an opportunity to kidnap the baby. And doing this he was going to get even with the world."[11]

Scaduto further explains, "Paul Wendel was a man who believed everybody in the world had done him wrong and he was going to show the world he was smarter than anyone else by kidnapping the baby of the world's hero, the Lindbergh baby."[12]

That might explain why he took the child, but why did he confess?

"Paul Wendel confessed because he had an urge to let the world know he kidnapped the Lindbergh child."[13]

If this is why Wendel confessed, then why did he wait three years to do it, and why did it take a severe beating to get it out of him? Moreover, if he was so proud of his achievement, why did he take back his confession the moment he got out of Parker Sr.'s clutches? Even Scaduto cannot explain this, and he does not try to. At the place in his book where this explanation should be, Scaduto diverts the reader's attention by attacking the police for believing Wendel's statement that he confessed because he had been kidnapped and was being beaten.[14]

Scaduto also believes that Bruno Richard Hauptmann was completely innocent, and that all of the prosecution's witnesses, including Colonel Lindbergh, lied under oath. According to Scaduto, Lindbergh's courtroom identification of Hauptmann's voice as the voice he had heard in the cemetery on the night of the ransom payoff, was a lie. Scaduto asserts that Lindbergh also lied when he denied giving gangster Mickey Rosner a copy of the nursery note, and he committed perjury when he testified that he trusted John F. Condon. Having convinced himself that Hauptmann was innocent and Lindbergh was a perjurer, Scaduto writes, "[A]ll of this makes it quite possible Charles Lindbergh was a willing participant in the wrongful execution of Richard Hauptmann."[15]

Again, why would Lindbergh, a world hero, stand by and allow the police to frame a man he knew was innocent? Scaduto has an answer for this as well: "Could it have been that his [Lindbergh's] wife was in such fragile emotional condition he felt it necessary to close out this case and this tormenting period in their lives, even if it meant convicting a man who was probably innocent?"[16]

It seems that if Mrs. Lindbergh was so fragile, and her husband so caring, he would not have put her through a six-week trial, a prolonged and unprecedented media circus, and an electrocution that probably haunted her the rest of her life.

On the subject of silly motives in support of stupid theories, why would Colonel Lindbergh, after having accidentally dropped and killed his baby while playing a practical joke on his wife, throw it into the woods and claim the baby had been kidnapped? Why would Lindbergh, an obsessively private man, invite the world to his doorstep? Authors Ahlgren and Monier explain it this way: "The 'kidnapping' was an effort to cover Lindbergh's stupidity."[17]

Paying fifty thousand dollars in the Great Depression to a con man; living ten weeks with an army of cops camped out in your garage, and a hundred reporters in your yard; putting your wife through hell; subjecting yourself to rumors that the baby was murdered because he was defective; then going to court, and before the entire civilized world, committing perjury—now that is stupid. On the other hand, accidentally killing your child while pulling a practical joke is not stupid. Killing your child that way is tragic, and forgivable.

In the motives department, Noel Behn has the biggest challenge of all. Why would Elisabeth Morrow throw her nephew out the nursery window? Why would the Lindbergh servants lie to the police and lie in court to protect her? Why would Colonel Henry Breckinridge do the same thing and risk a high-powered legal career? Why would Mrs. Lindbergh go to such lengths to protect the woman who had killed her son? And finally, why did Colonel Lindbergh orchestrate a phony kidnapping to hide the truth of his son's death?

Noel Behn quite intelligently avoids going deeply into the motivations for these actions. Instead, this is what he gives his readers: "It was to protect Elisabeth and the Lindbergh-Morrow family names that a conspiracy was conceived and carried out, the deception had been amazingly successful."[18]

Amazing indeed.

10 The Butler, the Maid, and the Baby's Nurse

In the beginning, Lindbergh case investigators had good reason to suspect that the kidnapper or kidnappers had inside help. This meant the domestic servants, twenty-nine in all, employed in the Lindbergh and Morrow households, were potential suspects. The police were especially interested in the servants closest to the baby, Oliver and Elsie Whately, the Lindbergh maid and butler; and the child's nursemaid, Betty Gow. Although Colonel Lindbergh publicly and privately defended the servants and refused to allow any of them to be tested on the polygraph, the New Jersey State Police, New York City Police, and the FBI conducted thorough investigations in America and Great Britain into the backgrounds of these employees, their family, and friends.

The idea that a servant had either furnished the kidnappers inside information or had actually participated in the crime was not farfetched. It seemed the kidnappers had known the Lindberghs were spending the night of the crime in Hopewell. Normally they would have been back at the Morrow estate in Englewood. And the fact the kidnapper had entered the one nursery window with the warped shutters that could not be latched might have been more than coincidence or good luck. Moreover, the crime had been perfectly timed. If the ladder had been laid against the house during the period Colonel Lindbergh was seated at his desk in his den, he would have seen it through the southeast window. The family dog, Wahgoosh, had not barked that night, fueling speculation that someone in the house had taken steps to see that the animal would not interfere with the kidnapping. There were other aspects of the crime that caused suspicion of an inside job. Why didn't the kidnappers wait until later in the night to snatch the baby? Why didn't they wait until everyone in the Lindbergh house was asleep? And why weren't there any latent fingerprints on the nursery window, the crib, or anywhere else in the room? Did someone wipe the room clean before the arrival of the police?

Eleven days after the kidnapping, the police invited a private fingerprint expert, a New York City physician named Dr. Erastus Mead Hudson, to the Lindbergh estate to help Corporal Frank A. Kelly of the New Jersey State Police develop fingerprints off the kidnap ladder. Dr. Hudson, a graduate of Harvard University and New York City's College of Physicians and Surgeons, had practiced medicine for twenty-four years, was a student of forensic science, and had studied fingerprint science at Scotland Yard, where, in 1901, the great master in the field, Francis Galton, started the world's first fingerprint identification bureau.

Dr. Hudson switched sides in the Lindbergh case when he learned that Hauptmann's fingerprints were not on the kidnap ladder. Believing Hauptmann innocent, he offered his services to Hauptmann's lawyers and even testified for the defense at Hauptmann's trial. When Governor Harold G. Hoffman entered the case on Hauptmann's behalf, Dr. Hudson joined the governor's team as a volunteer.

In a 1937 article for *Liberty* magazine, Dr. Hudson discussed his long and varied connection to the Lindbergh case, and why he believed the kidnapping was an inside job:

> A point of great importance rested in the absence of any fingerprints on the nursery window and its remarkably broad sill. Kelly had powdered it a few hours after the kidnapping. No prints were found, although Betty Gow, the child's nurse, and Mrs. Lindbergh had opened and closed the window that same night. Miss Gow had rubbed the child's chest with an ointment the oleaginous base of which would have augmented the secretion of the finger ridges in leaving clear prints. Of course there would have been older prints as well. The reason Kelly failed to get all these prints was because they must have been washed off. Some one with a pail of water and cloth undoubtedly bathed those spots where fingerprints must have been left. They did so between the time Betty Gow put the baby to bed and about four hours later, when Kelly began investigating.
>
> It is ludicrous to suppose that the kidnapper climbed the ladder with the pail and rag and descended with this in one hand and the baby in the other. It is equally unreasonable to suppose that any one alien to the household, wear-

ing gloves, as the prosecution contended the kidnapper did, would have any interest in eliminating the normal fingerprints to be found in the nursery.

Bluntly, the absence of fingerprints on the window proves conclusively that others than Hauptmann were involved; that the kidnapper had an accomplice probably within the Lindbergh household. Major Schoeffel of the state police called my attention to this fact when he told me, "Doctor, I cannot understand why the fingerprints of Betty Gow were not on that window." Miss Gow even showed Kelly where her hand was placed on the window. No reflection whatever is meant to be cast upon Miss Gow, least of all that she may have been an accomplice.

Hauptmann's counsel, during the trial, made a grievous error in attempting to belittle the fingerprint work of Sergeant [formerly Corporal] Kelly and Sgt. Louis Kubler, Kelly's associate, both of whom, considering their equipment and experience, did an excellent job.[1]

Dr. Hudson's conclusion that Hauptmann had never touched the kidnap ladder because his fingerprints were not found on it, was challenged by prosecutor David T. Wilentz during Hudson's cross-examination as a defense witness:

Q. Supposing the ladder were out in the open on a March night, when it rained and snowed the day before, and it was misty and moist, on damp ground, in the Sourland Mountains, and had been lying out there from a quarter after nine until one o'clock in the morning, in that sort of atmosphere and under those conditions would that affect any fingerprints on the ladder?

A. Not the conditions you stated, sir.

Q. It would have to pour on it or what?

A. Have to rain right on it.

Q. And the dampness and the snow on the ground, if there was any, the damp ground wouldn't affect it at all?

A. The air must be very damp, must be very humid.

Q. So that the part lying immediately on the ground would be affected by it, wouldn't it?

A. Yes, it would be wet.

Q. And if it was wet such fingerprints as were there would be obliterated or interfered with?

A. Yes sir.

Q. And if hundreds of people handled the ladder to such an extent that some of them, more than one of them we will say, put his finger prints and superimposed them over others, why, that would obliterate it, wouldn't it?

A. Yes, the photographs would show that.[2]

Sergeant Frank A. Kelly's trial testimony confirms Dr. Hudson's point about no fingerprints found in the nursery. Sergeant Kelly, when asked if he had attempted to find any fingerprints in the nursery answered: "I processed the window sill, the window, inside and out, the crib, the screen (a free-standing screen used to shade the crib), the light in back of the screen, the French windows, the window on the north side of the nursery, the bureau drawers, a little chair that was at the foot of the crib, everything in the room that it was possible to obtain a fingerprint from."

Q. Did you find any fingerprint upon those articles?
A. No, sir, I did not.[3]

The absence of the kidnapper's fingerprints in the nursery can be explained—he either wore gloves, wiped off what he touched, or his prints were smudged, smeared, or were merely partials; or the fingerprint technicians accidentally ruined them. Why there were no fingerprints in the room at all—assuming there were no smudges either—is tougher to explain and remains a mystery. It would have been helpful if Wilentz had clarified Kelly's answer by asking if he meant "no smudges" when he said "no fingerprints."

Inside-job theorists have a hard time believing that one man could have physically managed to get the baby out the window and down the ladder. They cite this fact in support of the theory that someone inside the house carried the baby down the back stairs and handed him to someone outside. The ladder, according to this scenario, was merely a diversion. Pulp writer Alan Hynd, an early Hauptmann revisionist whose ideas were later incorporated into Scaduto's book, questioned the orthodox version of the abduction in a 1935 article for *True Detective Mysteries*. About the ladder, Alan Hynd wrote:

> The top rung of the second section was exactly thirty inches below the window-sill. When Lieutenant Sweeney and several state troopers climbed the ladder, they had little difficulty in drawing themselves up through the window, but in coming out again, they were forced to use both hands to grip the window-sill while finding their footing on the top rung of the ladder, thirty inches below. If it was necessary to use both hands to do this, how had the kidnapper managed to hold the child?
>
> During the experiments several sleuths tried coming down the ladder with a package weighing thirty pounds—the weight of the Lindy child—and most of them were obliged to lay the package on the window-sill until they found

their footing, then pick it up. Two or three sleuths managed to get their footing on the ladder without letting go of the package, but they looked like contortionists when they did so. Had the actual kidnapper laid the baby on the window-sill until he found his footing on the ladder, then returned to the child—and all of this in the dark; or had he enacted a veritable contortionist's role in that inky night, and when the ladder gave way under his weight and that of the baby, fallen to the ground?[4]

The trial testimony of Lieutenant John P. Sweeney of the New Jersey State Police confirms that climbing into the nursery from the ladder, with the shutters closed, and the top of the ladder falling thirty inches below the window sill, took a certain amount of strength and skill. Getting back out of the window with the thirty-pound baby was even more awkward and difficult. It was certainly possible, however, and assuming that it wasn't, there is no reason not to believe that the kidnapper tossed the baby out the window before climbing down the ladder. The fact the baby had a fractured skull makes this a real possibility, a possibility Alan Hynd did not consider in his article.

As long as there was hope that the baby was alive, New Jersey State Police investigators took their orders from Colonel Lindbergh and his principal advisor, Colonel Henry Breckinridge. Investigatively, detectives were limited to following up leads in the form of "baby sightings" and to running down tips regarding suspicious persons. They were also doing investigations into the backgrounds of the Lindbergh-Morrow servants, treating each domestic as a possible suspect.

The discovery of the baby's corpse in the Mount Rose Heights woods a few miles from the Lindbergh estate changed everything investigatively. Colonel Schwarzkopf and his men were no longer restrained—from now on they would not have to worry about jeopardizing the child. They now had a free hand; the investigation had entered a new phase.

On May 13, 1932, the day following the discovery of the baby's corpse, Schwarzkopf's chief investigator, Lt. Arthur T. Keaten, questioned John F. Condon, the man who had paid the ransom to "Cemetery John" on April 2. Up until now, Condon, working secretly with Colonel Lindbergh and his advisors, had been off-limits to the police. With the baby dead, and Colonel Lindbergh out of the picture, Condon was up for grabs, and the police had a lot of questions. They were particularly interested in knowing if "Cemetery John" could have been connected in any way to one or more of the Lindbergh-Morrow employees. Lieutenant Keaten's questioning of Condon along this line went as follows:

Q. During any of your conversations with this man (Cemetery John) did he make any mention of how this child was actually stolen from its crib?

A. Yes, he did. I made the particular point to ask him where he got the child, how they got the child and he said that it was taken out of the window.

Q. You made mention also in your statement of the fact that there were five people involved in the crime, two of which were women, did he surrender any information that would lead to their identification or apprehension?

A. Not in the slightest degree except that the two women were innocent and the baby was in their care.

Q. Did he at any time make mention that any employee of the Morrow or Lindbergh family had any knowledge of the crime?

A. Never hinted at it, neither by hint or innuendo or any other way.

Q. Did he at any time reveal how he had selected you to act as their intermediary?

A. He said one of them knew me, then I asked him to bring that man to me or let me see that man and he said no, they would smack me out, I have told you too much already, I have to go.[5]

The nature of Lieutenant Keaten's questions indicates that the police were looking for several kidnappers and a possible connection to the Lindbergh-Morrow households. Although there were no servants free of suspicion, Lieutenant Keaten had focused on Betty Gow, the twenty-eight-year-old nursemaid from Glasgow, Scotland.

Miss Gow had been serving the Lindberghs since February 25, 1931. She had been hired on the recommendation of Mary Beattie, a lady maid employed by Mrs. Dwight Morrow. Miss Gow had come to America in May 1929. Slender, dark-haired, and pretty, Betty did not usually accompany the Lindberghs on their weekend excursions to the new estate in Hopewell.

Lieutenant Keaten's interest in Betty Gow, as a possible conspirator, was justified. She was the last person in the household to see the baby alive. She was also one of the few people who had known of the family's last-minute decision to stay in Hopewell, information she could have passed on to her boyfriend, Henry "Red" Johnson. Johnson had telephoned the Lindbergh estate at 8:30 that night, thirty minutes to an hour before the abduction. Perhaps this call had something to do with the kidnapping? When asked by Lieutenant Keaten to explain the phone call, Betty Gow said the following:

I tried to get Johnson on the telephone at Englewood before I left for Hopewell, but I couldn't reach him because he wasn't at his boardinghouse. So I left word for him to call me in the evening at Hopewell. We had intended seeing each other that evening. He called me from Englewood between eight and nine that night and I told him how it happened that I wasn't at the Morrow house. I told him the baby had a cold.[6]

Betty Gow had met the twenty-four-year-old Johnson in the summer of 1931 at North Haven, Maine, where she was taking care of the Lindbergh baby at the Morrow summer place. Johnson, a red-haired Norwegian, was working on a yacht owned by Thomas W. Lamant. When summer ended and Johnson was no longer employed on the ship, he continued visiting Betty at the Morrow estate in Englewood. When he was not working, he stayed with his brother John in West Hartford, Connecticut.

Betty herself had been working as a domestic since she was fourteen. Her first job after coming to the United States was in Detroit. Six months later she was working for a Mrs. Sullivan in Englewood. She had two brothers, Alexander and James, both living in Scotland. Keaten checked with the police in Detroit, who reported they were looking for a crook up there named "Scotty" Gow who was mixed up in the so-called "snatch racket." As it turned out, this man had no connection to Betty or the Lindbergh case.

Lieutenant Keaten was bothered by the sleeveless nightshirt Betty Gow had fashioned for the baby that night shortly before bedtime. Could she have known that the child would soon be exposed to the forty-degree night? Lieutenant Keaten had also talked to officer Charles E. Williamson of the Hopewell Police Department. Williamson and his partner, Harry Wolfe, were the first officers at the scene that night. In his police report, Williamson had written: "My observation of all those present, that is the family and servants were that the Colonel was collected; Mrs. Lindbergh very nervous and restless; the butler appeared to me to be depressed and nervous; and his wife was crying. The maid (Betty Gow) appeared to me to be the coolest of the lot."[7]

Three days after the kidnapping, the New Jersey State Police asked the Hartford Police to pick up Henry Johnson for questioning. Throughout the interrogation, Johnson denied any connection to the kidnapping. His answers were straightforward, matter-of-fact, and plausible. He did not seem anxious, nor did he act indignant. The police searched Johnson's green Chrysler coupe. A green car had been seen near the Lindbergh estate on the day of the kidnapping. But owning a green car did not make Johnson a prime suspect—the police had already checked the registrations of 374 such vehicles. In Johnson's car, however, the police found an empty milk bottle. It was lying in the rumble seat and was stamped "Wednesday." The bottle had been issued by a dairy in Newark. Johnson's interrogator asked him what a grown man was doing with an empty milk bottle in his car. Was it for the Lindbergh baby? Showing little emotion, Johnson said that he would not confess to something he did not do. He drank a lot of milk, often draining a bottle as he drove. When finished, he'd toss the empty bottle into the back seat of his car. Later, he would return the bottles for the two-cent deposit. He drank so much milk that he frequently told people that he was on a milk diet.[8]

Interrogators from Jersey City, at Colonel Schwarzkopf's request, went to Hartford to continue the grilling, but they could not shake Henry Johnson's story. In the meantime, Johnson's fingerprints were sent to the FBI's fingerprint bureau in Washington, D.C. A week later, with Johnson still in custody as a Lindbergh case suspect, the FBI discovered that five years earlier Johnson had entered the country illegally. The police could now hold him as an illegal alien.

On March 15, two weeks after the kidnapping, Colonel Schwarzkopf announced that Henry Johnson had been cleared of any wrongdoing in the Lindbergh case. He was still in federal custody as an illegal alien and could be deported. Schwarzkopf also declared that Betty Gow was no longer under investigation. She too had been cleared. Henry Johnson was not deported; he simply disappeared and was not to be heard of again.[9]

On March 10, 1932, a pair of detectives from the Newark Police Department, Sergeant McCrath and Detective Schiable, went to the Morrow home to question a twenty-eight-year-old maid named Violet Sharpe. All of the twenty-nine domestic servants in the Lindbergh-Morrow households were being routinely questioned. In 1929, Violet had come to America via Canada from the village of Tult's Clump in Bradfield, England. She had worked nine months in Toronto before moving to New York City, where she registered with an employment agency. Ten days later she was interviewed by Mrs. Cecil Craeme, of the Morrow staff, who recommended her for employment. The woman Violet had worked for in Toronto had described her as "sober, industrious, willing, and loyal."[10] Violet's sister Emily worked as a maid for Miss Constance Chilton. Miss Chilton and Elisabeth

Morrow, Anne Lindbergh's sister, were co-owners of a private school for children.

Although informally engaged to the Morrow butler, Septimus Banks, Violet dated other men. On occasion she would sneak an illegal beer at one of the local speakeasies. Violet had to be discreet, however, because Mrs. Morrow was old fashioned and straight laced, and Violet, in the midst of the Great Depression, could not afford to lose her job.

The detectives sent to question Violet expected her to be as cooperative and docile as the other servants they had talked to. But instead, she was sharp tongued and made it clear that she resented being questioned by the police. The only reason she was cooperating at all was because she felt she had no choice. Besides being abrasive and nervous, Violet was evasive in her responses to several pointed questions. After being pressed to account for her whereabouts before the kidnapping, Violet said that on the afternoon of Sunday, February 28, she and her sister Emily were walking along Lydecker Street in Englewood when a man drove by and waved to them. Believing she knew this man, Violet waved back, causing the driver to stop and offer them a ride home. As it turned out, the women did not know this man, but he seemed nice enough, so they climbed into his car. On the way home, Violet agreed to go out with the man at a later, but unspecified, date.

The detectives asked Violet if she had prior knowledge that the Lindberghs were not coming home as usual following that weekend. She replied that at 11:30 A.M. on the day of the kidnapping, she answered the Morrow telephone and it was Mrs. Lindbergh calling from Hopewell. Mrs. Lindbergh wanted to speak to Betty Gow. Later in the day, Betty told Violet that the baby was still suffering from his cold and that she, Betty, would be driven over to Hopewell to help look after him. At eight o'clock that night, the man she had met on Lydecker Street called and asked her out to the movies. He came to the house thirty minutes later to pick her up.

When Violet got to the car, she looked into the back seat and saw another man and his date. After the movie her date drove her back to the Morrow estate. It was 11:00. When pressed for names Violet drew a blank. Although she had agreed to a second date with this man, she could not remember his name. She could not recall the name of the other man or the identity of the woman with him. Violet was also unable to remember anything about the movie, and did not know the name or location of the theater.[11]

While the Newark detectives questioned Violet Sharpe at the Lindbergh home in Hopewell, detectives were searching her room at the Morrow estate across the state in Englewood. A couple of items found in Violet's room were of interest. She had a savings account in a New York City bank that showed a balance of sixteen hundred dollars. This was an incredible amount of money for a domestic employee who made a hundred dollars a month. The officers took into consideration the fact that Violet's room and board came with the job, allowing her to save almost everything she earned. The officers also found, in Violet's room, a small leather notebook that contained ribald, handwritten stories. There was also a slip of paper with the hand-written notation: "Banks promises to try to be straight for 12 months."[12] The Morrow butler had apparently been spending too much time at the local speakeasy. (It was common knowledge that Banks had a drinking problem and on several occasions had come close to losing his job.)

Violet Sharpe was questioned again on April 13, 1932. This time she was interrogated by Inspector Harry Walsh of the Jersey City Police Department. The hard-nosed detective, following some preliminary chitchat, asked the maid if she had since remembered the name of the movie she had seen on the night of the kidnapping. Violet told Inspector Walsh that she had been mistaken—she had not gone to a movie that night. Instead, she, her escort, and the other couple had driven to a roadhouse called the Peanut Grill. She could not say where the bar was exactly, except that it was an hour's drive from Englewood. Her date was named Ernie something and she still did not know who the other people were. She said she had not heard from Ernie since the kidnapping.[13]

Following the interview, Inspector Walsh told Captain John J. Lamb of the New Jersey State Police that he did not believe Violet Sharpe was telling the truth. Captain Lamb agreed and informed Walsh that on the day of the kidnapping, Violet's sister Emily had applied for a visa to return to England, and on April 6, just four days after the ransom payment, she had set sail for home. Emily had done this without notifying the police.

On May 9, three days before the Lindbergh baby was found, Violet was admitted to the Englewood Hospital with infected tonsils. The next day her tonsils and adenoids were removed. She was recovering from her surgery when she learned of the Lindbergh baby. Despondent and ill, she checked herself out of the hospital on May 14 against her doctor's advice.[14]

Inspector Walsh, eager to resolve his doubts about Violet Sharpe, questioned the maid, against the wishes of her doctor, on May 23 in the Morrow study. Present were Colonel Lindbergh, Colonel Schwarzkopf, and Lieutenant Keaten. Violet was nervous, but perhaps due to her illness, was docile. When Inspector Walsh asked about Ernie, he learned that Ernie had called Violet at the Morrow house at one in the afternoon on the day of the kidnapping. This meant that Ernie had called an hour and a half after Violet had learned that the Lindbergh baby would remain at the Hopewell estate that night. The implication was clear—Violet Sharpe could have informed Ernie of this and he would have had time to tell others—possibly the kidnappers.

Inspector Walsh asked Violet about the speakeasy and how she knew it was called the Peanut Grill—"Because I saw the name on a sign," she replied.[15]

Walsh asked Violet to explain her financial situation, which she did, then he asked for a detailed description of her friend Ernie. At the conclusion of the interview, Inspector Walsh declared that he still was not ready to clear Violet Sharpe. Colonel Schwarzkopf agreed. Colonel Lindbergh, on the other hand, explained that Violet had lied about the movie because she did not want Mrs. Morrow to know about the Peanut Grill. The maid was also ill and very upset about the baby. Lindbergh made it very clear that, in his opinion, Violet Sharpe had nothing to do with the kidnapping. As for her man Ernie, he could not be sure.[16]

On June 7, Violet, despondent and physically weak, penned a letter to her girlfriend back in England. She wrote:

Dearest Fan,

Just a hurried line. At last so glad to get your letter this morning. I hope you will forgive me for not writing before but really we have had so much trouble here over the Lindbergh baby. We have all been questioned by the police and I have been in hospital a week with a poisoned throat—had my tonsils out and I only weigh seven stones [98 pounds] the least I have ever been in my life and I just feel as weak as a rat. I want to come home so much but I can't leave the country or they will think I knew something about the baby. You have no idea what we have been through when the police had me for questioning. I fainted 2 in 2 hours so you can guess how weak I was. I was so sorry to hear about that little girl, Fan, gee, life is getting so sad I really don't think there is much to live for anymore.[17]

Violet Sharpe was questioned for the fourth time on June 9, two weeks after being questioned in front of Colonel Lindbergh in the Morrow study.

Inspector Walsh arrived at the Morrow estate at eleven o'clock in the morning carrying mug shots of a petty thief named Ernest Brinkert. Brinkert had operated the Fast Road Taxi Company in White Plains, New York, a firm that had been out of business for more than a year. Brinkert's business cards had been found in Violet's room, therefore Walsh wanted to ask Violet if Brinkert had driven her and the other couple to the Peanut Grill on the night of the kidnapping.

For the fourth time, Violet Sharpe described her activities on the night of the crime. She still had not recovered from her surgery, was obviously nervous, was hesitant in answering the inspector's questions, and seemed on the verge of tears. Inspector Walsh showed Violet a photograph of Ernest Brinkert and asked if he was the man who had taken her and the other people to the Peanut Grill. At first Violet said that he was, then qualified her identification by stating that Ernest Brinkert merely resembled the man. She could not, she said, make a positive identification. When Inspector Walsh pressed harder, Violet physically collapsed into uncontrollable sobbing. The Morrow family doctor had to be summoned to calm her down. After a cursory examination, the physician declared that Violet was on the verge of hysteria. Because of this and the fact her blood pressure was dangerously high, the doctor told Inspector Walsh that he would have to ask him to terminate the questioning. The doctor's order angered Walsh, who thought Violet was faking, "We'll call it quits for today," Walsh said. "But tomorrow we'll have you brought to our officers in Alpine for more questioning."[18]

Violet got to her feet and walked unaided out of the room. The Morrow secretary, Laura Hughes, was seated at the desk in the study. She was the one who had called the doctor. Laura looked up sympathetically as Violet passed by. To the secretary's utter amazement, Violet flashed a sly smile, then winked. Inspector Walsh did not see this, and neither did the doctor.[19]

Following his session with Violet Sharpe, Inspector Walsh drove to Trenton, where he reported to Colonel Schwarzkopf that Ernest Brinkert had taken Violet Sharpe to the Peanut Grill on the night of the kidnapping. Schwarzkopf immediately sent out an all-points bulletin describing the five-foot four-inch Brinkert and his car, a green 1926 Nash. He was to be arrested on sight.

That night, at the Morrow estate, Violet Sharpe was telling Betty Gow and some of the other servants about her ordeal with Inspector Walsh. In a state of near hysteria, she vowed that she would never let the police take her from the house.

The next morning, at ten o'clock, Inspector Walsh telephoned the Morrow house and asked Arthur Springer, Mrs. Morrow's personal secretary, to tell Violet that Lieutenant Arthur T. Keaten from the New Jersey State Police would be by the house in an hour to take Violet to Alpine for further questioning. Springer picked up the house phone and relayed the message to Violet, who, in a state of panic, ran to the pantry and pulled a large measuring glass off the shelf. With the glass in her hand, she scurried up the stairway to her room, and, from the top shelf of her wardrobe closet, took down a can containing a penciled-on warning: "Poison. Do not Unpack." She ran into the bathroom carrying this can and poured some of its contents, white powder in the form of crystals, into the measuring cup from the downstairs pantry. She filled the measuring cup with water then walked back to her room, where she gulped down the milky white liquid. She stepped out of her room and started down the stairs with the measuring cup dangling from her right hand. Except for the filigree of undissolved crystals on the bottom of the glass, it was empty. Once Violet reached the bottom of the stairs, she shuffled to the pantry where she met Emily Kampairien, another maid. Swaying back and forth, she tried to speak, but all she could manage was a gurgling sound. She collapsed to the floor and within minutes was dead.[20]

Some of the evidence of Violet's suicide was in her bedroom. The can containing the white crystals was still on the table next to her bed. The printed label read: "Cyanide chloride." Violet had brought the poison, used to clean silver, to the Morrow house two years earlier.

The next day, Ernest Brinkert was arrested in New Rochelle, New York. Given the third degree, he denied knowing Violet Sharpe. Dr. John F. Condon was summoned to the New Rochelle police station, and he declared that Brinkert was not "Cemetery John."

On June 11, 1932, a man named Ernest Miller from Closter, New Jersey, walked into the local police department and announced that he was the Ernie who had been out with Violet Sharpe on the night of the kidnapping. Attention shifted suddenly from Brinkert to Miller who told Lieutenant Keaten and others that he had met Violet and her sister Emily on the Sunday preceding the kidnapping. The women were walking along Lydecker

Street in Englewood that afternoon when he happened to drive by. They waved and he stopped to give them a lift back to the Morrow house. On the following Tuesday, the twenty-three-year-old bus driver called Violet and asked her for a date that night. He said he called the Morrow house at one o'clock in the afternoon. Around eight that night he and another couple, Elmer Johnson and Katherine Minners, picked up Violet at the Morrow estate. Miller drove the group to Orangeburg, New York, near Tappan, where they danced and had a few drinks at a place called the Peanut Grill. Around midnight Ernest drove Violet home. Miller said that he thought Violet had known his name and had no idea why she said Brinkert, who did not look anything like him, resembled the man who had taken her out that night.

The police questioned Katherine Minners, a stenographer from Palisades Park, New Jersey, and Elmer Johnson, her date that night. Their stories matched Miller's. Detectives also questioned Thomas Fay, Ernest Brinkert's former business partner. Fay reported that on March 1, 1932, he and Brinkert were in Bridgeport, Connecticut, playing cards. Albert S. Osborn, the renowned forensic documents examiner, studied samples of Brinkert's and Miller's handwriting and declared that these men had not written any of the ransom notes.[21]

Inspector Walsh, having strongly suspected that Violet Sharpe was the kidnapper's inside connection, was at a loss to explain her reaction to the police and her suicide. Speaking to a group of reporters about Sharpe, he said, "This is a peculiar turn of events. It is no fault of ours. I can't understand why Violet Sharpe, if she had nothing to do with the kidnapping, preferred death to revealing Miller's name. I cannot understand it at all."[22]

Inspector Walsh, until the day he died, was convinced that Violet Sharpe's suicide was in some way connected to the Lindbergh kidnapping.

At the time of the suicide, Violet's sister Emily was in England visiting her family. Detectives from Scotland Yard had questioned her and had cabled Schwarzkopf that Emily, a girl of excellent character, had no inside knowledge of the Lindbergh case.

On June 12, 1932, a Sunday, the newspapers were full of the Lindbergh case, including a statement by Emily Sharpe that would open the flood gates to a tidal wave of criticism of the New Jersey State Police. Her statement reads as follows:

Ever since the baby disappeared, Violet was badgered and was questioned until she did not know what she was saying or doing. She was driven nearly mad. After the baby was stolen Violet wrote me and I went to Englewood to see her. She was terribly distressed and said the police had been questioning her for hours. She asserted that she knew nothing about the child's disappearance, but she said the police would not believe her. It was all so cruel. Violet would never have done anything to the child or to anyone who wanted to find it.[23]

In Trenton, New Jersey, reporters asked Colonel Schwarzkopf, in view of Brinkert's alibi and Ernest Miller's statement, if he would publicly exonerate Violet Sharpe. Schwarzkopf said that Violet's guilt or innocence was a matter of opinion. "The fact remains," he said, "that conflicting statements were made, that a false identification was made, that the identity of Miller was concealed, and that truths were denied."[24] As to how Ernest Brinkert's business cards had gotten into Violet's room, Schwarzkopf did not have an answer. According to rumor, Inspector Walsh had planted the cards. The theory went something like this: Initially Walsh had no reason to connect his suspect, Brinkert, to Violet other than the fact his first name was Ernest and he had an arrest record. Taking Brinkert's photograph to Violet had been a long shot. Therefore, no one was more surprised than Walsh when Violet identified Brinkert as the man she had been out with on the night of the kidnapping. At that point, Walsh planted the cards to cement the connection between Brinkert and Sharpe in order to make it harder for Brinkert to deny he had been Violet's date that night. When it turned out that Brinkert, in fact, had not been out with Violet, the whole thing blew up in Walsh's face. When the real Ernie came forward, Brinkert's business cards in Violet's room suddenly became a mystery and an embarrassment.

If the real Ernest had not come forward with the truth, Ernest Brinkert would have been eventually inducted into the Lindbergh Suspect Hall of Fame along with the likes of John F. Condon, John H. Curtis, Isidor Fisch, Paul H. Wendel, Al Capone, Betty Gow, and, yes, Violet Sharpe.

The Violet Sharpe controversy put Colonel Lindbergh in an awkward position. He wanted to defend Colonel Schwarzkopf against the charges of incompetence and brutality, but could not. If he allowed himself to be drawn into the debate, he would have to publicize his opinion that Violet Sharpe was innocent of any wrongdoing in connection with the kidnapping. Knowing that Schwarzkopf had believed otherwise, and that a statement in support of the maid would weaken Schwarzkopf's position as head of the investigation, Lindbergh kept silent on the matter.

Violet Sharpe's suicide had a profound effect on Mrs. Lindbergh. Reflecting on the tragedy, she wrote, "terrible criticism of police, in papers: 'Bullied innocent girl to death.' Blaze of criticism in papers in England. Girl appears innocent. It is very sickening. What a crude, imperfect world—we understand nothing."[25]

Because Schwarzkopf harbored the belief that Violet Sharpe may have been Hauptmann's inside contact, his detectives continued to dig into her background after Hauptmann had been arrested, tried, and convicted. They even continued their inquiry beyond Hauptmann's execution in April 1936. (Revisionist Ludovic Kennedy's accusation that the police quit looking for other suspects or accomplices the minute they arrested Hauptmann is not supported by the record.) Four years after Violet's death, his detectives uncovered information that comes close to explaining her suicide. People they talked to said that while Violet was employed at the Morrow estate, she dated five men with whom she had been sexually intimate. One of these men, William O'Brien, was a soda jerk at Dr. Wilmer's Drug Store on the corner of Lexington Avenue and 39th Street in Manhattan. O'Brien had met Violet when she was living at the YWCA prior to working for the Morrow family.[26]

Violet Sharpe may have been afraid that the Lindbergh investigators would find out about her relationships with these men. If Mrs. Morrow had learned of these relationships, she might have fired Violet. The thought of being jobless and homeless with no one to recommend her in the midst of the Great Depression would have been frightening. Violet would have had no choice but to return in disgrace to her parent's tiny cottage in England. Violet may also have been thinking about Septimus Banks who had hoped to marry her. Worried about her job and future in America, sick and weak from her recent hospitalization, and under relentless attack from Inspector Walsh and others who believed she might have helped the Lindbergh kidnappers, Violet had ended her horrible situation by taking her life. Was her death related to the Lindbergh case? Yes. Was she a Lindbergh case conspirator? No. Violet Sharpe, like so many others in the case, was simply another victim of the Lindbergh crime.

Part 3 The Evidence

▌▌ Hard Evidence

Hauptmann died in the electric chair because experts said he wrote the ransom notes and made the kidnap ladder. If they were correct, a thousand alibi witnesses, and proof that John F. Condon, Colonel Lindbergh, Amandus Hochmuth, Millard Whited, and Joseph Perrone had lied on the witness stand, will not make Hauptmann innocent.

How strong is the handwriting evidence against Hauptmann? Is there any room for doubt?

Eight nationally known questioned-document examiners, from Los Angeles to New York City, both private and government employed, testified that Hauptmann wrote the ransom notes—the questioned documents.[1] The Lindbergh crime produced an enormous quantity of questioned writing, much more than examiners usually get to analyze. They also had plenty of known writing in the form of request writings—Albert S. Osborn's carefully constructed paragraphs dictated to Hauptmann by the police—and his conceded or "course of business" writings in the form of Hauptmann's personal notebooks and his auto registration, driver's license and insurance applications. The experts testified that Hauptmann's known writing looked like the writing in the ransom notes. They produced dozen of word charts for the jury that illustrated this clearly. Hauptmann and the ransom note writer had also misspelled certain words the same way. Four of the experts testified that Hauptmann had also addressed the package sent to John F. Condon, the one that contained the baby's sleeping suit.[2]

The questioned-document testimony in the Hauptmann trial took four days and produced eight hundred pages of trial transcript. Besides the eight experts who had taken the stand, the prosecution had four rebuttal experts who would have testified against Hauptmann had the defense put on a battery of their own handwriting witnesses.[3] As it turned out, they were not needed.

One of these rebuttal experts, John Vreeland Haring, later published a heavily illustrated book showing why he believed Hauptmann had written the ransom documents.[4] Haring made a special effort to illustrate the similarities between Hauptmann's writing and the ransom note left in the nursery. For comparison purposes, he used as known handwriting samples the two post-conviction letters Hauptmann had written to Governor Harold G. Hoffman.

In addition to the prosecution's eight handwriting witnesses and the four rebuttal experts, Charles A. Appel Jr., the head of the FBI Crime Lab, believed Hauptmann was the ransom note writer. Appel Jr., the Bureau's questioned-document examiner, testified before the Bronx Grand Jury.[5]

Hauptmann's defense attorney, Edward J. Reilly, asked seven document examiners to look at the handwriting evidence—the questioned documents. Three declared Hauptmann the ransom note writer, another three said the ransom notes had been altered after Hauptmann's arrest to look like his writing—thereby conceding that the writing was similar—and the seventh, John C. Trendley from St. Louis, actually testified for the defense as Hauptmann's sole handwriting witness.[6]

A reporter who covered the Hauptmann trial wrote this about Trendley: "He was a furtive, musty little codger who had the greatest difficulty establishing his claim to be an expert.... And his testimony was really pathetic."[7] Besides his background as a courtroom charlatan, Trendley's testimony was weakened by the fact he had not spent much time with the evidence. There were others who said Hauptmann did not write the ransom notes, but they were either graphologists, penmanship teachers, crackpots, or con artists.[8]

The handwriting evidence against Hauptmann was overwhelming; nevertheless, people with political, literary, and psychological axes to grind—people who must have Hauptmann innocent—employ a variety of ways to deal with this evidence. Ludovic Kennedy, for example, simply attacks the prosecution's experts, describing them as "Looking like senior members of an old folks' bowling club."[9]

Donald F. Doud, a highly respected forensic document examiner from Milwaukee, in reviewing Kennedy's book for the *Journal of Forensic Sci-*

ences, points out that "in fact, with the exception of Albert S. Osborn who was in his 70's, the document examiners were in the prime of life, all being in their 40's, 50's and 60's."[10] Kennedy's point is not only irrelevant to the question of who wrote the ransom notes, it is a factual misrepresentation.

Kennedy's fellow revisionist, Anthony Scaduto, simply dismisses questioned documents as a science: "American courts have held repeatedly that the testimony of so-called handwriting experts represents the lowest degree of evidence, and with good reason."[11] This of course, is not true either. Questioned-document experts have been testifying in court all over the world for more than a hundred years. "The members of this profession are scientists in the truest sense of that term," wrote Francis X. Busch, the renowned true-crime author and attorney.[12]

Hauptmann's supporters attack the handwriting evidence on another front by claiming—without proof—that the prosecution's experts were so intimidated by Albert S. Osborn, they obediently fell into line behind him. The revisionists also accuse Osborn's son, Albert D., of changing his opinion to please his father. To explain the damning misspellings in Hauptmann's request writings that help identify him as the ransom note writer, Hauptmann supporters have no recourse but to accuse the police of wrongdoing. They claim, again without proof, that these officers told Hauptmann to misspell certain words to make it appear he had written the ransom documents. The fact is, no one connected to the Lindbergh case has ever admitted doing such a thing, and no witness to it has ever come forward. If the police had in fact done what Scaduto and others say they had done, officers from three rival law enforcement agencies would have committed perjury, and dozens of other detectives would have known about it and kept silent.[13] Anyone familiar with law enforcement knows that this kind of cooperation between competing agencies is virtually impossible.

Hauptmann supporters must also confront the fact that in his personal papers unrelated to the case, Hauptmann had misspelled boat as "Boad," money as "mony," New York as "New-York," light as "lihgt," and seventy as "senvety." Hauptmann testified that the police told him to misspell signature as "singnature," so it would match the incorrectly spelled word in the nursery and other ransom notes. But in fact, the word signature was not included in the material dictated to Hauptmann by the police. Hauptmann lied.

Hauptmann defenders desperately need to disassociate him from the ransom note in the nursery because it places him at the scene of the kidnapping. But they cannot do it because Hauptmann, the clever fox, had fashioned the unique symbol that identified subsequent ransom letters as coming from the man who had left the note in the nursery. Therefore, if Hauptmann wrote one of the letters, he wrote them all, including the one at the scene of the crime. Notwithstanding powerful evidence to the contrary, those who support Hauptmann point to the nursery note as a weak link in the prosecution's handwriting case. Six months after Hauptmann's execution, John F. Tyrrell, one of the prosecution's handwriting experts, wrote a letter to James Clark Sellers, another expert who had testified against Hauptmann, about this so-called weak link in the handwriting evidence. Tyrrell wrote:

> Last year Lloyd Fisher, Hauptmann's attorney, wrote to Walter Winchell a lengthy communication in part as follows:
>
> "Do you recollect that the only word taken for comparison by any of the handwriting experts in the state's side of the case, from the nursery note, was the word 'is.' and that aside from that they disregard the original ransom note completely? . . . "
>
> Mr. Fisher furnished a whole column just like this in a letter to Mr. Winchell. . . . When I read this communication . . . I had recourse to the copy of my testimony and I found that I had taken particular pains to link the cradle note with other notes and had made, as I recall now, some fifteen comparisons between the cradle note and the subsequent notes.[14]

Since the 1976 publication of Scaduto's book, five forensic scientists, all members of the American Society of Document Examiners, have studied the handwriting in the Lindbergh case. If Hauptmann were tried today, these five experts would testify that he had written the ransom notes.[15]

In his 1985 book, Ludovic Kennedy reports that "a leading British handwriting expert" named Gunter Haas concluded that Hauptmann *did not* write the ransom notes.[16] But according to Robert W. Radley, a private document examiner in Reading, England, Kennedy had asked a colleague of Radley's, handwriting expert Derek Davis, to examine the Lindbergh evidence. Kennedy figured correctly that Davis, a highly regarded British document examiner, would not be influenced by the Albert S. Osborn legacy and could be counted on to give an unbiased, scientific opinion. And that is exactly what Davis did when, according to Radley, he reported that Hauptmann had, in fact, written the ransom notes.[17] As a result, one does not find Davis's name in Kennedy's book. Kennedy, in need of a different opinion, found Gunter Haas.

So who is Gunter Haas, and what are his credentials? None of the document examiners in America who were asked this question had heard of Haas.

Robert W. Radley had not heard of Haas either, but after making a few inquiries in England, reported the following comments, which had been made to him from a number of associates he had contacted:

> It appears that he (Haas) died two or three years ago but was not a recognized forensic document examiner. He was unknown to both the Home Office Forensic Science Laboratory and the Metropolitan Police Laboratory and having dealt with over 5,000 cases myself, this is the only occasion on which his name has arisen.
>
> Further investigation into his background reveals quite clearly that he is a graphologist i.e. assessed character from handwriting and would not therefore have been qualified to identify handwriting.[18]

When asked about Gunter Haas, Dr. Alan Filby, the head of the Questioned Document section of the Metropolitan Police Laboratory in London, said that if Haas was a graphologist, as indicated by Radley's inquiry, Haas would not be qualified to identify handwriting forensically.[19]

In 1981, Anna Hauptmann's attorney, Robert S. Bryan, asked Gus R. Lesnevich, a private document examiner in Philadelphia, to compare samples of her husband's "course of business" writings with the ransom notes. Lesnevich did not examine Hauptmann's request writings because he believes they had been written under duress and "doctored" by the police, who told Hauptmann how to misspell certain words.[20] Lesnevich's findings are published as follows in Kennedy's book: "An examination, comparison and analysis of the questioned ransom notes and known writings not used by the police, along with the additional known writings has resulted in the conclusion that Mr. Richard Hauptmann did not write the questioned ransom notes."[21]

Nine years later, attorney Bryan asked Roy A. Huber, a Canadian document examiner, to study the handwriting in the Lindbergh case. Huber declined.[22]

So, as it now stands, without the graphologists, writing teachers, crack-pots, and charlatans—the handwriting experts are against Hauptmann twenty-one to one. In the game of revisionist crime writing, this is called a tie.

Jan Beck, a respected Seattle document examiner, in a letter to a client who was concerned about a law review article questioning the scientific validity of the field itself, explains how Michael J. Saks, one of the authors of that article, attempts to discredit the handwriting evidence in the Lindbergh case:

> The attack on the "father" of document examination, Albert S. Osborn, is cleverly set up by using a kind of psycho-history combined with not-so-subtle items of disparagement. An example is the Hauptmann case on which Mr. Saks comments: "The evidence against Hauptmann was flimsy and circumstantial, but a ransom note linked the defendant to the kidnapping." For one thing, it is an error of fact to refer to a ransom note in the singular, since there were at least nine ransom notes with some amounts of handwriting that was really identified as Hauptmann's.
>
> And I find it very hard to believe that a person of Osborn's ability and integrity would have failed to recognize Hauptmann's handwriting in the notes, or that he would have changed his opinion after learning of some circumstantial fact. The important point here is that the authors' source for the Osborn dig is the book by Ludovic Kennedy, *The Airman and the Carpenter,* a hatchet-job that has been thoroughly rebutted by forensic scientists who have reviewed the evidence from 1935.
>
> The Kennedy book is germane because the present authors apparently belong to the same coterie of late 20th century revisionists who have been trying to show the world that the evidence against Bruno Hauptmann, Alger Hiss and Sacco and Vanzetti was "flimsy and circumstantial." The common theme in all such attempts at discrediting the state's evidence in these much-debated cases is that when the critics encountered the mute but damning *physical* evidence they have to resort to charges of incompetence, fabrication and conspiracy on the part of the state and the experts.
>
> The fact of the matter in these cases is that the physical evidence is visible, demonstrable and convincing to a reasonable observer; the handwriting in the Hauptmann case; the handwriting and typewriting in the Hiss case; and the bullets and cartridge cases in the Sacco-Vanzetti case. And I have noticed over a period of years that those who have not looked closely into these matters

are usually unaware that Hauptmann's defense did put one expert on the stand saying the notes were not in Hauptmann's handwriting but that he was discredited. . . .

There is an odd populist theme of anti-expertism in the article, which implies that lay persons can deal with handwriting problems without the help of experts. Such anti-expertism is not new but seems to have had a strong revival in recent years, especially in the age group influenced by the anti-authority and anti-establishment sentiments of the 1960's.[23]

For people who need Hauptmann innocent, evidence to the contrary just gets in the way. Trying to change their minds with hard evidence and rational analysis is as futile as using dental charts to prove to certain Elvis Presley fans that the "King" is dead. In a world without science, Elvis Presley can live as long as his fans need him, and Bruno Richard Hauptmann can be transformed into the image created by his widow. There is no room, in a place like this, for the science of questioned documents.

No one disputes the fact that Hauptmann was caught with the ransom money hidden in his garage. He also matched the description of "Cemetery John." While this evidence relates directly to the extortion aspect of the crime, the homemade ladder found at the scene was used in the actual abduction. If Hauptmann, the extortionist, had also made the kidnap ladder, how can he not be guilty of kidnapping and murder?

The evidence connecting Hauptmann to the kidnap ladder, although circumstantial, is powerful and convincing. Aside from being a carpenter by trade, the prosecution linked Hauptmann to the ladder in four ways:

1. Pieces of the ladder had been purchased at a store where Hauptmann bought his wood.
2. One of his notebooks contained a partial sketch of a ladder and a dowel pin.
3. The ladder contained unique and distinct tool marks made by Hauptmann's chisel and handplane.
4. A section of the ladder, rail sixteen, had been a floor plank in Hauptmann's attic.

At the trial, Arthur Koehler, a federally employed wood expert, identified Hauptmann's tool marks, and matched rail sixteen to the board in Hauptmann's attic. In two ways he identified rail sixteen as coming from the attic: the nail holes on rail sixteen lined up with the holes in the attic joists, and when rail sixteen was laid in the gap in the attic floor, it *looked* as though it had been cut from the remaining plank.

This evidence is so demonstrably incriminating, Hauptmann supporters have no choice but to claim it was fabricated—a charge that is easy to make, but on close examination, difficult to sell.

There are two ways the wood evidence could have been fabricated against Hauptmann. One method would have involved taking rail sixteen to Hauptmann's attic and driving nails through it into the floor joists. In his book, Anthony Scaduto claims this is what happened.[24] Although this explains how the nail holes happened to line up, it does not explain the obvious grain similarity between rail sixteen and the sawed off board in the attic. It is only a partial frame-up, and it is not enough. Perhaps that is why, in a 1993 magazine article, Scaduto suggests a more ambitious fabrication: "The suspicion is strong that Bornmann threw away one piece (rail 16) of the kidnap ladder and submitted the board he himself had cut from the attic floor."[25]

Throwing away the original rail sixteen, and substituting a board from Hauptmann's attic, is the only way the wood evidence could have been fabricated against Hauptmann. Had Hauptmann been arrested the day after the kidnapping, when only a few detectives from New Jersey had seen the kidnap ladder, then police may have gotten away with this. But Hauptmann was not identified as a suspect until two and a half years after the crime. During that period, thousands of people looked at the kidnap ladder and had seen the holes in rail sixteen. If the switch had been made after Hauptmann's arrest, hundreds of people, friendly and hostile to the prosecution, would have noticed that rail sixteen suddenly had nail holes.

Ludovic Kennedy in arguing that the original rail sixteen did not have holes, quotes the following from one of Governor Harold G. Hoffman's *Liberty* magazine articles: "I [Governor Hoffman] have in my possession . . . a photograph of the ladder made the day after the commission of the crime . . . and rail sixteen can be easily identified; but neither in the original [photo] nor in a copy magnified ten times can the alleged nail holes be found."[26]

Where is this photograph? It is certainly not in Kennedy's book, nor anywhere else, for that matter.

On March 8, 1932, Corporal George G. Wilton of the New Jersey State Police took fourteen photographs of the kidnap ladder. Two of these photographs show the nail holes in rail sixteen. Wilton developed these pictures himself. He testified at Hauptmann's trial and these two photographs—marked s-302 and s-303—were introduced into evidence.[27]

Harold S. Betts, a thirty-year employee of the U.S. Forest Service, examined rail sixteen on May 23, 1932, and filed a report dated June 1, 1932. At the trial, Betts testified that rail sixteen had four holes made by "old fashioned cut nails," and that "two of the nail holes were at an angle."[28]

Hauptmann's defense attorneys were not fools, they knew the police could not have planted a phony rail sixteen. That is why they were forced into putting a housewrecker, then a millworker on the stand to say that the grain in rail sixteen and the attic plank did not match. Since the jury was not blind, it ignored both witnesses.[29]

Dr. Harold Dearden, the British author and criminal psychologist, characterizes the ladder evidence in the Lindbergh case as follows: "It was unanswerable. There was nothing in it to be denied or explained. . . . And it damned him."[30]

Dr. Dearden was right. But forty-two years after he wrote this, not that many cared.

12 Red Herrings, Pseudologic, and Misinformation

When speaking of the Lindbergh case, Hauptmann supporters are quick to point out that the poor man was beaten by the police, unfairly tried, and convicted without fingerprint evidence. But do these aspects of the case make Hauptmann innocent? If they do not, then they are nothing more than red herrings—irrelevant points of information used to divert attention away from evidence that is clear and strong, evidence that is damning.

Perhaps nothing is more phony than Hauptmann's so-called alibi for the day of the crime. Anthony Scaduto, and later Ludovic Kennedy, accuse the authorities of altering a payroll ledger to make it look as though Hauptmann had not worked at the Majestic Apartments in Manhattan on March 1, 1932. They say he did work there that day until 5:00 or 6:00 P.M. Scaduto repeats this allegation of evidence tampering in his recent article, and so does Kennedy, in his 1989 autobiography.[1]

If the authorities had tampered with the payroll ledger, they were fools, because Hauptmann never said he worked at the Majestic Apartments on the day of the crime. At his extradition hearing in the Bronx, he was asked: "After you left your wife at the store [bakery] . . . at about seven o'clock in the morning on the first of March 1932, what did you do after that?"

Hauptmann answered: "I brought the car home in the garage."

He was asked: "Then what did you do the rest of the day?"

Hauptmann answered: "That I cannot exactly remember."[2]

At his trial, Hauptmann, on direct examination, testified that on March 1, 1932, he drove his wife to work at the lunchroom-bakery at seven in the morning then returned home to put his car away. He then took the subway to the Majestic Apartments to see about starting work as a carpenter.

"I was down eight o'clock in the morning," he said. The rest of his testimony went as follows:

Q. 1932?
A. Yes.
Q. And when you got down there to the place did you go to work?
A. I got to see the superintendent first.
Q. Did you see him?
A. I saw him. I got to wait a little while, about a half hour. Then he said he couldn't put me to work and I got to come back on the 15th of February, because he said he only hires men on the first and on the 15th.
Q. How do you mean the 15th of February or the 15th of March?
A. The 15th of March, I mean. Excuse me.[3]

The following day, on direct examination, the subject of Hauptmann's activities on the day of the crime came up again:

Q. And then where did you go?
A. I went to the Majestic Hotel.
Q. And when you arrived there did you see anybody?
A. Well, I went to the carpenter shop. Of course, my tools was down there already. I took the tools down the day before and was going to start work. The foreman said I got to see the superintendent first.
Q. Now, do you recall the name of the foreman?
A. I can't.
Q. All right. Continue your movements.
A. When I saw the superintendent he said I can't start. Well, I showed him the letter from the agency. [The employment agency Hauptmann had used to get the job.] He said, "I am sorry, it is filled up." So I left the tools right in the Majestic and took the letter and went down to the employment agency where I get the job trying to get them ten dollars back what I paid for it. I couldn't get it then ten dollars and he said, "Come around next day, maybe something else coming in." And after that I went to another agency and I went over to Radio City which was under construction, trying to get a job over there, but I couldn't.[4]

In other words, Hauptmann, on the day of the kidnapping, was not working at the Majestic Apartments and really could not account for himself after nine or ten in the morning.

When questioned by the police on the day of his arrest, Hauptmann could not account for his activities on the *night* of the crime either:

Q. And you remember the night the baby was kidnapped? It was a very dismal night.

A. I do not remember.

Q. You do not remember that night at all?

A. I do not remember.

Q. You do not remember that night at all?

A. No.[5]

So, before Hauptmann had a chance to make up an alibi, he had no choice but to tell the truth, and the business about the altered payroll records, the centerpiece of Scaduto's book, is not only a red herring; it is at odds with the facts.

Shortly after Hauptmann's arrest, Inspector Henry D. Bruckman of the New York City Police Department asked Mrs. Hauptmann if she knew what her husband was doing on the night of March 1, 1932. Mrs. Hauptmann replied that she did not, it was too far back for her to remember.[6]

In the weeks that followed, during Hauptmann's incarceration at the Hunterdon County Jail in Flemington, Mrs. Hauptmann visited her husband on a regular basis, at which time they struggled to concoct an alibi for the night of the kidnapping.

When Mrs. Hauptmann visited her husband on November 26, 1934, his birthday, she was frustrated. She said, in German, "I saw yesterday [in the newspaper] where the state has seventy-five people who are supposed to be our friends and they said that they didn't see you that night." Later in the conversation, she asked: "Do you remember the night we were looking for my niece, I mean paying her a visit and when we got there we found out that she had moved?"

Hauptmann: "I don't seem to remember that night, was that on March the first?"

Mrs. Hauptmann: "Yes, don't you remember you rang the doorbell and a strange woman came out and we thought we were in the wrong apartment, and the woman told us that my niece had moved away."

Hauptmann: "Yes I do remember now."

Mrs. Hauptmann: "And we went over to Mrs. Hahn and had supper there that night." [Marie and Frederick Hahn owned Fred's Restaurant on Webster Avenue in the Bronx. The Hauptmann's were frequent patrons.]

Hauptmann: "That is very important. See if you can locate that woman."[7]

Two weeks later, the Hauptmanns were still fishing for an alibi when Hauptmann asked, "Do you remember that day in March? It was when we were with Maria just before she moved when she had her things packed?"

Mrs. Hauptmann: "No, I don't remember."
Hauptmann: "Don't you remember it was around the time I was sick?"
Mrs. Hauptmann: "No, I cannot remember."[8]

A week later Mrs. Hauptmann was still at it: "The first of that month was on Friday. I remember because the Sunday previous was Easter Sunday. When we went over to Maria's the furniture was all packed and she was ready to move, and when we went there the next Sunday she was staying with Edna and the furniture was stored."

Hauptmann: "I am not sure about that date."[9]

A week after the above conversation, Mrs. Hauptmann had given up on that alibi and was trying something else: "When was it that you were working on those different jobs? I mean the building jobs?"

Hauptmann: "I was at Rosenbaum's and Schweigler's during 1928 and 1929 for quite a long while. From there I went to Croseet's. I quit there after a short stay. I remember that when I worked at Rosenbaum's I had had my car for only a short time."
Mrs. Hauptmann: "I thought you were working at one of those places around the time." ["Around the time" was the Hauptmann code for the night of the kidnapping.]
Hauptmann: "You know I was with you then and we played cards."[10]

The day after Christmas 1934, the Hauptmanns were still fishing for an alibi.

Mrs. Hauptmann: "Do you remember that sometime around then you were working for your uncle for about a week or more?"
Hauptmann: "Yes. I remember going to work on a Monday."
Mrs. Hauptmann: "And I came out a week later. Do you remember that *around that time* a fireman died and you went to the funeral? You were in a car with Maria and some other people."
Hauptmann: "Yes. I remember that occasion."

Mrs. Hauptmann: "Was it before or after *that time* when you first came to know that person?"

Hauptmann: "It was after. It was sometime in April" (italics added).[11]

The Hauptmanns finally concocted an alibi and it was this: when the baby was kidnapped, they were together at the lunchroom-bakery in the Bronx where Mrs. Hauptmann worked. Bruno had picked Mrs. Hauptmann up at 7:00 that night, and at 9:30, they rode home in the car.

At the close of the prosecution's case, the burden had shifted to Hauptmann to prove that he *was not* at the Lindbergh home on the night of March 1, 1932. The owners of the lunchroom-bakery at 3815 Dyre Avenue, Christian and Katie Fredericksen, testified that Hauptmann usually came to the store on Tuesday nights to pick up his wife. They could not, however, place him there on the night of the crime.

An interesting side note to Mrs. Fredericksen and her willingness to testify as an alibi witness relates to the fact she was robbed and assaulted by a man with a gun as she left the bakery at closing time one night in the middle of March 1932. The crime occurred after the kidnapping, but prior to the ransom payoff. Mr. Fredericksen was attending a lodge meeting at the time. As Mrs. Fredericksen turned out the store light, a man with an athletic build rushed into the bakery and said, "Hands up." Mrs. Fredericksen did not get a good look at the robber's face because it was dark and his cap was pulled down and his coat collar turned up. The man forced her into the washroom, where he knocked her unconscious with a hard instrument. Several hours later she woke up to find $140 missing from the money bag she had been carrying. She rushed to the forty-seventh Precinct Police Station on 229th Street and Webster Avenue, where she reported the crime. She told the police the man who robbed her was aware of her habits and movements at the bakery and knew that Mr. Fredericksen was absent from the store that night.

Nearly three years following the robbery and assault, shortly after Mrs. Fredericksen had testified for the Hauptmann defense, she was questioned by Detectives William J. Wallace of the New York City Police Department and Claude Patterson of the New Jersey State Police. According to Detective Patterson's report:

> She [Mrs. Fredericksen] stated that at that time she had no suspicions of who the hold-up man was but after reading of Hauptmann's arrest she thought it

over and believed it possible that he may have been the one and suggested this to her husband. She further stated it was a man about his build, which she describes as athletic. . . .

It is our opinion that Mrs. Fredericksen could probably identify Richard Hauptmann as the man who held her up but will not due to her actions and her reluctancy in giving information concerning this hold-up. During the interview she stated that this man had enough trouble and that she did not want to cause him anymore.[12]

Anna Hauptmann took the stand as an alibi witness, but her testimony was so self-serving, and weak because of earlier contradictory statements, it carried no weight. There were, however, four witnesses who took the stand and testified they had seen the defendant in the bakery that night. The first man got his dates mixed up; the second admitted he had not laid eyes on Hauptmann until the night in question; the third, a man who said he had seen Hauptmann walking the dog that night, was a small-time vice operator; and the fourth, was mentally retarded.[13] As alibi defenses go, and they usually do not go very well, Hauptmann's was weak. It was not Reilly's fault; a defense attorney has to play the cards he is dealt, and Reilly had a losing hand.

In celebrated cases under revision, time can help make evidence disappear and a guilty man Innocent. Fifty years after Hauptmann's trial, his widow's attorney, Robert S. Bryan, announced that he had discovered, among Lindbergh case documents once possessed by Governor Hoffman, "deliberately suppressed evidence that would have cleared Hauptmann."[14]

According to Bryan, the authorities hid the existence of a witness, Frieda von Valta, who would have testified that she rode the subway home with Hauptmann from Manhattan to the Bronx on the night of the kidnapping. Bryan said, "This would have verified not only that Richard Hauptmann was in New York on the night of the kidnapping, but also that he had worked that day in New York."[15]

Bryan bases the above conclusions upon an affidavit signed by Frieda von Valta on January 10, 1936. He uses this document, slightly more than one page long, to prove three specific propositions:

1. Lindbergh case investigators maliciously coerced Mrs. von Valta into not testifying.

2. von Valta's statement supports Hauptmann's alibi for the night of the kidnapping.
3. The affidavit is proof that Hauptmann was working at the Majestic Apartments on the day of the crime.

In truth, the von Valta statement does not prove any of these things. First, von Valta was not kept out of the witness box by the police. According to her signed statement: "I was threatened by the Hoboken Police in case I should go Flemington to testify for Bruno Richard Hauptmann. In spite of these threats I went to Flemington to offer myself as a witness to the chief counselor Reilly who refused me."[16]

Secondly, von Valta's statement does not give support to Hauptmann's alibi. According to her statement, she saw Hauptmann that night between 6:00 and 6:30 P.M. Since the kidnapping occurred sometime between 9:00 and 9:30, Hauptmann would have had time to kidnap the baby in New Jersey. Reilly rejected von Valta because he needed witnesses who could place Hauptmann in New York after 8:00 P.M.

Thirdly, Mrs. von Valta swore she saw Hauptmann riding the subway after working hours. In this regard, her statement supports Hauptmann's testimony that he did not work at the Majestic Apartments that day, a fact supported by the payroll records that indicate Hauptmann did not start work there until March 21.

Frieda von Valta owned a rooming house on 11th Street in Hoboken. The seventy-year-old widow had been married to a man named Buttkis, and was known to the Hoboken police, who had made hundreds of nuisance calls to her rooming house. It seemed that Frieda spent much of her time spying on her tenants and then reporting them to the police for crimes that occurred in her imagination. The police in Hoboken, von Valta's renters, and her neighbors considered the woman mentally unsound. On January 3, 1935, just as the Hauptmann trial was getting under way, von Valta called the Hoboken police and reported that she had information that would clear Bruno Richard Hauptmann. When Lt. William Christie arrived at her house, von Valta showed him a photograph of Hauptmann that appeared in the German newspaper *The New York Zeitung* and said, "Ain't he a fine lookin' man, the poor fellow."[17] A week later von Valta signed the affidavit regarding seeing Hauptmann that day on the subway.

It is no wonder that defense attorney Reilly, up to his eyeballs in crackpots, charlatans and nut cases, sent Frieda von Valta packing. She was not good enough for Reilly, but after the passage of all this time, she was just right for Attorney Robert S. Bryan. For one thing, dead witnesses do not embarrass. In the court of public opinion, witnesses do not have to be alive, put under oath, cross-examined, or face a real jury. Reilly, by wisely keeping this woman out of the witness box, had saved her for Bryan. When revisionists use so-called witnesses like Frieda von Valta, Albert Hamilton, Gunter Haas, and Murray Bleefeld, nothing in history is safe.

Hauptmann was caught with $14,600 of the Lindbergh money hidden in his garage, cash he had been spending secretly since supposedly finding fifteen thousand dollars in a shoe box left behind by the dead Isidor Fisch. Hauptmann said he had found the money in his kitchen closet three weeks before his arrest. According to Hauptmann, Fisch had left the shoe box in Hauptmann's care on December 2, 1933, shortly before sailing to Germany where, four months later, he died of tuberculosis. This is the famous "Fisch Story."

Besides being incredibly convenient, and otherwise hard to believe, the prosecution produced a credible witness named Cecile Barr, who ripped the Fisch Story to shreds. Mrs. Barr testified that on November 26, 1933, about a week before Hauptmann claimed to have received the shoe box from Isidor Fisch, and nine months before he said he had found the gold notes inside it, Hauptmann handed her, a cashier at a Greenwich Village theater, a five-dollar ransom bill. This gold note was folded into eighths like many of the ransom bills that had been passed earlier around the city.

Cecile Barr's testimony is so devastating, Hauptmann supporters have to attack it. And they do, ferociously—and dishonestly. For example, in his 1993 article, Scaduto writes:

> The jury believed Cecil Barr [sic]. But she lied. When she was first questioned by police about the ransom bill, the man she described didn't resemble Hauptmann physically. More important, she said the man wasn't a foreigner; he'd had, she said, "an American accent." Hauptmann's accent was heavily German.
>
> Barr's original statement never reached Hauptmann's lawyer. The lie was given to the jury.[18]

Apparently Barr's original statement to Detective William F. Horn of the New Jersey State Police never reached Scaduto. When interviewed on

November 27, 1933, eleven months prior to Hauptmann's arrest, Mrs. Barr described the passer of the five-dollar ransom bill as follows: "Thirty years old [Hauptmann had just turned thirty-four], slender [Hauptmann was 170 pounds], 5 feet eight or nine inches [Hauptmann was five feet ten inches], light brown hair [Hauptmann's hair was light brown], and '*apparently American*'" (italics added).[19]

Nowhere in Detective Horn's report does Cecile Barr mention this man's accent. This is not surprising since Hauptmann, according to Barr's trial testimony, only spoke two words.[20]

Another problem with the Fisch Story was Fisch himself. If he had the ransom money all those months, why was he so poor? The FBI located Fisch's bank account and learned "that the largest deposit he ever made was $750 and the smallest was $400 and there are only three or four deposits."[21] It was a different story with Hauptmann. FBI accountant Joseph A. Genau studied Hauptmann's bank and brokerage transactions and concluded that between the time of the ransom payment and Hauptmann's arrest, he had deposited $26,016.[22] (Although Agent Genau made a detailed investigation of Hauptmann's finances, before and after the ransom payoff, documenting his findings in a sixty-three-page report, he was not called to testify at Hauptmann's trial.)

According to another FBI document: Isidor Fisch, "in the spring of 1933, was virtually penniless and was sleeping in park benches in New York City."[23]

Did Bruno Richard Hauptmann get a fair trial? Those who believe he was innocent also think he was railroaded. Does it necessarily follow that all wrongfully convicted defendants are innocent? In American jurisprudence, the chief goal of a trial is not truth, but justice. Hauptmann may arguably have been denied justice, but was he guilty? Unless one believes Scaduto's general claim that all of the physical evidence was fabricated, and every key prosecution witness lied, the question of fairness and guilt are separate issues. Therefore, when the question has to do with guilt or innocence, the so-called unfairness of the trial is a red herring.

Was Hauptmann's trial truly unfair? He had an experienced, objective and lenient judge, and the jury was made up of honest, common sense people. Although Edward J. Reilly had a drinking problem, he was experienced, knew how to cross-examine experts, and was aided by C. Lloyd Fisher and three other able and dedicated attorneys. In the midst of the Hauptmann trial, the *New Yorker* published a lengthy and flattering profile of Reilly that presented him as a successful and talented defense attorney.[24] The article described Reilly's courtroom technique, which squares with his methods at the Hauptmann trial:

> Ordinarily, he does not bother with elaborate preparation. He comes before the bar with little more than a cursory knowledge of the matter at hand, staking everything on his quick-wittedness, his sharpness at cross-examination, his intuitive feeling for the weakest juror, his slightly fly-blown eloquence. His courtroom manner is reminiscent of William J. Fallon and Earl Rogers, for he frequently tries a litigation without taking a note, holding in mind perfectly as did these master defenders, the most complicated and indigestible slabs of testimony.[25]

After Reilly had won acquittals for a pair of New York City racketeers, he refused to shake their hands. From this it seems that Reilly did not have to like, or even believe in his clients, to give them his best defense.[26]

Trials are won or lost on the facts presented, not on the law. In Hauptmann's case, as evidenced by the witnesses who came forward on his behalf, all the factual evidence was on the other side. Therefore, F. Lee Bailey, on his best day, could not have gotten Hauptmann off the hook. William M. Kunstler, an equally successful trial lawyer, wrote; "Wilentz had so much incriminating evidence against Hauptmann that he almost fell over his own feet trying to get it all in."[27]

Had Wilentz foreseen that decades later his bones would be picked by revisionist vultures, he may not have put Millard Whited, Ben Lupica, Joseph Perrone, and Amandus Hochmuth on the stand. Wilentz did not need these witnesses because the physical evidence proved Hauptmann's guilt. These so-called eyewitnesses, particularly Hochmuth and Whited, turned out to be an embarrassment. By using these people, Wilentz gave Hauptmann supporters something to shoot at. It is a lot easier ridiculing Hochmuth than explaining away the handwriting, the ransom money, and the wood evidence.

Dr. John F. Condon and Colonel Lindbergh are also easy targets for the revisionists. Condon because he was an eccentric showboat who waffled when it came time to pick Hauptmann out of the line-up, and Lindbergh because he identified Hauptmann by voice at the cemetery. What is lost in all of the shouting is this: Condon's description of "Cemetery John," long before anyone heard of Hauptmann, is a very close match. And Colonel Lindbergh, whether you like him or not, was not a liar.

Much has been made of the circuslike atmosphere surrounding the trial in Flemington and how it influenced the jury against Hauptmann. It is true that the trial was a huge and spectacular media event, but the stories of ugly, blood-thirsty, anti-German mobs calling for Hauptmann's death are highly exaggerated, and not supported by the facts. Ethel Stockton, one of the Hauptmann jurors, had this to say about the effect all of this had on the jury:

> I'm sure the other jurors and myself were not influenced by all the goings on. We were kept to ourselves by the constables assigned to us and were confined much of the time to our rooms in the Union Hotel across from the courthouse when trial was not in session.
>
> Of course, we met for dinner and three or us women slept in the same room so there was plenty of talk—mostly about the trial. But we weren't allowed to see any newspapers, didn't know about the celebrities who were visiting Flemington or have any idea of how the case was being handled in the press or on the radio.[28]

In dismissing the bulk of Mrs. Hauptmann's lawsuit filed in 1981, federal judge Frederick B. Lacey, in addressing the so-called anti-German sentiment against defendant Hauptmann, wrote the following:

> German emigrants to the United States have not been the victims of "historically pervasive discrimination." Plaintiff portrays Richard Hauptmann as a victim of the anti-German sentiment occasioned by the rise of Nazism. Plaintiff's allegations, however, are not grounded in historical fact. The nature of the Nazi regime, tragically, was not widely known in 1935. The acts of aggression that began to reveal the regime's nature, and then only slowly— the *Anschluss* with Austria, the annexation of the Sudetenland, the war with Poland—occurred long after Hauptmann's execution in 1936. World War II certainly aroused widespread anti-German feeling. Such sentiment, however, did not exist at the time of Hauptmann's trial.[29]

Mrs. Hauptmann herself, in her unpublished autobiography written in 1935, contradicts the conventional wisdom on this issue:

The newspapers have published stories of the feeling of the crowd toward my husband and me. They spoke of the crowd demanding the life of my husband. I never heard one single utterance against my husband and myself. On the contrary, throughout the entire case the crowds encouraged me, cheered me, and seemed always to be in favor of my husband. To my mind, as I approached the courthouse that night, the crowd seemed to be for me. They shouted words of encouragement.[30]

Hauptmann was indicted twice, given an extradition hearing, five defense attorneys, a six-week trial, two appeals before the Court of Pardons, stays of execution, appeals to state and federal appellate courts, and a pair of constitutional lawyers who filed, on Hauptmann's behalf, a *writ of certiari* to the U.S. Supreme Court. More than four decades later, Hauptmann's wife twice pleaded his case in Federal court. These two decisions were then reviewed, on appeal, by the Third Circuit Court of Appeals. If Hauptmann, an illegal alien, has been shortchanged by the American courts, then every prisoner in America should be set free immediately.

Perhaps the most outlandish red herring in the Hauptmann debate is the argument that Hauptmann, a carpenter, would not have built a ladder so crude. This is an excellent example of how, with just the right spin, severely incriminating reality can be turned into evidence that actually exonerates. But consider this: How many second-story kidnappers would construct their own portable, three-piece extension ladder? Would Al Capone have built one? Hauptmann was an unemployed carpenter, exactly the kind of kidnapper who would make his own ladder. But the foolishness does not end here. Would, the question goes, Hauptmann have spaced the rungs so far apart? The answer is yes if he wanted to get up and down the ladder fast. The ladder had to be light, therefore it was crude, and rickety. Hauptmann made the ladder to abduct the Lindbergh baby, not to paint his garage.

Those who defend Hauptmann make much of the fact he was roughed up at the Greenwich Police Station in New York City. Had Hauptmann confessed, the trustworthiness of his statement would, under this circumstance, be in question. But Hauptmann did not confess, therefore his treatment at the hands of the police is not relevant to the issue of his guilt or innocence. It is another red herring.

Hauptmann could have saved his life by confessing, but he chose, it is said, to go to the electric chair rather than to admit to a crime he did not commit. Why, at the last moment, didn't Hauptmann confess?

Hauptmann did not confess because he did not think that Governor Hoffman, who had been on his side, would allow his execution. "Richard never thought he would go to the chair," said Mrs. Hauptmann. "We never talked of it, when I visited him there in the jail."[31] By the time Hauptmann realized they were actually going to electrocute him, he was in no condition to confess. It was too late. "His silence fed doubts," wrote FBI agent Leon G. Turrou in 1949, "and the doubts are voiced today all over the world. But it is my opinion that Hauptmann died justly."[32]

Why didn't Hauptmann confess following his arrest? Most men, even hardened criminals, confronted with so much evidence, and subjected to relentless interrogation, would have broken down—not Hauptmann.

Hauptmann was not legally insane, but he was defective and incomplete as a human. On the surface, Hauptmann looked and behaved like an ordinary man, but beneath the facade there was no conscience, no insight, no imagination, no perspective, and no feelings except greed and anger. The contents of the ransom notes reflect a man who is naive, foolhardy, simpleminded, and cruel. According to Leon G. Turrou, an FBI agent who spent a lot of time with Hauptmann, "He [Hauptmann] had a low bovine mentality, a surly disposition, and was one of the most colorless men I have ever met."[33]

In 1934, following Hauptmann's arrest, the president of the American Association of Consulting Psychologists, opined that Hauptmann's most outstanding trait was his dogged persistence indicated by his determination to reach America as a stowaway. This psychologist, Dr. Richard H. Paynter, believed this trait came out at the trial when Hauptmann, under grueling and withering cross-examination, calmly protested his innocence.[34]

Hauptmann never blustered or became outraged or indignant when accused of killing the Lindbergh baby. According to the psychologists and psychiatrists who studied him, that's because Hauptmann never *felt* guilty about committing the crime. Dr. Dudley D. Shoenfeld, the New York City psychiatrist who, in 1932, psychoanalyzed the kidnapper by studying the ransom notes, predicted that the ransom note writer was not the kind of man who would confess. Dr. Shoenfeld attended Hauptmann's trial, and in his book on the case, states that Hauptmann possessed an omnipotent attitude. Hauptmann was also argumentative, secretive, and was the type of egomaniac who would never admit defeat by confessing—even in the face of overwhelming evidence.[35] Hauptmann was, in short, a sociopath—a Jekyll and Hyde.

Thomas H. Sisk, the principal Lindbergh case investigator for the FBI, was so exhausted by Hauptmann's prolonged interrogation, he nodded off during the questioning. Special Agent Sisk woke up with a start and looked around to find the other four interrogators sound asleep in their chairs. "The only two people awake," he said, "were the prisoner and the prisoner's guard."[36] Hauptmann, it seemed, had worn down his interrogators.

None of the latent fingerprints recovered from the ransom notes and the kidnap ladder were Hauptmann's. His prints were not found in the nursery either. This must have distressed Wilentz, because had there been prints linking Hauptmann to the crime, the defendant might have been forced to confess.

When a person touches an object, an identifiable latent is not always left on the thing touched. Moreover, an unskilled fingerprint technician working with out-of-date equipment could easily ruin otherwise good finger marks. It does not necessarily follow, then, that because Hauptmann's fingerprints were not recovered at the scene, he had not been there. In the Lindbergh case, the absence of fingerprints means either that Hauptmann wore gloves, the fingerprint man blew the job, or the police were just unlucky.

When Eleanor Roosevelt was asked about Hauptmann's conviction, she said she was a bit worried that he had been found guilty on circumstantial evidence. Her statement reflects the commonly held view that circumstantial evidence is weak, second-rate proof. Those who believe Hauptmann innocent also point out, quite correctly, that he was convicted solely on this kind of evidence. Circumstantial evidence suffers from a bad reputation, a reputation it does not always deserve.

Hauptmann was convicted on physical evidence, which is, by definition, circumstantial. The safe burglar's fingerprint on the money chest merely proves he touched it. That he also broke into it must be inferred from this circumstance. The fingerprint itself, therefore, does not directly prove this man's guilt. Still, the suspect's fingerprint on the safe is solid and incriminating evidence. Direct evidence, on the other hand, particularly in the form of eyewitness testimony, is often unreliable. Even confessions, another kind of direct proof, are often suspect.

In his book, *Studies in Murder*, Edmund Pearson writes that: "The brief, classic definition of circumstantial evidence is the footprint seen on the beach by Robinson Crusoe. He knew from that circumstance that there had been a stranger on his island. He wouldn't have cared for the direct evidence to the contrary of any number of people."[37]

Of all the circumstantial evidence presented by the prosecution in the Lindbergh case, rail sixteen was perhaps the most damaging. Hauptmann defenders ask a very pointed question: If Hauptmann was such a cunning criminal, why would he connect himself to the kidnap ladder by using a board from his attic? The general answer, although not very satisfying, is simple: Just because someone does something that does not make sense does not mean it did not happen. Why did Hauptmann pick the Lindbergh baby to kidnap and murder? Why did John H. Curtis, a respectable businessman, subject the Lindberghs to such an elaborate and cruel hoax?

Because Hauptmann did not confess, no one will ever know why he used rail sixteen. There might, however, be a reasonable explanation. At the risk of adding one more harebrained theory to the Lindbergh case, try this:

Hauptmann had been planning the kidnapping for a year but had not set a date. It would not be long until the Lindberghs moved into their new home in Hopewell. If Hauptmann did not act soon, he'd miss the chance to snatch the baby out of his crib at the Morrow estate in Englewood, just across the river from the Bronx.[38] He would have to commit the crime on a Tuesday night, one of the days his wife, Anna, worked late at the bakery-lunchroom. She also worked late on Fridays, but Fridays were out because the Lindberghs had been going to Hopewell on the weekends. Hauptmann would have plenty of time to drive to Englewood, get the baby out of his room, dispose of the corpse, and get back to the Bronx in time to pick up his wife after work.

On Tuesday, March 1, Hauptmann expected to be working at the Majestic Apartments in Manhattan. But when he showed up for work that morning, the boss told him to come back in a couple of weeks. Hauptmann was free the rest of the day, his wife was working until nine, and when he picked up the morning paper, he read that Colonel Lindbergh would be in New York City that night speaking to a group at New York University.

Hauptmann decided this would be the day he would kidnap, and murder, the Lindbergh baby.

The nineteen pieces of Hauptmann's homemade ladder—the eleven rungs, six side rails, and two dowel pins—were hidden away in his garage. Hauptmann would spend the rest of the morning in his garage nailing it together. The three-piece ladder, fully extended, would reach just below the baby's window at the Morrow estate.

When Hauptmann nailed the bottom rung to the top section of the ladder—just above the 1³/₈-inch hole for the dowel pin, one of the side rails, the one made of yellow pine, split. This rail would have to be replaced. Being a careful man, Hauptmann did not want to walk into a store and risk buying a piece of wood for the kidnap ladder on the day of the crime. The attic floor above his rented apartment was made of pine and had not been completed. To get up to that attic, one had to climb a ladder through a ceiling hatch inside a linen closet.[39] Hauptmann could take a board from this place and no one would ever miss it. The board he took was rail sixteen, the plank that would help pave his way to the electric chair.

Hauptmann was careful, but he was not immune to bad luck—on that particular Tuesday, the Lindberghs were still in Hopewell. But it was too late to turn back now—the ladder was assembled, Anna was at work, and Colonel Lindbergh was in New York City. Determined to carry out his mission, Hauptmann drove across New Jersey to the Lindbergh estate where, using the bottom two sections of his ladder (that fell thirty inches below the window), he snatched the baby from the nursery. That night, two hours later than usual, just as the first police officers were arriving in Hopewell, Hauptmann picked up his wife at the bakery-lunchroom and they drove home.[40]

A month later Hauptmann received the ransom money and began living the life he had always dreamed of. But the Lindbergh cash, his own handwriting, and the homemade ladder he left behind that night in the rain, finally caught up to him, and sealed his fate.

The jurors at Hauptmann's trial did not care why Hauptmann had gone to his attic for rail sixteen—they just needed to know that he had.

13 New Evidence

One cannot make a case for Hauptmann without alleging prosecutorial wrongdoing. This tactic works because it puts the government on trial and takes the evidence out of the debate. Moreover, how can anyone prove that the evidence *was not* fabricated? Proving a negative is difficult, if not impossible, particularly sixty years after the fact. The only way to shift the debate back to the evidence is to present evidence that is new: statements, findings, and clues, not the product of police misconduct that did not reach the Hauptmann jury. This new evidence, coupled with the facts of the case not in dispute, proves beyond a reasonable doubt that Bruno Richard Hauptmann was guilty as charged.

Hauptmann's sudden and unexplained affluence between the time of the ransom payoff and his arrest is a problem for his supporters. By his own admission, Hauptmann did not earn a wage during this period. He said he made his money in the stock market, but according to his bank and brokerage accounts, he lost thousands of dollars. So where did Hauptmann get the money? The Fisch story explains the money in his garage, but it does not account for his wealth from the time of the ransom payoff to the day he said he discovered Fisch's shoe box in his kitchen closet. That is a period of more than two years, a time when most of the nation's banks were closed and 25 percent of the American people were unemployed. A month after Hauptmann's arrest, Assistant District Attorney Breslin, in the company of detectives from New Jersey and New York, questioned Frederick Hahn in District Attorney Sam Foley's office in the Bronx. Hahn and his wife, Marie, owned Fred's Lunch Bar and Restaurant at 1816 Webster Avenue. The Hahns had met Hauptmann when he first patronized their restaurant and had known him for three years. Hahn, in June 1932, two and a half months following the ransom payoff, and shortly after Mrs. Hauptmann's trip to Germany, visited Hauptmann in his apartment.

The following is Hahn's edited recollection of that visit as told to Prosecutor Breslin:

Q. What happened up there?

A. Well he showed me his apartment and then . . . he showed me this victrola. He opened it and there I seen the two bags of money.

Q. Two what?

A. Two paper bags with money.

Q. Two paper bags with money?

A. Yes. One bag was on the right side when he lifted the cover and the other was on the left side where the victrola runs.

Q. And you saw two packages of money?

A. Yes.

Q. One on either side?

A. When it was opened I could see what it was.

Q. A bag, what kind of bag?

A. A paper bag. I figured it was a 5-pound paper bag. We call it a #5 paper bag.

Q. It was a brown paper bag?

A. Brown paper bag yes and it was open.

Q. At one end?

A. Yes and I could see the stack of money at that time like that.

Q. About four inches high?

A. Yes.

Q. That was on the right?

A. Yes on the right, where the big cover was on.

Q. On the other side of the disk?

A. The disk, yes, and on the side of the disk between the partition and disk was another bag, but it was closed.

Q. What did he say?

A. Well he said, "It is not my money. I don't care for that money. It belongs to Fisch," and I said, "Who is Fisch?" And he said, "It is a man living down the block next to a church and some of this money belongs to me."

Q. Did Hauptmann tell you how much was there?

A. No, he didn't tell me the amount. I said, "It is a lot of money if it is large bills," and he said, "Yes," but he didn't tell me how much money there is.[1]

Hauptmann's possession of this cash, more than two years before the Fisch story kicks in, is incriminating. Moreover, Hahn's interview reveals that Hauptmann, when asked about the bundles of money, said he was holding the cash for Isidor Fisch, the story he would give the police twenty-seven months later when they asked him about the money hidden in his garage.

Breslin also questioned Marie Hahn that day. She had not been with her husband the day he saw the money in the victrola, but had visited Mrs. Hauptmann shortly before she left for Germany. The following is an edited excerpt of her interview:

Q. How did you happen to go up there?
A. . . . She came to me and said she was taking a trip to Germany. . . . And she said, "Mrs. Hahn, will you come and take a look at my wardrobe? Why don't you come one afternoon while my husband is not here." . . . And then about six or seven o'clock in the evening her husband came back. . . . And I said, "When the Mrs. is away what are you going to do?" And he never looked at me and he said, "Well, I suppose I got to give her some money along." And I say, "She has a very nice wardrobe." I was surprised, she comes from a place in the country. She bought evening gowns and she had all good clothes. They all came from good stores. There was no dress under $20. She had fifteen or sixteen of them.
Q. Where had she bought them?
A. I don't know. . . . I said, "What are you doing with evening clothes?" She said, "I probably going here and there," and I thought ain't it funny where she goes she needs evening clothes. Then I asked him, "Well Mr. Hauptmann, how much you give the Mrs. when she takes the trip?" And he said, "I think $1,000 enough for her." And I said, "She got ticket already and got such nice clothes and he give her $1,000, and $1,000, it is very good," and then there was nothing said and I went home.

Marie Hahn stated that she and her husband visited Hauptmann once during the time Mrs. Hauptmann was in Germany:

Q. What happened that time when you stopped in the house?
A. Well when we went in there he showed us what he had. First he brought a radio, a Stromberg-Carlson, and he showed us it was the latest with phonograph and I said, "My, you must have paid pretty good price?" And he said something about $600 or $675 or something like that. He brought us down and showed us the garage and he showed us electric installment

when he brought us back to his bedroom. He showed us he had lights made to the garage from the bedroom where the bed and some electric buttons and it would light up the garage in case somebody was break in or anything happen he showed us that.

Q. Did he show you where you press the button?

A. Yes. He said, "See I don't even have to get out of bed. If anything should happen I push the button and it light up the whole outside."

Q. From the bedroom you could look out and see the garage?

A. Yes.

Q. Did you see it lit up?

A. Yes, I didn't see inside of garage lit up but all the surrounding.[2]

Hauptmann had gone to great lengths to alarm his garage with a protective lighting system. It seems that he was protecting something in there.[3]

Frederick and Marie Hahn received subpoenas to testify at Hauptmann's trial but did not take the stand.[4] They were scheduled to appear on January 18, the thirteenth day of the trial, which saw fifteen witnesses testify for the state.[5] Although the Hahns did not testify, Prosecutor Wilentz used what he had learned from their interviews as ammunition in the final stages of his cross-examination of a battered and discredited Hauptmann:

Q. Did you ever put any money in that victrola for safekeeping?

A. No.

Q. Particularly in the months of April, May, June or July of 1932, did you keep any money in that victrola?

A. There is a possibility I keep the rent in it.

Q. I don't mean the rent, I mean money, lots of money?

A. No, never.

Q. Packages of money?

A. Never, never got packages of money.

Q. Is it not a fact that during some of these months, particularly after April the second, 1932, that you opened that victrola and when you opened it in the presence of Fritz [Frederick] Hahn, the restaurant man I spoke to you about yesterday. . . .

A. Yes.

Q. . . . that there were in that victrola right on top two envelopes about eleven inches long, maybe fourteen inches long, a few inches thick of money, two packages, two envelopes? It is not a fact?

A. No, absolutely not.

Q. Absolutely not?

A. No.

Q. And didn't Mr. Hahn ask you about the money?

A. No, I really can't remember Mr. Hahn was ever in our house, but I will not say, "No," but I really can't remember he was in my house.

Q. Let me ask you just to refresh your recollection—you don't ever remember him being in your house.

A. No.

Q. You remember when you took him to Rye Beach?

A. That, yes, I remember.

Q. On your way home did you stop at your house with Mr. Hahn?

A. I know it was Mr. Hahn, Mrs. Hahn and a little boy.

Q. Yes.

A. But I really can't remember if we stopped in our house, because my wife wasn't home this time.

Q. No.

A. She was in Europe.

Q. But you had taken Mr. Hahn and Mrs. Hahn to Rye Beach hadn't you?

A. That is right.

Q. They were friends of yours?

A. Yes.

Q. The Hahns don't owe you any money they don't pay you, do they?

A. No.

Q. You have had no trouble with them at all?

A. No trouble.

Q. And you say now that when Mr. Hahn was in your home in 1932, after April the second, 1932, that you did not open the victrola and there in his presence he saw those two bundles and called to your attention bundles of money?

A. Well, you said envelopes before.

Q. Yes, that's right, envelopes, bundles, bundled, up with money.

A. No.

Q. All right. Did you open the victrola while Mr. Hahn was there?

A. Well, I didn't know if Mr. Hahn was ever in our house.

Q. Don't you remember when you got to the bedroom you said, "This room you cannot go in?"

A. No.

Q. You don't remember that?

A. No, I didn't say that.

Q. You didn't say that?

A. No.

Q. You won't say Mr. Hahn was not in your house, will you?

A. That's what I say. I can't remember he was at our house.

Q. You won't say he was not at your house.

A. No, I can't say that either.

Q. Didn't you say on your way back from Rye Beach, "C'mon, I want to show you my new radio?"

A. No.

Q. Didn't he say to you, when you got in the house, "My, this is a swell radio, it must have cost a lot of money." Don't you remember that?

A. I got the impression you are making up a big story here.

Q. Well, we will see about that. Who told you to say that, about your impression?

A. That's my impression.

Q. One of your advisors?

A. No, that's—

Q. Weren't you told last night to say that?

A. No, sir.

Q. You weren't?

A. No, sir.[6]

Following Hauptmann's arrest, FBI agents interviewed many of Hauptmann's acquaintances. One such person was Louise Wollenberg, a long-time friend of Mrs. Hauptmann. The two women had come from the same village in Germany. Wollenberg and her husband, Otto, had visited the Hauptmann apartment shortly before Mrs. Hauptmann's trip to Germany and had seen Hauptmann's new Stromberg-Carlson radio.

In July 1932, with Mrs. Hauptmann still in Germany, Bruno took the Wollenbergs to Hunters Island. According to an FBI report,

> It was about this time that Hauptmann first told Wollenberg that he was interested in the stock market—said he made a lot of money; that for a while he made $2,000 a week; that if he had not been on Hunters Island one day he could have made $50,000.
>
> One evening at about this time, Hauptmann called on the Wollenbergs and said he was going home early to write to his wife to tell her that it would be all right for her to pay $125 for some silverware she wanted to buy in Germany.
>
> Mr. Wollenberg went with Hauptmann to see the Schmeling-Mickey Walker fight at the Long Island City Bowl. . . . Hauptmann had a pair of field glasses— said he had just purchased them, and paid over $100 for them; that he had

to buy them to replace some which his wife had brought over from Germany and which were stolen out of his automobile a few days before.

. . . Shortly before Mrs. Hauptmann returned from Germany, Mrs. Wollenberg, at Hauptmann's request, spent three days cleaning the Hauptmann apartment. . . . She scrubbed the wood work, windows, etc. but received no payment or present for this work. He purchased a plant for $16, and many other flowers, for his wife's return.

Hauptmann bought ring-side tickets for the Schmeling-Sharkey fight . . . he paid $40 for two tickets. Hauptmann was always talking about the stock market at this time. Sometime later the Hauptmanns went to Florida.[7]

At the height of the great depression, when most people were poor, the Hauptmanns could afford nice clothes, fancy silverware, trips to Germany and Florida, expensive field glasses, a new radio, ringside seats at sporting events, and welcome-home floral bouquets.

Besides evidence of Hauptmann's general wealth, Wilentz possessed, but did not use, solid evidence that Hauptmann was in possession of the ransom money before he said he had taken the shoe box from Isidor Fisch. Had Wilentz put this witness on the stand, it would have taken some of the heat off Cecile Barr, the cashier at the Greenwich Village Theatre who had connected Hauptmann to the money prior to when he said he got it out of the shoe box.

On March 3, 1933, a ten-dollar ransom bill turned up at the Guaranty Trust Company at 180 Broadway. An investigation by the FBI determined that this gold note had been passed on March 1, 1933, at the United Cigar Store, 504 Third Avenue. The manager of the store, Philip Alsofrom, described the bill passer as a white male, about six foot tall, about forty years of age, with a light complexion and a long, thin face. The man was wearing a "soft hat and dark clothes." A year and a half later, Hauptmann was arrested. Alsofrom saw Hauptmann's photograph in the newspaper and immediately recognized him as the man who had passed the gold note in his store. On October 2, 1934, Special Agent Leon G. Turrou showed Alsofrom additional photographs of Hauptmann. Upon viewing these pictures, Alsofrom stated once again that it was Hauptmann who had passed the ransom bill.[8]

The Hahns and Alsofrom would have made excellent rebuttal witnesses had Wilentz needed them. But he did not, because the Hauptmann defense was so pathetic. Hauptmann's seventeen hours of testimony, spread over four days, sealed his fate. When he finally got off the hot seat, there was not a person in the courtroom, except maybe Hauptmann's wife and his lawyers, who did not know he was a liar, and that the Fisch story was as bogus as his alibi.[9]

It was Wilentz's job to get a murder conviction, and that is what he did. That the Lindbergh case would later be rewritten by junk historians, tabloid journalists, and political activists was not the prosecutor's concern.

Wilentz had at his disposal, but did not use, scientific evidence that would have destroyed the Fisch Story. Hauptmann said that after finding Fisch's shoe box, he hid the gold notes in his garage where, a few weeks later, the police found his stash. If Hauptmann's account of this is true, the ransom money had only been in his garage a couple of weeks.

At the trial, FBI special agent Thomas H. Sisk recalled finding an empty crock buried under Hauptmann's garage. Sisk testified as follows:

A. Well, Lieutenant Arthur Keaten of the New Jersey State Police and Inspector John Lyons of the New York Police, and myself went to down into that garage to search it. And we found that the two middle planks on the floor of the garage were loose, and we took a crowbar and we pried them up. And underneath them was some freshly disturbed dirt, as though someone had been digging. So we got a shovel and we dug down and found a crock. . . . It was covered with dirt and had a lid on it and at the bottom was about two or three inches of water.

Q. Did you find any money in there?

A. No, sir. We questioned Hauptmann as to that jug. He denied knowing anything about it, but the next day when we questioned him, he admitted that he had that money in there three weeks before he was arrested.

Q. In the jug?

A. In that jug.

At this point in Agent Sisk's testimony, Hauptmann jumped to his feet and yelled, "Mister, Mister, you stop lying. You are telling a story!"[10]

According to Stanley P. Keith, a metallurgical engineer hired by the prosecution as a scientific consultant, the water in that crock contained traces of camphor produced by mothballs. The mothballs had been in the crock to keep out moths and other vermin. Keith had examined some of the ransom bills found in Hauptmann's garage and noticed they had a distinctive odor. When he examined these bills under a microscope, he saw crystals of camphor. From this, Keith concluded that the person who had buried this money had put it away for a long time, and that ground water had soaked this money, not water from a leaking closet. Keith also concluded that Hauptmann, seeing where Agent Sisk's testimony was heading, had no choice but to create a scene.[11] As it turned out, Wilentz had other fish to fry, making Hauptmann's outburst unnecessary.

Prosecutor Wilentz, by connecting Hauptmann to the kidnap ladder through his carpenter tools, attic floor board, notebook sketch, and purchase place of the wood, proved he was at least in some way connected to the kidnapping. By denying any association with the ladder, Hauptmann raised the stakes and the importance of this evidence.

Because the tool mark evidence and the rail sixteen match-up is so obvious, irrefutable, and demonstrable, Hauptmann crusaders have no choice but to claim foul play. Had Wilentz foreseen Governor Hoffman's bizarre post-trial allegiance to the Hauptmann defense, and the resultant charges of perjury, evidence suppression, and outright fabrication, he might have presented the jury with additional evidence that Hauptmann had built the ladder.

In March 1933, a year and a half before Hauptmann became a suspect, the Internal Revenue Service (IRS) identified the Pittsburgh Steel Company in Monessen, Pennsylvania, as the maker of the nails used in the kidnap ladder. Because the nail heads were well centered on the shank and symmetrically rounded, it was determined they had been manufactured sometime within the previous two years. Moreover, the trade symbol "P" stamped on each nail identified the Pittsburgh Steel Company as the manufacturer.[12]

Following Hauptmann's arrest in September 1934, Stanley P. Keith, the former metallurgical engineer at Bethlehem Steel, identified and compared three sets of nails: forty-four from the kidnap ladder; the unused nails from the hundred-pound keg in Hauptmann's garage; and the nails Hauptmann had used in October 1931, to build his garage. Keith determined that all of these nails had been made at the Pittsburgh Steel Company by the same set of eight machines. This was indicated by the eight distinct die impressions on each nail shank. Keith also discovered that Hauptmann's keg was one of a sixteen-keg batch containing nails bearing these distinct impressions.[13] In other words, the nails in the kidnap ladder and Hauptmann's garage either came from the keg in his garage, or from one of fifteen other kegs. Considering the vast number of nails that are sold, what are the chances that Hauptmann did not build the ladder, but unfortunately happened to have a keg of nails that came from the same container as the kidnapper's nails? Because the IRS had identified the ladder nails before Hauptmann's arrest, and the police would not have been able to find two-year-old nails from this same tiny group, this evidence could not have been planted. Hauptmann's stubborn insistence that he had nothing to do with the ladder was obviously untrue, and the jury knew it. Although Wilentz did not need this evidence in 1935, and the revisionists will find some way to explain it away, it is still worth mentioning.

Hauptmann slipped into America illegally in 1923 to escape the consequences of his crimes and to get rich. He planned on returning to Germany some day, but not as a common criminal. He would go back a rich and respected man. That was his dream. Two years later he married a plain, country-bred woman named Anna Schoeffler. Hauptmann appears to have married her because she *was* frugal, worked hard, and had $2,500 in the bank.

During the first five years of their marriage, the Hauptmanns worked hard and saved most of what they earned. By 1930, the depression had made carpenter jobs scarce, and Hauptmann was out of work. This is when he began dabbling in the stock market, using money his wife did not know he had—$3,500 he kept hidden in a locked trunk in his living room closet.[14]

Hauptmann lost money in the stock market, and by March, 1932, he was unemployed and broke. In Germany, when he got financially desperate, Hauptmann had turned to crime—grand larceny, receiving stolen property, house burglary, escape, and armed robbery.[15]

Hauptmann's apologists have done a good, albeit dishonest, job of minimizing his criminal history, which was varied, prolonged, and very serious. "Ja, he stole a loaf of bread," said Anna Hauptmann in 1988. "This is the kind of criminal was my Richard."[16] In referring to the Hauptmanns, one writer allowed the following statement: "Both were German immigrants, he an illegal one with some scrapes with the law in his youth."[17] Another writer dismissed Hauptmann's criminal record like this: "Hauptmann, a carpenter with a record of petty crime in Germany."[18] A police official from Berlin, in a letter to J. Edgar Hoover, had a more realistic view of Hauptmann: "Immediately after having served his time [in 1923] he again committed acts for burglary in Kamenz. He absconded during the course of his trial in the lower courts of Kamenz and has since disappeared from Germany. In any event, he had the worst possible reputation in Kamenz and was known to be a dangerous criminal."[19]

In America, in 1932, criminals who wanted a lot of money turned to kidnapping. And so did Hauptmann.

By June of 1932, Hauptmann had the money he had wanted so badly. It was hidden in his garage, and like the money he had rat-holed in his trunk, his wife did not know it was there. Hauptmann was now ready to return to Germany, but he was not sure if it was safe, so he sent his wife to find out. It was a costly trip, but it was something, thanks to Colonel Lindbergh, Hauptmann could now afford. Mrs. Hauptmann was gone all summer that year, the summer Hauptmann, the successful stock manipulator, took up with Gerta Henkel.[20] It was also during this period that Hauptmann confided to a clerk at his brokerage house, Steiner, Rouse, & Company, that he could not live with his wife any more.[21]

Mrs. Hauptmann returned from Europe with bad news—the German police still wanted Bruno Richard—he could not go home. Hauptmann had some bad news for her, he had met a friend named Gerta. Mrs. Hauptmann was not comfortable with Richard's new friends, his playboy life style, and his new persona as a Wall Street wizard. Anna liked him better as an ordinary working man.[22] But Bruno, with Colonel Lindbergh's money buried safely in his garage, could play big man on Wall Street. From now on he would wear suits instead of coveralls, buy nice things for himself, and hang out at brokerage houses with men who made money the easy way. He would not do physical work ever again and, except for a little blood, get his hands dirty.

By January 1934, nearly two years following the ransom pay off, Hauptmann was seriously planning his permanent return to Germany. He had written his mother and Isidor Fisch about coming home. His mother had checked with the German authorities, who said it was now safe because the statute of limitations had run out on all of Hauptmann's crimes.[23] Bruno Richard's wife knew nothing of his plan to return to Germany. Hauptmann was leaving her behind. Although everybody believed Hauptmann was making a killing on Wall Street, he had been losing money and had spent too much during the past twenty-two months. Hauptmann still had more than fifteen thousand dollars stashed in his garage, but all of these bills were gold notes, which should have been exchanged for greenbacks when President Roosevelt took the country off the gold standard. Hauptmann had spent the five-dollar bills, about half the tens, and still had ten thousand dollars worth of twenties — big bills made even more conspicuous because they were gold notes. The money in his garage was getting hotter by the day, his wife was driving him crazy, and he still could not get a handle on the stock market. Without new money, Hauptmann could not return to Germany. In the past, when things looked hopeless, Hauptmann had turned to crime. In Germany, he had gotten caught and sent to prison, but in America, he had picked Lindbergh clean and had outfoxed the police.

In America, getting away with crime was a tradition. There had been twenty-seven major kidnappings in 1933 alone. In January of 1934, as Hauptmann agonized over his predicament, a gang or kidnappers abducted Edward Bremer, the president of a St. Paul, Minnesota, bank. A ransom note demanding two hundred thousand dollars for his return was sent to the victim's father, Joseph Schmidt, the owner of a successful brewing company. Schmidt paid the ransom and the kidnappers released his son. This case made the front pages of every newspaper in the country and would not have escaped Hauptmann.[24]

Sometime in January 1934, the month of the Bremer kidnapping, when Hauptmann was thinking seriously about Germany and his dwindling resources in America, a man walked into the Raabe Pharmacy at 3981 White Plains Avenue in the Bronx and purchased a three-ounce bottle of ether. This man told the owner of the store, Max Schaffer, he was a dentist. (In 1934, ether, a colorless, highly flammable liquid, was the most commonly used anesthetic in America. Rarely causing death, it was considered relatively safe.)[25] When Schaffer ran into this man on the street sometime later, he identified himself as a cobbler, denying he was the dentist who had purchased the ether. The anesthetic was in a bottle with a green, screw-type cap containing a Raabe Pharmacy label bearing Schaffer's handwriting. The sale was unusual because ether was normally sold in sealed cans, not in small bottles. Eight months later, this bottle, containing two ounces of ether, was found by FBI agent L. F. Malone in Hauptmann's garage following the discovery of the ransom money.[26]

The FBI's discovery of Hauptmann's ether was written up in a memo simply entitled:

Because this report gave no hint of this startling find, it has been one of
the best kept secrets in the history of the Lindbergh case. Notwithstanding millions of words in newspapers, magazines, and books, not one reference to this evidence can be found elsewhere in print. Not only that,
Hauptmann's possession of the anesthetic did not surface at his trial, his
extradition proceeding, or the two Grand Jury hearings. Had Wilentz
known about the ether, he would have at least dropped this bomb when
he cross-examined Hauptmann.

How could this evidence have been so completely missed? The simplest
and most plausible explanation is this: nobody read far enough into the FBI
memoranda. During the week following Hauptmann's arrest, dozens of
memos, letters, and reports were written every day by investigators and
administrators from the FBI, the New York City Police, and the New Jersey State Police. There was so much going on at one time, and so many
reports and memos, the ether evidence got buried in the paperwork. It stayed
buried until the summer of 1991 when a New Jersey high school teacher
and Lindbergh case researcher named Frank Pizzichillo came across it while
digging aimlessly through the Lindbergh case archives.[27] Pizzichillo did not
realize the significance of the FBI memo until he got to page four where,
half way down the page, he read this paragraph:

> During the searching of the garage at 1279 East 222nd Street, in the Bronx,
> Special Agent L. F. Malone found a 3-ounce bottle with a green screw type
> stopper which contained about two fluid ounces of ether. The marking on the
> bottle shows the word "Ether" written on a druggist's label marked "Poison",
> and the label indicates that it had been sold by William Raabe, pharmacist, 3981
> White Plains Avenue, between 225 and 226th Streets, Bronx, New York.[28]

The first three and a half pages of this memorandum had nothing to
do with the garage search, and there was no heading or other indicator
in the memo to direct the reader's attention to this discovery. FBI special
agent John L. Geraghty, the writer of the memo, did not intentionally hide
this needle in the bureau haystack; he was just reporting, chronologically,
what he and others had done in the investigation. It just happened that

the ether business fell in the middle of the memo. In big, complex crimes like the Lindbergh case, bits and pieces of information get lost because investigators are only concerned with their small, sometimes isolated, roles in the case.

The big question, of course, is why Hauptmann was hiding a small bottle of highly flammable ether in his garage. What does it mean, and how does it relate to the Lindbergh kidnapping? The fact that ether was purchased at the time Hauptmann began seriously planning his return to Germany, a time when his financial situation was beginning to look hopeless, suggests he was also planning another kidnapping. Crime writer Alan Hynd, long before he ghostwrote Governor Hoffman's *Liberty* magazine articles, knew exactly how the Lindbergh kidnapper may have used an anesthetic in committing an abduction: "Undoubtedly, he [the kidnapper] took some means to prevent the baby from crying out. A chloroform-soaked handkerchief would have turned the trick."[29]

Prosecutor Wilentz, in his courtroom summation, asked the jury to consider the possibility that the Lindbergh baby had been either strangled, smothered or choked to death in his crib, a vision of the crime that is not consistent with the use of an anesthetic to get the baby quietly out of the house. Had Wilentz known about the ether in Hauptmann's garage, he may have painted a slightly different picture, one closer to Alan Hynd's theory of the abduction. Although this particular ether was purchased after the Lindbergh kidnapping, Wilentz might have used it to suggest Hauptmann's *modus operandi* in the Lindbergh case.

Wilentz's version of the baby's death may have been correct. As things turned out, having killed the baby nearly ruined Hauptmann's chance of getting the ransom money. If it had been up to John F. Condon, Colonel Lindbergh's ransom intermediary, Hauptmann would not have gotten the money because he could not prove that the child was alive. There may have been a lesson in this for Hauptmann. The next time he grabbed a baby for ransom, he would at least keep it alive until he got the ransom. That meant he would need a way to get the baby quietly out of the house, and that is where the ether would have fit in.

Before Edward J. Reilly came into the picture, Hauptmann was represented by an attorney from Brooklyn named James M. Fawcett. With the evidence mounting against his client. Fawcett, contemplating an insanity plea, arranged to have Hauptmann examined by a team of five psychiatrists, then called alienists.[30]

The psychiatrists examined Hauptmann in District Attorney Foley's office in the Bronx on the third and fourth of October 1934. They spent five hours with Hauptmann, and on October 7, the chief psychiatrist, Dr. James H. Huddleson of Manhattan, submitted a twenty-three-page report to Attorney Fawcett. Several weeks later, when Fawcett was fired, he said he would not turn his work product over to the Hauptmann's new attorney until his bill was paid. Reilly sued, and the court ruled that Fawcett could retain his data, including the psychiatric report, until the Hauptmanns paid Fawcett's fee.[31] Reilly appealed, and on July 20, 1935, the court ordered Fawcett to turn his papers over to Reilly.[32] By this time, the Hauptmann trial was half over, and it is doubtful there was anything in Fawcett's papers that would have helped Reilly. However, from a historical point of view, the most important item Fawcett turned over to Reilly was Dr. Huddleson's psychiatric report, a document that never saw the light until September of 1991. That fall, Dr. John T. Huddleson (Dr. James H. Huddleson's son), while attending one of the Hauptmann trial reenactments in Flemington, New Jersey, told cast member Frank Pizzichillo that he had this long-lost document. A few days later, thanks to Dr. Huddleson, Frank Pizzichillo had a copy of the report.[33]

If Fawcett planned an insanity defense, he was disappointed in Dr. Huddleson's report. The five psychiatrists who studied Hauptmann agreed he was "sane in every respect, understanding the nature and quality of his acts, right and wrong, cause and effect, etc."[34] That did not mean, however, that the doctors had found Hauptmann perfectly normal. Like others who would come to know the defendant, they marveled at his lack of feeling: "The most noticeable fact of the examinee's attitude were his low voice, sometimes practically inaudible, his apathy and low level of interest throughout, his failure to show excitement, resentment, grief, or any other emotion to the extent that would be expected in a man of his experience and mental capacity."[35]

That Hauptmann was legally sane, but defective, is hardly a surprise. The most revealing, and extremely meaningful part of the Huddleson report has to do with a childhood speech defect and related writing tic, that proves, beyond a reasonable doubt, that Hauptmann wrote all of the ransom documents.[36] It is no wonder that Huddleson's report, in the hands of Hauptmann's defense attorneys, never saw the light.

Hauptmann suffered from a peculiar and unique form of agraphia—an inability to write properly—that caused him to add the letter "e" onto words he otherwise knew how to spell. He did not do it all the time, only when he was not consciously making an effort not to.

In the report, Dr. Huddleson writes:

Asked about his childhood, the examinee . . . describes at length and under detailed questioning a type of speech defect, says, "I couldn't speak, my mother, she was afraid the school would not take me;" adds that he entered school at six. Asked when he learned to speak, says, "I learned it in school." He denies stammering or other speech defects, but states that for a long while in school *he would add* "e" to the *end of words where* it did *not belong*, e.g., "iche" for "ich" and "menschene" instead of "menschen"; says the boys made fun of him in school, so that he did learn to correct this peculiarity *but that even now "if I don't think on it, I do it."*[37] Asked to translate a short sentence from English to German in which the word "menschen" occurred, the examinee does so, pronouncing "menschen" correctly without the erroneous final "e," but his speech is more deliberate than one would expect for a man using his native tongue. Later in the examination, when asked if he added the 'e' singing, Hauptmann said, "In singing I can't remember putting an 'e' on; only in speaking" (italics added).[38]

Dr. Huddleson sums up Hauptmann's speech and writing oddity with the following comment: "It is noteworthy that the examinee was retarded in his mental development in childhood. From the fact his speech was so little developed as late as the age of six. The adding of an 'e' to the ends of words also indicates some mental peculiarity."[39]

Since the German language is phonetic—it is written as it is spoken—the writing of an "e" at the end of a word where it does not belong is not a matter of bad spelling. Put another way, there are no silent "e's" in German. If one pronounces the inappropriate "e" as Hauptmann says he did, and was laughed at because it sounded funny, this unwanted "e" would also surface from time to time in the way he spelled these words.[40]

The extortionist who wrote the Lindbergh ransom documents, comprised of letters, notes, envelopes, and a package wrapper—1,400 words contained in twenty-two items—placed in ten documents an inappropriate "e" (a total of twenty-six times) onto the ends of nine different words. In addition to the other similarities between Hauptmann's writing and the ransom notes, the ransom note writer and Hauptmann also shared this very peculiar writing tic. For example, the word "not," an easy word to spell, appears twenty-one times in the ransom letters and is misspelled seventeen times as "note." The nursery note contains "gute" for "gut" (German for good) and is spelled "gut" in a subsequent letter. "Be" shows up nine times and is misspelled "bee" twice. Other "e" words are "hase" (has), "cane" (can) "gete" (get), "transfare" (transfer), "fore" (for), and "finde" (find).[41]

In Hauptmann's known handwriting, in the form of samples requested by the police following his arrest, the "e" problem is also evident. The police dictated to Hauptmann a paragraph drafted by Albert S. Osborn that contains many of the words and phrases found in the ransom notes. In four of these paragraphs, totaling 480 words, the "e" is tacked onto four words, a total of fourteen times. But as in the ransom notes, the word "not," although misspelled "note" seven times, was spelled correctly on three occasions. Had the police instructed Hauptmann to misspell "not" with the "e," they were extremely clever because they were careful not to make him misspell it this way every time. The same is true for the words "bee" (be) and "cane" (can).[42] It is interesting to note that the fourth "e" word in the requested writings— "Halle" for "hall"—is not in any of the ransom documents. That being the case, why would the police tell Hauptmann to add the "e" to this word? Explaining the evidence away by claiming police wrong doing, in this instance, assumes a cleverness and knowledge that was clearly beyond these officers.

Although there is no evidence other than Hauptmann's own testimony that the police told him to misspell certain words, the mere fact it could have happened weakens this evidence. Therefore, the best evidence of Hauptmann's telltale writing tic would comprise what the experts call conceded, or course-or-business writing, writing known to be Hauptmann's, but not requested by the police. To be certain that Hauptmann had carried this writing oddity into his adulthood, it would be best to examine things he had written after his arrest and trial, a time when he would be careful not to duplicate the writing in the ransom notes. Fortunately, there is such a document in the form of a five-hundred-word, handwritten letter by Hauptmann, dated March 31, 1936, to Governor Harold G. Hoffman. In writing this letter, Hauptmann took great pains not to misspell the words he had misspelled in the ransom notes—words like "police," "money," "case," "innocent," and "everything." He was also careful not to add the letter "e" to "not," "be," and "can." It was Hauptmann's habit, as was the ransom note writer's, not to dot his "i's" or cross his "t's." In his letter to Governor Hoffman, however, every "i" was dotted, and there was not one uncrossed "t." In spite of Hauptmann's effort not to reveal himself as the writer of the ransom notes, he gave himself away.

In the middle of the second page of the letter to Governor Hoffman, Hauptmann wrote: "You know it was not true, a *halfe* hour after my conviction . . ." (italics added). There it was, the telltale "e." Hauptmann did not add it to "not," he was too clever for that, and he was careful not to misspell "hour" as "houer." When he wrote "half"—a word he had not used in the ransom notes—he slipped up.

Earlier in the Hauptmann letter, Hauptmann had written the following: "I know in my *one* sense of justice" (italics added). Hauptmann meant my *own* sense of justice, spelling "own" as "on" with the added "e."

The police did not write the ransom documents, they did not know of Hauptmann's writing tic, and they did not pen the letter to Governor Hoffman. This damning connection to the ransom notes cannot be brushed aside by accusing the police of evidence tampering. It does raise an interesting question, however. How could Mrs. Hauptmann not have known of this peculiarity and not have seen it in the ransom letters? Few have questioned Mrs. Hauptmann's unflagging belief in her husband's innocence. Assuming that she's sincere, the scope and depth of her denial is as bizarre and tragic as the crime itself.

Since the publication of Scaduto's *Scapegoat* in 1976, the Hauptmann revisionists have been on the offensive. Applying an outrageous double standard of proof, they have pinned the crime on people conveniently dead and thus safe to defame. There is probably no such thing as enough evidence to convince true believing Hauptmannites that he was, in fact, guilty of a terrible crime. But in this author's opinion, the evidence not in dispute coupled with the new evidence revealed in this book is enough to prove, beyond a reasonable doubt, that Bruno Richard Hauptmann kidnapped and killed the Lindbergh baby. No one saw him snatch the baby from the crib, and no one, save the killer, witnessed the child's death. Hauptmann did not confess. Nevertheless, it is reasonable to infer that he did it for the money and as hard as it is to accept, he did it alone.

Notes   Bibliography   Index

Notes

3. Bruno and the Governor

1. *New York Times*, 18 Jan. 1936, p. 1.
2. Governor Harold G. Hoffman to Colonel Schwarzkopf, 28 Feb. 1936, Lindbergh Collection, New Jersey State Police Museum and Learning Center, West Trenton, New Jersey (hereafter cited as Lindbergh Collection).

4. The Aftermath

1. Sidney B. Whipple, *The Lindbergh Crime* (New York: Blue Ribbon Books, 1935); *The Trial of Bruno Richard Hauptmann: Edited with a History of the Case* (1937; reprint, with an introduction by Alan M. Dershowitz, Notable Trials Library, Gryphon Editions, Inc. Birmingham, Ala.: Doubleday, Doran and Company, 1989).
2. John F. Condon, *Jafsie Tells All!* (New York: Jonathan Lee, 1936). "Jafsie Tells All!" parts 1–10, *Liberty* 13 (18 Jan. 1936): p. 51; (25 Jan.): p. 7; (1 Feb.): p. 19; (8 Feb.): p. 21; (15 Feb.): p. 30; (22 Feb.): p. 28; (29 Feb.): p. 50; (7 Mar.): p. 47; (14 Mar.): p. 13; (21 Mar.): p. 20.
3. Dudley David Shoenfeld, *The Crime and the Criminal: A Psychiatric Study of the Lindbergh Case* (New York: Covici-Friede, 1936).
4. John Vreeland Haring, *The Hand of Hauptmann: The Handwriting Expert Tells the Story of the Lindbergh Case* (Plainfield, N.J.: Hamer Publishing, 1937).
5. George Waller, *Kidnap: The Story of the Lindbergh Case* (New York: Dial Press, 1961). The English edition was published by Hamish Hamilton in 1961.
6. Harold Olson's story and his quest to prove his true identity as the Lindbergh child as originally published in Theon Wright, *In Search of the Lindbergh Baby* (New York: Tower Books, 1981). See also George DeWan, "The Lindbergh Case

Just Won't Go Away," *Newsday* 56 (15 Dec. 1987): pp. 16–20.

7. Associated Press, "Man Claims Documents Will Prove He's Heir to Aviator Lindbergh," *USA Today,* 23 Oct. 1985.

8. Harold Olson also made his DNA request on WOR-TV's *Evening Magazine,* which aired on 1 March 1988.

9. Associated Press, 23 Oct. 1985.

10. The seven experts who presented papers at the Lindbergh Plenary Session were as follows: Dr. Michael M. Baden (the autopsy), Paul A. Osborn (questioned documents), John P. Osborn (questioned documents), Lucien Haag (the wood evidence), Dr. Emanuel Taney (psychiatric evidence), James F. Starrs (legal aspects), and Jim Horan (the general investigation). The session's findings are published as follows: Michael M. Baden, ed., "The Lindbergh Kidnapping: Review of the Autopsy Evidence," *Journal of Forensic Sciences* 28 (1983): pp. 1035–83.

5. New Age Revisions

1. Three other Lindbergh baby claimants are Don A. Stager, Kenneth Kerwin, and Bill Simons.

2. *Hauptmann v. Wilentz,* 570 F. supp, 351 at 395 (1983).

3. In Ludovic Kennedy, *The Airman and the Carpenter: The Lindbergh Kidnapping and the Framing of Richard Hauptmann* (New York: Viking Press, 1985), p. 416, Kennedy writes: "Supporters of the Kerwin/Olson theory have never faced up to the consequences of their own logic, which necessitates a belief not in one kidnapping but two. . . . Does anyone think such a bizarre scenario likely?"

4. Ronald Goldfarb, "He Had to Be Guilty," *New York Times Book Review,* 17 June 1985, p. 28.

5. Jeffrey Hart, "An American Tragedy," *National Review* 40 (1985): p. 52.

6. Some of these private investigators were George H. Foster, Leon Ho-Age, Robert W. Hicks, Julius B. Braun, Winslow P. Humphrey, Leo F. Meade, and Harold C. Keyes. Hoffman Papers, Lindbergh Collection, New Jersey State Police Museum and Learning Center, West Trenton, New Jersey (hereafter cited as Hoffman Papers).

7. *Hauptmann v. Bornmann et al.* 573 F. supp. 419 at 421 (1986). See also Lee Seglem, "Judge Rejects Effort by Hauptmann Widow to Clear Her Husband," Gannett News Service, 24 Sept. 1987.

8. Associated Press, 12 Sept. 1986.

9. Associated Press, 12 Sept. 1986.

10. See Associated Press, 13 June 1990; Michael Vitez, "Hauptmann Widow Turns to Florio to Clear Her Husband," *Philadelphia Inquirer,* 13 June 1990, p.

7; and Tony Scaduto, "The Lindbergh Case: Is History's Verdict Wrong?" *Crime Beat*, Apr. 1993, p. 51. J. P. Miller, *The Lindbergh Case* (NBC, 1976), docudrama. The movie starred Anthony Hopkins as Hauptmann, Clifford DeYoung as Colonel Lindbergh, and Joseph Cotton as "Jafsie."

11. Michael Vitez, "Hauptmann Widow," p. 7.

12. Lee McDonald, "Hauptmann Widow, 92, Seeks Reprieve in Lindbergh Case," *Courier-News* (Bridgewater, N.J.), 5 Oct. 1991, p. 1. In 1990, a Flemington, New Jersey, playwright, Harry Kazman, wrote a play called *Lindbergh and Hauptmann: The Trial of the Century*. Directed and produced by Kazman and his wife, Reva, the play, drawn from the Hauptmann trial transcripts, is essentially an edited reenactment of the trial. Kazman and a cast of talented actors from the New Jersey area perform twelve shows each fall.

13. Leslie Guttman, "Attorney Battles History's Verdict," *San Francisco Chronicle*, 29 Mar. 1992, p. 2. Guttman quotes Christopher Florentz, a spokesman for the New Jersey Attorney General's Office, as saying there was "no evidence raised in those papers [Bryan's] that would indicate that the conviction . . . of Mr. Hauptmann was anything other than appropriate and correct" (p. 2).

14. Guttman, "Attorney Battles," p. 3.

15. Vitez, "Widow of the Century," *Philadelphia Inquirer*, 19 Jan. 1992, p. 12. Robert S. Bryan was national chairman of the Coalition Against the Death Penalty.

16. Vitez, "Widow of the Century," p. 12.

17. Max Allan Collins, *Stolen Away: A Novel of the Lindbergh Kidnapping* (New York: Bantam, 1991).

18. Gregory Ahlgren and Stephen Monier, *Crime of the Century: The Lindbergh Kidnapping Hoax* (Boston: Branden Books, 1993).

19. Alan Hynd, "Everyone Wanted to Get into the Act," *True Magazine*, Mar. 1949, p. 77. Hynd's article was later reprinted, under a variety of titles, in numerous true-crime anthologies. Ahlgren and Monier, *Crime of the Century*, p. 264.

20. Gloria Negri, "New Hampshire Writers Say Lindbergh Responsible in Kidnapping," *Boston Globe*, 17 Mar. 1993, p. 26.

21. Geoffrey C. Ward, "Cols. Lindbergh and Mustard," *American Heritage* 45 (Apr. 1994): p. 12.

22. Noel Behn, *Lindbergh, the Crime* (New York: Atlantic Monthly Press, 1994).

23. Ward, "Cols. Lindbergh and Mustard," p. 12.

24. "A Half-Century of Heartache" was produced by David Lee Miller.

25. John Logan, *Hauptmann*, dir. Terry McCabe, opened in New York in May 1992 at the Cherry Lane Theater in Greenwich Village. For a review of the play,

see Mel Gussow, "Was Hauptmann Guilty in the Lindbergh Case?" *New York Times*, 29 May 1992, p. 28. See also John Logan, "Hauptmann," *Playbill* 92 (June 1992): p. 23.

26. Carrie Stetler and Bill Gannon, "Hauptmann's Wife Dies a True Believer," *Star-Ledger*, 19 Oct. 1994, p. 1.

27. Barbara D. Phillips, "TV Reopens the Lindbergh Case," *Wall Street Journal*, 9 Sept. 1996, p. 2.

28. Whipple, *The Trial*, p. i.

6. How Many Conspirators Does It Take to Steal a Baby?

1. A few lone assassin cases include the murders of the following: Pres. James A. Garfield, 1881; Pres. William McKinley, 1901; Sen. Huey P. Long, 1935; Pres. John F. Kennedy, 1963; Dr. Martin Luther King Jr., 1968; and Sen. Robert F. Kennedy, 1968. Unsuccessful murders by lone assassins include the following targets: Pres. Franklin D. Roosevelt, 1933; Gov. George Wallace, 1972; Pres. Gerald Ford, 1975 (twice); and Pres. Ronald Reagan, 1981. Lone ransom kidnappers include the following: Pat Crowe (Edward A. Cudahy, victim), 1900; Edward Hickman (Marion Parker, victim), 1927; John Henry Seadlund (Charles S. Ross, victim), 1937; Angfelo John LaMarca (Peter Weinberger, victim), 1956; and Gary Steven Krist (Barbara Jane Mackle, victim), 1968.

2. Ward, "The Most Durable Assassination Theory: Oswald Did It Alone," *New York Times Book Review*, 21 Nov. 1993, p. 21.

3. Gerald Posner, *Case Closed: Lee Harvey Oswald and the Assassination of John F. Kennedy* (New York: Random House, 1993), p. x.

4. Ward, "Most Durable," p. 21.

5. Joseph A. Wolf, "Major Initial Report," 1 Mar. 1932, Lindbergh Collection, p. 2.

6. For Joseph A. Wolf's testimony regarding crime scene footprints, see Hauptmann trial transcript, Day 3, Lindbergh Collection, pp. 785, 790, 792, 795, 797, 809. A photograph of the man's shoe impression seen near where the kidnap ladder had been placed was introduced into evidence as Exhibit S-31.

7. FBI summary report (62–3057), 16 Feb. 1932, FBI Freedom of Information Reading Room, 9th Street and Pennsylvania Avenue, N.W., Washington, D.C. (hereafter referred to as FBI Freedom of Information Reading Room), pp. 51, 52, 106.

8. Hynd, "Untold Facts in the Lindbergh Kidnapping," *True Detective Mysteries* 19 (Dec. 1932): p. 46.

9. Lewis J. Bornmann, "Investigative Report," 13 Mar. 1932, Lindbergh Collection, p. 1.

10. P. W. Wilson, "The Lindbergh Case," *North American Review,* Jan. 1934, p. 55.

11. Scaduto, *Scapegoat: The Lonesome Death of Bruno Richard Hauptmann* (New York: G. P. Putnam's Sons, 1976), p. 397.

12. Scaduto, *Scapegoat,* pp. 315–19.

13. Condon, *Jafsie Tells All!* p. 59.

14. Condon, *Jafsie Tells All!* pp. 121–22.

15. Condon, *Jafsie Tells All!* p. 21.

16. John Tyrrell to Albert S. Osborn, 19 June 1935, author's collection.

17. W. W. Williams, *The Lindbergh Case* (Portland, Or.: W. W. Williams, 1936), pp. 40, 42, 53, 54. A photocopy of this twenty-five-cent booklet is with the Hoffman Papers.

18. *Newsweek Magazine,* 29 Sept. 1934, p. 7.

19. Paul G. Clancy, "Did the Lindbergh Kidnapping Stop a War?" *Astrological Forecast,* Mar. 1938, p. 9.

20. Scaduto, *Scapegoat,* pp. 44, 45.

21. Nuncio DeGaetano, 14 Mar. 1932, Lindbergh Collection, p. 3.

22. Posner, *Case Closed,* p. xi.

23. Regarding the politicians and bureaucrats who rushed to the Lindbergh crime limelight, Mrs. Lindbergh said, "There were people who fluttered around the flame of publicity, politicians who came and posed for pictures next to the kidnapper's ladder" (Anne Morrow Lindbergh, *Hour of Gold, Hour of Lead: Diaries and Letters of Anne Morrow Lindbergh, 1929–1932* [New York: Harcourt Brace Jovanovich, 1973], p. 238.) Perhaps the best known public figures fighting to get into the act were New Jersey governor Harold G. Hoffman and FBI director J. Edgar Hoover.

24. John F. Condon, Evalyn McLean, and Reverend Dobson Peacock, among dozens of others.

25. John Hughes Curtis and Gaston Means are the most famous hoaxers and con men.

26. The following are the most notable confessors: Gaston Means, who confessed on Mar. 30, 1936; Paul H. Wendel; and Frank Parzych, who confessed on May 17, 1932. There were hundreds of confessions.

27. Lieutenant James Finn of the New York City Police Department wrote a series of articles about how he had solved the crime of the century. Ellis Parker Sr. did his best to further his law enforcement career by sabotaging Colonel H. Norman Schwarzkopf of the New Jersey State Police. This was also true of J. Edgar Hoover. There were many others.

28. The list of false witnesses in the Lindbergh case is endless. A few of the ones who testified follow: Louis Kiss, Elvert Carlstrom, Benjamin Heier, Philip Moses, Sam Streppone, Walter Manley, and Berta Hoff.

29. Albert Hamilton, W. W. Williams, Jesse William Pelletreau, John C. Trendley, Robert W. Hicks, Hilda Braunlich, Erastus Mead Hudson, and Charles J. DeBisschop.

30. Frieda von Valta, Arthur Jones, George Michael Paulin, and hundreds of others.

31. Among those who have pointed the finger of guilt at John F. Condon are Edward J. Reilly, Governor Harold G. Hoffman, Anthony Scaduto, Ludovic Kennedy, Anna Hauptmann, and Robert S. Bryan.

32. *New York Times,* 23 Sept. 1934, p. 25; 24 Sept. 1934, p. 2; *Newsweek Magazine,* 29 Sept. 1934, p. 7.

33. *New York Times,* 24 Sept. 1934, p. 2.

34. *New York Times,* 23 Sept. 1924, p. 25.

35. Joyce Milton, *Loss of Eden: A Biography of Charles and Anne Morrow Lindbergh* (New York: Harper Collins, 1993).

36. Milton, *Loss of Eden,* p. 321.

37. Milton, *Loss of Eden,* pp. 315, 316.

38. Milton, *Loss of Eden,* pp. 315–19.

39. Statement of J. R. Russell, FBI file number 7-1-5096, 5 Oct. 1934, FBI Freedom of Information Reading Room.

7. Father Kallok: The Forgotten Story

1. Reverend Dobson Peacock was embarrassed about his involvement with the Lindbergh hoaxer, John H. Curtis. Reverend Vincent S. Burns interrupted Hauptmann's trial on February 12, 1935, by announcing from his seat in the courtroom that Hauptmann was an innocent man. Court officers had to haul Burns out of the courthouse. Reverends D. C. Werner and J. Mathiesen were defrocked as a result of their publicly stated views that Hauptmann was innocent. Reverend Mathiesen disobeyed his superiors by attending Hauptmann's funeral (*New York Times,* 29 Feb. 1936, p. 7).

2. Just Another Republican to Governor Harold G. Hoffman, 2 Jan. 1936, Lindbergh Collection. This letter, as well as all of the Kallok material herein cited, is with the Lindbergh Collection. Father Kallok's story was published in the *Milwaukee Sentinel,* 7 Apr. 1935, pp. 1, 2, 4 and in the *New York Times,* 7 Apr. 1935, p. 37.

3. Mrs. Hauptmann's suicide threat was reported in the *New York Times,* 25 Mar. 1935, p. 46.

4. J. G. Laubenheimer to Colonel H. Norman Schwarzkopf, 30 Jan. 1936, Lindbergh Collection.

5. Detective William F. Horn, report, 12 Feb. 1936, Lindbergh Collection.

6. State of New Jersey Certificate of Death, 5 Sept. 1931. This document is part of the 12 Feb. 1936 report of Corporal William F. Horn, New Jersey State Police. Lindbergh Collection.

7. John F. Tyrrell to Charles Evans, 12 Jan. 1937, author's collection.

8. Other Voices, Other Stories

1. Henry Bryan, "Hauptmann Witness Comes Forward," *Sunday Times Advertiser* (Trenton, N.J.), 14 Nov. 1976, p. 1.

2. Becky Taylor, "Hauptmann Placed at Kidnap Scene," *Sunday Times Advertiser,* 14 Nov. 1976, p. 1.

3. These examples of false leads and investigative wild-goose chases in the initial stages of the crime are from newspaper reportage during the first two weeks of March 1932 and from Edward Dean Sullivan, *The Snatch Racket* (New York: Vanguard Press, 1932).

4. This comes from the following four-page report: Frank J. Carr and Thomas J. Ritchie, 12 Mar. 1932, Lindbergh Collection. Carr and Ritchie are detectives in the New Jersey State Police department.

5. Nuncio DeGaetano, 18 Dec. 1932, Lindbergh Collection. This is a one-page report by Detective DeGaetano of the New Jersey State Police.

6. Unsigned report, F-4, Lindbergh Collection.

7. *New York Times,* 4 Mar. 1936.

9. The Lindberghs: Victims or Suspects?

1. Leon G. Turrou, *Where My Shadow Falls: Two Decades of Crime Detection* (Garden City, N.Y.: Doubleday and Co., 1949), pp. 107, 108.

2. Anne Morrow Lindbergh, *Hour of Gold,* p. 212.

3. Mary Belle Spencer, No. 2310, *Criminal File Exposed! Aviator's Baby Was Never Kidnapped or Murdered* (Chicago: Confidential News Syndicate, 1933), p. 10.

4. Memo from private investigator William Lewis (Red Bank, New Jersey) to Governor Harold G. Hoffman, 28 Feb. 1936, Hoffman Papers, Lindbergh Collection.

5. Jeffrey Newman, "Charles Lindbergh Planned His Baby Son's Kidnapping—He Didn't Want the Child Because It was Malformed," *National Enquirer,* 12 Oct. 1976, p. 71.

6. Newman, "Charles Lindbergh," p. 71.

7. Murray Bleefeld was convicted federally in 1937 for kidnapping Paul H. Wendel, the disbarred lawyer who confessed to kidnapping the Lindbergh baby

after being beaten by his captors. The moment he was released, Wendel took back his "confession." In 1973, the seventy-eight-year-old Bleefeld told author Anthony Scaduto that Paul H. Wendel had kidnapped the Lindbergh baby even though he had taken back his confession.

In 1986 Harry Green, an attorney and former "associate" of Governor Harold G. Hoffman, told writer Noel Behn (Green was then ninety-three) that Mrs. Morrow's chauffeur believed Elisabeth Morrow had killed the Lindbergh baby.

8. Ahlgren and Monier, *Crime of the Century,* p. 202.

9. Behn, *Lindbergh, the Crime,* p. 10.

10. Behn, *Lindbergh, the Crime,* p. 389.

11. Scaduto, *Scapegoat,* p. 241.

12. Scaduto, *Scapegoat,* p. 15.

13. Scaduto, *Scapegoat,* p. 249.

14. Scaduto, *Scapegoat,* p. 252.

15. Scaduto, *Scapegoat,* p. 322.

16. Scaduto, *Scapegoat,* p. 322.

17. Ahlgren and Monier, *Crime of the Century,* p. 237.

18. Behn, *Lindbergh, the Crime,* p. 398.

10. The Butler, the Maid, and the Baby's Nurse

1. Erastus Mead Hudson, "A Scientific Verdict in the Lindbergh-Hauptmann Riddle," *Liberty* 14 (3 Apr. 1937): pp. 34, 35.

2. Hauptmann trial transcript, Day 27, Lindbergh Collection, pp. 6522–26, 6540.

3. Hauptmann trial transcript, Day 4, Lindbergh Collection, p. 856.

4. Alan Hynd, "The Real Story behind the Lindbergh Capture, Part Three," *True Detective Mysteries* 19 (Mar. 1935): p. 78.

5. Five-page statement of John F. Condon to Lieutenant Arthur T. Keaten, 13 May 1932, Lindbergh Collection.

6. Statement of Betty Gow to Lieutenant Arthur T. Keaten, 3 Mar. 1932, Lindbergh Collection.

7. Charles E. Williamson, report (Hopewell Police Department), 2 Mar. 1932, Lindbergh Collection.

8. Whipple, *The Lindbergh Crime,* p. 34.

9. Ray Doyle, "Eight Years after the Lindbergh Case," *Look* (Mar. 1940), p. 19.

10. Jim Fisher, *The Lindbergh Case* (New Brunswick, N.J.: Rutgers University Press, 1987), p. 47.

11. Statement of Violet Sharpe, 10 Mar. 1932, Lindbergh Collection.

12. Violet Sharpe's notebook and the slip of paper regarding her notation about Septimus Banks are part of the Lindbergh Collection.

13. Statement of Violet Sharpe, 13 Apr. 1932, Lindbergh Collection.

14. The medical data concerning Violet Sharpe are based upon a statement by her surgeon, Dr. Walter Philips, 16 June 1932, Lindbergh Collection.

15. Statement of Violet Sharpe, 23 May 1932, Lindbergh Collection.

16. Colonel Lindbergh's defense of Violet Sharpe and Colonel Schwarzkopf's skepticism are based on the following sources: Harry W. Walsh and E. Collins, "Hunt for the Kidnappers: Inside Story of the Lindbergh Case," *Jersey Journal,* 17 Nov. 1932, pp. 17, 18; "Morrow Maid Ends Life; Suspected in Kidnapping," New York Times, 11 June 1932, p. 1.

17. Letter from Violet Sharpe to Fan Simons, 7 June 1932, Lindbergh Collection. Violet Sharpe's letter has not been altered other than to add punctuation for clarity.

18. Statement of Violet Sharpe, 9 June 1932, Lindbergh Collection. This is Violet Sharpe's fourth statement. See also Walsh and Collins, "Hunt for the Kidnappers," 16 Nov. 1932, pp. 1, 10.

19. On the day following Violet Sharpe's suicide, Laura Hughes told the police about Violet's smile and wink following her identification of Ernest Brinkert's photograph. This portion of Hughes's statement was published in the *New York Times,* 12 June 1932, p. 3.

20. The account of Violet Sharpe's suicide is based upon the following sources: Walsh and Collins, 16 Nov. 1932, p. 17; *New York Times,* 11 June 1932, p. 1; and Waller, *Kidnap,* p. 150.

21. *New York Times,* 12 June 1932, p. 1; and *White Plains Daily Reporter,* 13 June 1932, p. 3.

22. "Brinkert Supported in Kidnapping Alibi: Next Figure in Case," *New York Times,* 12 June 1932, p. 1.

23. Emily Sharpe's statement to the British press was reported in *New York Times,* 12 June 1932, p. 3.

24. *White Plains Daily Reporter,* 13 June 1932, p. 3.

25. Anne Morrow Lindbergh, *Hour of Gold,* p. 272.

26. Sergeant A. E. Norman, New Jersey State Police report, 10 Feb. 1936, Lindbergh Collection; Detective Sergeant E. A. Haussling, New Jersey State Police report, 21 Feb. 1936, Lindbergh Collection.

11. Hard Evidence

1. In order of their appearance on the witness stand, the experts were: Albert S. Osborn, Eldridge W. Stein, John F. Tyrrell, Herbert J. Walker, Harry E. Cassidy, Dr. Wilmer Souder, Albert D. Osborn, and James Clark Sellers.

2. These experts were Harry E. Cassidy, Albert D. Osborn, Dr. Wilmer Souder, and James Clark Sellers.

3. The rebuttal witnesses were Joseph Schulhafer, Bert C. Farrar, John Vreeland Haring, and J. Howard Haring.

4. John Vreeland Haring, *The Hand of Hauptmann.*

5. Charles A. Appel Jr.'s Grand Jury questioned-document testimony comprises seven pages of transcript and is with the Lindbergh Case Papers, New York City Archives, Room 103, Surrogate Court Building, Manhattan (hereafter referred to as the Lindbergh Case Papers). A photograph of Charles A. Appel Jr.'s word chart is from David Battan, *Handwriting Analysis* (San Luis Obispo, Cal.: Padre Productions, 1984), p. 254.

6. The three experts agreeing with the prosecution were Samuel C. Malone, John Vreeland Haring, and Arthur P. Meyers. The three who said the ransom notes had been altered were Mrs. Charles Foster, Julia Farr, and Hilda Braunlich (President of the Handwriting Experts' Association of Europe, an organization she founded.)

7. Leigh Matteson, "Lone Wolf vs. Lone Eagle," unpublished manuscript, Lindbergh Collection, pp. 138, 139.

8. Included in this group were Samuel Small, W. W. Williams, Aaron Lewis, H. Gropius, and Jesse William Pelletreau. Samuel Small called himself an "expert penman." His four-page report, "Handwriting in the Lindbergh Case," on the Lindbergh case handwriting evidence, is on file with the Hoffman Papers. See also *New York Daily News*, 4 Feb. 1935, p. 12. W. W. Williams was a handwriting teacher from Portland, Oregon. In the late 1930s he self-published a sixty-six-page booklet on his handwriting findings: see Williams, *The Lindbergh Case.* A photocopy of this booklet is with the Hoffman Papers.

9. Ludovic Kennedy, *The Airman,* p. 277.

10. Donald F. Doud, "Literary Retrials of Notable Forensic Science Cases—Convoluted History for Sale," *Journal of Forensic Sciences* 33 (Jan. 1988): p. 316.

11. Scaduto, *Scapegoat,* p. 142.

12. Francis X. Busch, *Prisoners at the Bar* (London: Arco, 1957), p. 243.

13. The New York City Police officers who would have had to have committed perjury are Lieutenant James J. Finn, Inspector John A. Lyons, and Detective James M. Cashman. The New Jersey State Police officers are Detective Corporal William F. Horn, Colonel H. Norman Schwarzkopf, Sergeant Thomas J. Ritchie, and Detective John B. Wallace. The other New York officers are Detective Philip G. Creamer, Sergeant William Grafenecker, and Detective John A. McNamara.

14. Letter from John F. Tyrrell to James Clark Sellers, 24 Nov. 1936, John F. Tyrrell Papers, Donald F. Doud, Milwaukee, Wisc.

15. The modern-day forensic document examiners are Donald F. Doud, Richard Tidey, Bill Burke, Paul A. Osborn, and John P. Osborn.

16. Kennedy, *The Airman,* pp. 417, 418.

17. The author spoke to Robert W. Radley on 24 August 1992, in Milwaukee, at which time Radley advised that Derek Davis died from cancer in February 1991 at the age of fifty-six.

18. Further, Robert W. Radley spoke to Derek Davis's widow, who confirmed the fact her husband had reported to Ludovic Kennedy that, in his opinion, Hauptmann had written all of the ransom notes in the Lindbergh case. This information is contained in a letter from Radley to the author, 7 September 1992.

19. Dr. Alan Filby has a Ph.D. in chemistry. The author talked to him on 22 August 1992 at the Pfister Hotel in Milwaukee.

20. The author interviewed Gus R. Lesnevich by telephone on 23 Oct. 1992.

21. Kennedy, *The Airman,* pp. 417, 418.

22. The author interviewed Roy A. Huber, 24 August 1992, Milwaukee.

23. Letter from Jan Beck, 13 July 1989 (author's collection), was in response D. Michael Resinger, et al., "Exorcism of Ignorance as a Proxy for Rational Knowledge: The Lessons of Handwriting Identification 'Expertise,'" *University of Pennsylvania Law Review* 137 (1989):p. 731.

24. Scaduto, *Scapegoat,* pp. 384, 385.

25. Scaduto, "The Lindbergh Case," p. 55.

26. Kennedy, *The Airman,* p. 390. Kennedy also offers this as evidence of a rail sixteen switch: "But the most startling piece of Hudson's evidence was his absolute insistence that when he examined the ladder minutely in 1932 there was only one nail hole in rail 16. He stuck to this view like a limpet, even after Wilentz had shown him a picture of rail 16 showing four nail holes, which he claimed had been taken in 1932" (p. 317).

27. For Corporal George G. Wilton's testimony, see Hauptmann trial transcript, Day 28, Lindbergh Collection, pp. 6928–47.

28. See Hauptmann trial transcript, Day 28, Lindbergh Collection, p. 6949.

29. Charles J. DeBisschop and Edward Mielk.

30. Harold Dearden, *Aspects of Murder* (London: Staples Press, 1951), p. 53.

12. Red Herrings, Pseudologic, and Misinformation

1. Scaduto, "The Lindbergh Case," pp. 51, 52. See also Ludovic Kennedy, *On My Way to the Club: An Autobiography* (London: Collins, 1989), p. 391.

2. Hauptmann's extradition hearing in the Bronx before Judge Ernest F. Hammer, 15 Oct. 1934, Lindbergh Collection, p. 7.

3. See Hauptmann trial transcript, Day 17, Lindbergh Collection, p. 4176.

4. See Hauptmann trial transcript, Day 18, Lindbergh Collection, p. 4204.

5. Hauptmann police interrogation transcript, 19 Sept. 1934, Greenwich Po-

lice Station, New York City, p. 35. In Leon G. Turrou, *Where My Shadow Falls,* p. 121, FBI agent Turrou writes: "We continued to puncture his story at every turn. This was simple, because he could scarcely think clearly, much less lie logically, and his groping, confused answers gave the impression that he had blundered into our arms without a prepared alibi."

6. See Hauptmann trial transcript, Day 21, Lindbergh Collection, pp. 5944–46.

7. Report of Hugo Stockburger, 26 Nov. 1934, Lindbergh Collection, p. 58. (Stockburger was one of the two German-speaking New Jersey State Police officers planted in the cell next to Hauptmann's to overhear the prisoner's conversations with his wife and others.)

8. Report of Lieutenant A. L. Smith, 8 Dec. 1934, Lindbergh Collection, p. 1. (Lieutenant Smith was the other German-speaking trooper in the cell next to Hauptmann's.)

9. Report of Lieutenant A. L. Smith, 15 Dec. 1934, Lindbergh Collection, p. 1.

10. Report of Lieutenant A. L. Smith, 22 Dec. 1934, Lindbergh Collection, p. 1.

11. Report of Lieutenant A. L. Smith, 26 Dec. 1934, Lindbergh Collection, p. 1.

12. Investigative report by Detective Claude Patterson, New Jersey State Police, 25 Jan. 1935, Lindbergh Collection, p. 1. See also report of Detective Sergeant A. H. Albrecht, New Jersey State Police, 4 Feb. 1935, Lindbergh Collection, p. 1.

13. These witnesses were Louis Kiss, Walter Manley, August Van Henke, and Elvert Carlstrom. Hauptmann did not tell the story about walking the dog that night when he testified before the Bronx Grand Jury. That part of the alibi did not evolve until much later. See Hauptmann trial transcript, Day 20, Lindbergh Collection, p. 4674.

14. Steve Wilstein, "Lindbergh Case to Be Reopened," Associated Press, 20 Nov. 1986.

15. Guttman, "Attorney Battles," p. 7.

16. von Valta affidavit, 10 Jan. 1936, Hoffman Papers.

17. Lieutenant William Christie, Hoboken Police report, Lindbergh Collection, p. 1. For additional background regarding Frieda von Valta, see a letter to Walter Winchell, 14 Jan. 1935, Lindbergh Collection. The letter is from people who knew her and considered her crazy. Winchell forwarded this letter to David T. Wilentz. Both documents are on file with the Lindbergh Collection.

18. Scaduto, "The Lindbergh Case," p. 52. Scaduto is referring to the report of Lieutenant James J. Finn of the New York City Police Department. In his book, *Scapegoat,* p. 324, Scaduto says: "[I]n a report by Lieutenant Finn, who questioned her, she is quoted as saying the customer was *'apparently an American'*" (italics

added). This contradicts his article and is in line with how Detective Horn reported the Barr interview. In writing his article, Scaduto must have failed to consult his own book.

19. Report by Detective William F. Horn, 27 Nov. 1933, Lindbergh Collection.

20. See Hauptmann trial transcript, Day 14, Lindbergh Collection, p. 3336. The two words spoken by the bill passer were, "one forty," meaning one forty-cent theater ticket. According to Scaduto, this man spoke a dozen words (*Scapegoat,* p. 324). This characterization does not square with the evidence.

21. E. A. Tamm, Memorandum for the Director, 22 Sept. 1934, FBI Freedom of Information Reading Room, p. 1.

22. J. A. Genau, FBI accounting report, 18 Oct. 1934, FBI Freedom of Information Reading Room, p. 20.

23. Special Agent John L. Geraghty, FBI memorandum, 24 Sept. 1934, FBI Freedom of Information Reading Room, p. 1

24. Milton MacKaye, "For the Defense," *New Yorker,* 12 Jan. 1935, p. 51.

25. MacKaye, "For the Defense," p. 30. Reilly, as an inexperienced, young trial attorney, lost a string of capital cases and for a period was known in the underworld as "Electrocution Reilly." University of Delaware Criminal Justice professor Dr. John Kelly has studied Reilly's career as reported in his hometown paper, the *Brooklyn Eagle.* Dr. Kelly reports that the nickname "Death House" Reilly does not appear in that newspaper.

26. MacKaye, "For the Defense," p. 30.

27. William M. Kunstler, *First Degree* (New York: Oceana Publications, 1960), p. 145.

28. Ed Mack, "Hauptmann Juror Curious about New 'Evidence,'" *Hunterdon County Democrat,* 18 Mar. 1982, p. 1.

29. *Hauptmann v. Wilentz,* 570 F. supp, 351 at 395 (1983).

30. Anna Hauptmann, "Story of Anna Hauptmann," 1935, Lindbergh Collection, p. 90.

31. Jeanette Smits, "What Anna Hauptmann Believes Now!" *Philadelphia Record,* 18 Feb. 1940, p. 17.

In Quentin Reynolds, *Courtroom: The Story of Samuel S. Leibowitz* (New York: Farrar, Straus, 1950), p. 333, a bibliography of attorney Samuel S. Leibowitz, the man who tried to get Hauptmann to confess, Reynolds agrees that Hauptmann did not realize his situation until it was too late. Reynolds quotes Leibowitz on this as follows: "I don't believe that Hauptmann thinks there is one chance in a million of his going to the chair. Perhaps the governor's interest in him, as borne out by the governor's personal visit to his death cell at midnight, has given him this overwhelming confidence."

According to Quentin Reynolds, "Leibowitz is convinced that this cunning, defiant desperate criminal would have confessed if the Hoffman, Fisher, and Parker crutches had been knocked from under him" (p. 338).

32. Turrou, *Where My Shadow Falls*, p. 128.

33. Turrou, *Where My Shadow Falls*, p. 121.

34. *New York Times*, 6 Feb. 1935, p. 12.

35. Shoenfeld, *The Crime and the Criminal*.

36. Tamm, memorandum, p. 1.

37. Edmund Pearson, *Studies in Murder* (New York: Random House, Modern Library Editions, 1938), p. 2.

38. The possibility that Hauptmann had planned to kidnap the baby from the Morrow estate in Englewood was rejected because it was believed Hauptmann's three-piece ladder did not reach the nursery window. On 15 April 1932, Inspector Harry Walsh reported as follows:

> Measured the distance between the ground and the top of the coping just outside the Lindbergh baby's nursery window in the Morrow home for the purpose of ascertaining whether or not it would have been possible for the kidnapers to have perpetrated this crime at the Morrow estate. The distance between the ground and that window is 25 feet 9 inches and in as much the three sections of the ladder used at Hopewell in the kidnapping of the Lindbergh baby measures only 20 feet overall, I have concluded that the kidnappers never intended to use this ladder in the abduction of that baby from the Morrow home, if they had any intent of committing that crime in Englewood (Lindbergh Collection, p. 1).

Inspector Walsh either measured wrong, or did not know where the baby slept. The baby's room was on the west wing, occupied by the Lindberghs. Hauptmann could have entered one of the three windows to the nursery. Two of these windows were about twenty feet above the ground while the third sat seven feet above the roof of the walkway connecting the Lindbergh wing to the main house. The easiest entrance would have involved using the bottom two sections of the ladder to climb to the low-pitched roof of the walkway—a height of twelve feet—then, using the top section, to climb the remaining distance to the nursery window directly above. The Morrow house is not only remote, its physical layout would have allowed easy access to the nursery. The Morrow night watchman, sixty-five-year-old George Marshall, came on duty at 8:30 P.M. but only made rounds inside the house. The author, Frank Pizzichillo (a Lindbergh case researcher), and James D. Fisher studied this entry possibility at the Morrow estate on August 11, 1992.

39. New Jersey State Police detective Lewis J. Bornmann, in a report dated 9 October 1934 (Lindbergh Collection, p. 1), noted the following regarding access to Hauptmann's attic: "[I]t is gained only through a small linen closet approxi-

mately 8 foot high, 28 inches deep with an inside width of 22½ inches and a door 15½ wide, this door having a knob lock. It would be impossible for anyone other than the occupants of the apartment to gain access to the attic."

40. According to the testimony of Christian Fredericksen, owner of the lunch-room-bakery where Mrs. Hauptmann worked, he baked all night, keeping the store "open as long as I expect customers, sometimes it was open until one o'clock." (Hauptmann trial transcript, Day 17, Lindbergh Collection, p. 4136) Hauptmann could have arrived at the lunchroom-bakery hours late on the night of the crime, and his wife would have still been working there.

Author P. J. O'Brien, in his book, *The Lindberghs: The Story of a Distinguished Family* (New York: International Press, 1935), p. 53, offers this interesting theory about the kidnap ladder:

On the lawn near the house lay the ladder, which had been used by the kid-napper. It was of rough lumber, built in three sections. Two were rather care-fully made but the third was hastily, even clumsily thrown together. This led investigators to believe an earlier attempt had been made to steal the baby and that the two sections were found too short. The third, they assumed, was quickly constructed.

13. New Evidence

1. Interview transcript of Frederick Hahn, 19 Nov. 1934, Lindbergh Case Papers, 28 pages. Present at the questioning were the following: from New Jersey, David T. Wilentz, Colonel Schwarzkopf, Captain Lamb, and Lieutenant Arthur T. Keaten. Detective Madden from the New York City Police Department was also present.

2. Statement of Marie Hahn, 19 Nov. 1934, Lindbergh Case Papers, 12 pages.

3. Marie Hahn is not the only person to have mentioned Hauptmann's garage alarm to the police. It seemed that Hauptmann liked showing it off. See "Hoarded Ransom Guarded by the Alarm," New York Times, 28 Sept. 1934, p. 8.

4. Frederick and Marie Hahn are included on a list of witnesses subpoenaed by the state of New Jersey in the Hauptmann trial (Prosecution Witness List, Lindbergh Collection, p. 1).

5. Frederick Hahn's anticipated testimony was noted in the *New York Times,* 18 Jan. 1935, p. 1.

6. See Hauptmann trial transcript, Day 20, Lindbergh Collection, pp. 4665–72. This testimony was heard on 29 Jan. 1935.

7. The Wollenbergs testified at Hauptmann's trial for the defense. Both said they had attended Fisch's farewell party on December 2, 1933, the night Fisch left

Hauptmann the shoe box that supposedly contained fifteen thousand dollars in gold notes. Wilentz's brief cross-examination was limited to the events of that evening. See Hauptmann trial transcript, Day 25, Lindbergh Collection, pp. 6003–16. See also Special Agent J. E. Seykora, FBI memorandum for file, 9 Oct. 1934, FBI Freedom of Information Reading Room, p. 1.

8. Special Agent Leon G. Turrou, FBI report, 3 Oct. 1934, FBI Freedom of Information Reading Room, p. 1.

9. The jurors were not the only ones in the courtroom unimpressed by Hauptmann. Youngstown, Ohio *Vindicator* columnist Esther Hamilton told Associated Press correspondent Samuel G. Blackman: "I didn't like Hauptmann. He was sneaky. He got better than he deserved." Samuel G. Blackman, "Lindbergh Kidnapping: 'Crime of the Century,'" (Youngstown, Ohio) *Vindicator,* 21 Feb. 1982, p. 6. In Adela Rogers St. Johns, "I Covered the Lindbergh Kidnapping," *Modern Maturity,* Apr.–May 1982, p. 60, St. Johns writes: "So for five weeks, through 31 days of testimony, I sat there watching Hauptmann. And as I watched I began to feel in my stomach, in my woman's intuition, in my visceral reaction, in my reporter's sixth sense, that this was the man who did it."

10. See Hauptmann trial transcript, Day 12, Lindbergh Collection, pp. 2803–6. FBI agent Sisk's account of this search is Lieutenant corroborated in Turrou, FBI report, 13 Oct. 1934, Lindbergh Collection.

11. Although Keith testified at the trial, he was on the stand less than five minutes, and his testimony had to do with a procedural legal point regarding the chain of custody of the kidnap ladder. (Hauptmann trial transcript, Day 13, Lindbergh Collection, pp. 2992–96). Keith's findings were backed-up by another scientist, Dr. Alexander O. Gettler, Chief Toxicologist of New York City. "I have found," Dr. Gettler said, "that most of this money has a musty smell, as though it has been long buried or secreted somewhere the air could not reach it." (*New York Times,* 22 Sept. 1934, p. 3). Dr. Gettler did not testify at Hauptmann's trial.

12. Letter Spec. Agt. Robert W. Corey, IRS Philadelphia, to Agt. Frank J. Wilson, IRS New York, 18 Mar. 1933, Lindbergh Case Papers. On 25 October 1934, Corporal Samuel J. Leon, New Jersey State Police, determined that nails from the Pittsburgh Steel Company were sold by the Great National Millwork and Lumber Company—a store where Hauptmann purchased building supplies.

13. Keith, "Bruno's Nails Built the Kidnap Ladder," King Features Syndicate, 1935, n.p. Keith also published his findings in "Identification of the Lindbergh Ladder Nails," *Iron Age 144* (17 Oct. 1935): p. 41.

14. This is by Hauptmann's own admission. See his testimony, Hauptmann trial transcript, Day 19, Lindbergh Collection, pp. 4459–67.

15. At one time or another, in moments of candor, Hauptmann revealed the true

extent of his criminal past. He talked about his crimes at his Bureau of Immigration deportation hearing on July 14, 1923, after being caught in New York City as a stowaway. He also admitted his past crimes to the psychiatrists hired by James M. Fawcett, his first attorney, after his Lindbergh arrest. German police records from Berlin, Seconsen, Kamenz, Dresden, and Bautzen document his criminality in that country.

16. Jay Maeder, "The Resurrection of Richard Hauptmann: Continuing the Arguments in the Case That Won't Go Away," *New York Daily News Magazine,* 3 Apr. 1988, p. 16.

17. "Anna Hauptmann: Lindbergh Kidnapping's Final Victim," *U.S. News and World Report,* 4 Nov. 1985, p. 41.

18. Guttman, "He's Certain Hauptmann Was Innocent," *Milwaukee Journal,* 2 May 1992, p. 1.

19. Letter from police, Berlin, Germany, to J. Edgar Hoover, 15 Nov. 1934, Lindbergh Collection.

20. Regarding Hauptmann's relationship with Gerta Henkel, see his testimony, Hauptmann trial transcript, Day 19, Lindbergh Collection, pp. 4530–36, and Mrs. Henkel's testimony, Hauptmann trial transcript, Day 26, Lindbergh Collection, pp. 6404–10. In a memo from FBI agent M. A. Taylor to J. Edgar Hoover (22 Sept. 1934, FBI Freedom of Information Reading Room), Taylor wrote, "that investigation had disclosed that suspect Hauptmann had been friendly, probably intimate with a Mrs. Hinkle [*sic*] and was accustomed to go to the Hinkel [*sic*] home mornings around 8:30 after the woman's husband had gone to his work (about 6:30 or 7:00 am)."

21. The Steiner, Rouse, and Company employee was a Mr. Brent. See Hauptmann trial transcript, Day 19, Lindbergh Collection, pp. 4498–99. Brent gave statements to the New York City Police and the FBI regarding Hauptmann's comments to him about Anna Hauptmann.

22. See Hauptmann trial transcript, Day 19, Lindbergh Collection, pp. 4534–35.

23. See Hauptmann trial transcript, Day 20, Lindbergh Collection, pp. 4728–29.

24. Ernest Kahlar Alix, *Ransom Kidnapping in America, 1874–1974: The Creation of a Capital Crime* (Carbondale: Southern Illinois University Press, 1978). The Bremer members of the Alvin Karpis-Ma Barker gang, were eventually caught.

25. LeMoyne Snyder, *Homicide Investigation* (Springfield, Ill: Charles C. Thomas, 1944), p. 117.

26. The discovery of the ether in Hauptmann's garage and the subsequent investigation into its origin are reported in Special Agent John L. Geraghty, FBI

memorandum, 23 Sept. 1934, Lindbergh Collection, pp. 4–6. The FBI narrowed the time of purchase to January 1934 in three ways: (1) The man who wrote "ether" on the Raabe label had recently purchased the pharmacy, opening it for business in January 1934. (2) The label itself was of the kind used by the former owner. After January 1934, these labels were no longer used. (3) The time of purchase was corroborated by the fact the bottle's screw-type cap did not exist until the latter part of 1933.

27. Frank Pizzichillo informed the author of the Geraghty report in August 1992. Pizzichillo has spent months at the New Jersey State Police Museum and Learning Center working his way through this massive collection of information. Finding the ether reference in Agent Geraghty's report was like finding a needle in a haystack.

28. Geraghty, FBI memorandum, p. 4.

29. Hynd, "Untold Facts," p. 77.

30. The psychiatrists were Dr. S. Philip Goodhart and Dr. Richard Hoffman from the Bronx. Drs. Connally and Spradley from New Jersey, and Dr. James H. Huddleson from Manhattan.

31. *New York Times,* 22 Dec. 1934, p. 32.

32. *New York Times,* 20 Jan. 1935, p. 12.

33. The author first saw Dr. Huddleson's report in the summer of 1992 while visiting Frank Pizzichillo at his home in New Jersey.

34. James H. Huddleson, report, Frank Pizzichillo files, author's collection, p. 16.

35. Huddleson, report, p. 9.

36. On August 23, 1992, the author spoke with two eminent forensic scientists about the Huddleson report, Hauptmann's writing tic, and how it ties Hauptmann to the Lindbergh ransom documents. Jan Beck, a Seattle examiner of questioned documents who speaks fluent German, stated that Hauptmann's speech-writing problem was quite unusual and rare. Dr. David A. Crown, a forensic document examiner with offices in Fairfax, Virginia, and Sanibel, Florida, stated that because German is a phonetic language, it is difficult to be a bad speller of that tongue. Both experts considered Hauptmann's writing tic, under the circumstances presented by the author, as highly incriminating.

37. Huddleson, report, pp. 1, 2.

38. Huddleson, report, p. 6.

39. Huddleson, report, p. 8.

40. Interviews of Jan Beck and Dr. David A. Crown, 23 Aug. 1992.

41. In Ahlgren and Monier, *Crime of the Century,* p. 176, the authors, in attempting to show that Hauptmann had not written the nursery note, made the fol-

lowing observation "In the original nursery note the 'sir' in the greeting 'Dear Sir!' is spelled correctly. In the March 12 note to Jafsie 'Sir' is misspelled with an 'e' at the end: 'Dear Sire!' Yet no one mentioned that to the jury."

This author has looked at the March 12 note to Jafsie and does not see that particular "e," but if Ahlgren and Monier are correct, considering the word "gute" in the nursery note, they unwittingly hammered another nail into Hauptmann's coffin.

42. In the known handwriting samples, the word "be" appears eight times and is misspelled as "bee" twice. The word "can" was misspelled as "cane" twice.

Bibliography

BOOKS

Ahlgren, Gregory, and Stephen Monier. *Crime of the Century: The Lindbergh Kidnapping, Hoax.* Boston: Branden Books, 1993.

Alix, Ernest Kahlar. *Ransom Kidnapping in America, 1874–1974: The Creation of a Capital Crime.* Carbondale: Southern Illinois University Press, 1978.

Battan, David. *Handwriting Analysis.* San Luis Obispo, Calif.: Padre Productions, 1984.

Behn, Noel. *Lindbergh, the Crime.* New York: Atlantic Monthly Press, 1994.

Berg, A. Scott. *Lindbergh.* New York: G. P. Putnam's Sons, 1998.

Boorstin, Daniel J. *Hidden Histories.* New York: Harper and Row, 1987.

Brant, John, and Edith Renauld. *True Story of the Lindbergh Kidnapping.* New York: Kroy Wen, 1932.

Busch, Francis X. *Prisoners at the Bar.* London: Arco, 1957.

Coakley, Leo J. *Jersey Troopers.* New Brunswick, N.J.: Rutgers University Press, 1971.

Collins, Max Allan. *Stolen Away: A Novel of the Lindbergh Kidnapping.* New York: Bantam, 1991.

Condon, John F. *Jafsie Tells All!* New York: Jonathan Lee, 1936.

Davis, Kenneth. *The Hero: Charles A. Lindbergh and the American Dream.* Garden City, N.Y.: Doubleday and Co., 1954.

Dearden, Harold. *Aspects of Murder.* London: Staples Press, 1951.

Demaris, Ovid. *The Lindbergh Kidnapping Case: The True Story of the Crime that Shocked the World.* Derby, Conn.: Monarch Books, 1961.

Dutch, Andrew K. *Hysteria: The Lindbergh Kidnap Case.* Philadelphia: Dorrance, 1975.

Elliott, Robert G., and Albert R. Beatty. *Agent of Death: The Memoirs of an Executioner.* New York: E. P. Dutton, 1940.

Fisher, Jim. *The Lindbergh Case*. 1987. Reprint, with a new preface, New Brunswick, N.J.: Rutgers University Press, 1998.

Goodman, Jonathan. *The Modern Murder Yearbook*. London: Robinson, 1994.

Gramling, Oliver. *AP: The Story of News*. New York: Farrar and Rinehart, 1940.

Haldeman-Julius, Marcet. *The Lindbergh-Hauptmann Kidnap-Murder Case*. Girard, Kans.: Haldeman-Julius Publications, 1937.

Haring, John Vreeland. *The Hand of Hauptmann: The Handwriting Expert Tells the Story of the Lindbergh Case*. Plainfield, N.J.: Hamer Publishing, 1937.

Hauptmann, Anna. "Story of Anna Hauptmann." 1935, Lindbergh Collection, New Jersey State Police Museum and Learning Center, West Trenton, N.J.

Herrmann, Dorothy. *Anne Morrow Lindbergh: A Gift for Life*. New York: Ticknor and Fields, 1993.

Hoyt, Edwin. *Spectacular Rogue: Gaston B. Means*. Indianapolis: Bobbs-Merrill, 1963.

Hynd, Alan. *The Giant Killers*. New York: Robert M. McBride, 1945.

——. *Murder, Mayhem, and Mystery*. New York: A. S. Barnes, 1958.

Irey, Elmer L., and William J. Slocum. *The Tax Dodgers*. New York: Greenberg, 1948.

Jones, Wayne. *Murder of Justice—New Jersey's Greatest Shame*. New York: Vantage Press, 1997.

Kennedy, Ludovic. *The Airman and the Carpenter: The Lindbergh Kidnapping and the Framing of Richard Hauptmann*. New York: Viking Press, 1985.

——. *On My Way to the Club: An Autobiography*. London: Collins, 1989.

Kunstler, William M. *First Degree*. New York: Oceana Publications, 1960.

Leighton, Isabel, ed. *The Aspirin Age: 1919–1941*. New York: Simon and Schuster, 1949.

Lewis, Jerry D., ed. *Crusade Against Crime*. New York: Brenard Geis Associations, 1962.

Lindbergh, Anne Morrow. *Hour of Gold, Hour of Lead: Diaries and Letters of Anne Morrow Lindbergh, 1929–1932*. New York: Harcourt Brace Jovanovich, 1973.

Lindbergh, Charles A. *Autobiography of Values*. Edited by William Jovanovich and Judith A. Schiff. New York: Harcourt Brace Jovanovich, 1977.

Marston, William M. *The Lie Detector Test*. New York: Richard B. Smith, 1938.

Matteson, Leigh. "Lone Wolf vs. Lone Eagle." Lindbergh Collection, New Jersey State Police Museum and Learning Center, West Trenton, N.J.: N.p., n.d.

McArdle, Phil, and Karen McArdle. *Fatal Fascinations: Where Facts Meets Fiction in Police Work*. Boston: Houghton Mifflin, 1988.

Milton, Joyce. *Loss of Eden: A Biography of Charles and Anne Morrow Lindbergh*. New York: Harper Collins, 1993.

Mosley, Leonard. *Lindbergh: A Biography*. Garden City, N.Y.: Doubleday and Co., 1976.

Mott, Frank Luther, ed. *Headlining America*. Boston: Houghton Mifflin, 1937.

Nicolson, Nigel, ed. *Harold Nicolson: Diaries and Letters 1930–1939*. New York: Atheneum, 1966.

O'Brien, P. J. *The Lindberghs: The Story of a Distinguished Family*. New York: International Press, 1935.

Osborn, Albert D. *Questioned Documents Problems*. Albany: Boyd Printing, 1944.

Osterburgh, James W. *The Crime Laboratory: Case Studies of Scientific Criminal Investigations*. 2d ed. New York: Clark Boardman, 1982.

Pearson, Edmund. *Studies in Murder*. Modern Library Editions. New York: Random House, 1938.

Pease, Frank. The "Hole" in the Hauptmann Case? New York: Frank Pease, 1936.

Posner, Gerald. *Case Closed: Lee Harvey Oswald and the Assassination of John F. Kennedy*. New York: Random House, 1993.

Powers, Richard Gid. *Secrecy and Power: The Life of J. Edgar Hoover*. New York: Free Press, 1987.

Radelet, Michael L., et. al. *In Spite of Innocence: Erroneous Convictions in Capital Cases*. Boston: Northeastern University Press, 1992.

Radin, Edward D. *Twelve Against Crime*. New York: G. P. Putnam's Sons, 1950.

Reynolds, Quentin. *Courtroom: The Story of Samuel S. Leibowitz*. New York: Farrar, Straus, 1950.

Robinson, Henry. *Science Catches the Criminal*. Indianapolis: Bobbs-Merrill, 1935.

Ross, Walter. *The Last Hero: Charles A. Lindbergh*. Rev. and enl. ed., New York: Harper and Row, 1976.

Scaduto, Anthony. *Scapegoat: The Lonesome Death of Bruno Richard Hauptmann*. New York: G. P. Putnam's Sons, 1976.

Sheridan, Lew W. *I Killed for the Law*. New York: Stackpole Sons, 1938.

Shoenfeld, Dudley David. *The Crime and the Criminal: A Psychiatric Study of the Lindbergh Case*. New York: Covici-Friede, 1936.

Snyder, LeMoyne. *Homicide Investigation*. Springfield, Ill.: Charles C. Thomas, 1944.

Spencer, Mary Belle. *No. 2310, Criminal File Exposed! Aviator's Baby Was Never Kidnapped or Murdered*. Chicago: Confidential News Syndicate, 1933.

Still, Charles. *Styles in Crime*. Philadelphia: J. B. Lippincott, 1938.

Sullivan, Edward Dean. *The Snatch Racket*. New York: Vanguard Press, 1932.

Tully, Andrew. *Treasury Agent: The Inside Story*. New York: Simon and Schuster, 1958.

Turrou, Leon G. *Where My Shadow Falls: Two Decades of Crime Detection*. Garden City, N.Y.: Doubleday and Co., 1949.

Veron, John. *Lindbergh's Son.* New York: Viking Press, 1987.

Vitray, Laura. *The Great Lindbergh Hullabaloo: An Unorthodox Account.* New York: William Faro, 1932.

Waller, George. *Kidnap: The Story of the Lindbergh Case.* New York: Dial Press, 1961.

Wendel, Paul H. *The Lindbergh-Hauptmann Aftermath.* New York: Loft, 1940.

Whipple, Sidney B. *The Lindbergh Crime.* New York: Blue Ribbon Books, 1935.

———, ed. *The Trial of Bruno Richard Hauptmann: Edited with a History of the Case.* 1937. Reprint, with an introduction by Alan M. Dershowitz. Notable Trials Library. Gryphon Editions, Inc. Birmingham, Ala.: Doubleday, Doran and Co., 1989.

Williams, W. W. *The Lindbergh Case.* Portland, Ore.: W. W. Williams, 1936.

Wilson, Frank J., and Beth Day. *Special Agent: A Quarter Century with the Treasury Department and the Secret Services.* New York: Holt, Rinehart, and Winston, 1956.

Wright, Theon. *In Search of the Lindbergh Baby.* New York: Tower Books, 1981.

ARTICLES

Adams, Jean. "The Untold Truth about Hauptmann's Wife." *True Detective Mysteries,* September 1936, p. 6.

Allen, Neal. "They Called It the Crime of the Century." *Woman's World,* 6 Mar. 1990, p. 44.

Allhoff, Fred. "What Happened to Ellis Parker?" Parts 1–8. *Liberty* 15 (7 May 1938): p. 19; (14 May): p. 51; (21 May): p. 17; (28 May): p. 12; (4 June): p. 38; (11 June): p. 55; (18 June): p. 40; (25 June): p. 42.

"Anna Hauptmann: Lindbergh Kidnapping's Final Victim," *U.S. News and World Report,* 4 Nov. 1985, p. 41.

Associated Press. "Man Claims Documents Will Prove He's Heir to Aviator Lindbergh." *USA Today,* 23 Oct. 1985.

———. 12 Sept. 1986; 13 June 1990.

Baden, Michael M., ed. "The Lindbergh Kidnapping: Review of the Autopsy Evidence." *Journal of Forensic Sciences* 28 (1983): pp. 1035–83.

Barnes, Harry E. "The Deeper Lesson of the Lindbergh Kidnapping." *Survey* 47 (1932): p. 31.

Bedau, Hugo A., and Michael L. Radelet. "Miscarriages of Justice in Potentially Capital Cases." *Stanford Law Review* 40 (Nov. 1987): pp. 21–179.

Blackman, Samuel G. "The Case That Shook the World." *Milwaukee Journal,* 3 Feb. 1992.

——. "Hauptmann Trial Gripped the U.S. Half Century Ago." (Youngstown, Ohio) *Vindicator*, 10 Feb. 1985.

——. "Lindbergh Kidnapping: 'Crime of the Century.'" (Youngstown, Ohio) *Vindicator*, 21 Feb. 1982.

Boehn, Sid. "Hauptmann—A Jersey Industry." *Easy Money*, June 1936, pp. 1–4.

Bryan, Henry. "Hauptmann Witness Comes Forward." *Sunday Times Advertiser* (Trenton, N.J.), 14 Nov. 1976.

Carnes, Cecil. "Let's Finish the Lindbergh Case." *Bluebook Magazine* 4 (Aug. 1952): p. 17.

Christensen, Donna J. "Lindbergh Kidnapping: The Ladder Link." *Forest and People* 27 (1977): p. 38.

Clancy, Paul G. "Did the Lindbergh Kidnapping Stop a War?" *Astrological Forecast*, Mar. 1938, p. 9.

Collins, Frederick L. "What Will Happen Next in the Lindbergh Case?" *Liberty* 13 (7 Nov. 1936): p. 18.

Condon, John F. "Jafsie Tells All!" Parts 1–10. *Liberty* 13 (18 Jan. 1936): p. 51; (25 Jan.): p. 7; (1 Feb.): p. 19; (8 Feb.): p. 21; (15 Feb.): p. 30; (22 Feb.): p. 28; (29 Feb.): p. 50; (7 Mar.): p. 47; (14 Mar.): p. 13; (21 Mar.): p. 20.

Curtin, D. Thomas. "What Hauptmann Did with the Missing Money." *Liberty* 13 (9 May 1936): p. 40.

Curtin, D. Thomas, and James J. Finn. "How I Captured Hauptmann." Parts 1–7. *Liberty* 12 (12 Oct. 1935): p. 5; (19 Oct.): p. 24; (26 Oct.): p. 13; (2 Nov.): p. 28; (9 Nov.): p. 14; (16 Nov.): p. 51; (23 Nov.): p. 17.

Daley, Yvonne. "For Lindberghs, Fame Has Its Price." *Boston Globe*, 28 Mar. 1933.

Davidson, David D. "The Story of the Century," *American Heritage*, Feb. 1976, p. 22.

DeWan, George. "The Lindbergh Case Just Won't Go Away." *Newsday* 56 (15 Dec. 1987): pp. 16–20.

Doud, Donald F. "Literary Retrials of Notable Forensic Science Cases—Convoluted History for Sale." *Journal of Forensic Sciences* 33 (1988): p. 316.

——. "A Review of The Lindbergh Case." *Journal of Forensic Sciences* 34 (1989): p. 276.

Doyle, Ray. "Eight Years after the Lindbergh Case." *Look*, Mar. 1940, p. 19.

Ducan, Gerald. "Unsolved Mysteries of the Lindbergh Case." *New York Daily News*, 29 Nov. 1935.

Dunlap, Al. "Was the Body of the Lindbergh Baby Really Found?" *Startling Detective*, May 1932, p. 48.

——. "Why No Lie Detector for the Lindbergh Case?" *Detective*, Sept. 1932. Reprinted in: Dilworth, Donald. C., ed. *Silent Witness*. Gaitherburg, Md.: International Association of Chiefs of Police, 1977.

Earle, Robert. "Find the Lindy Killers!" *Startling Detective,* Aug. 1932, p. 22.

Elliot, Robert G., and Albert R. Beatty. "And May God Have Mercy on Your Soul." *Collier's,* 24 Sept. 1938, p. 44.

Feld, Rose C. "Circumstantial Evidence: How Strong?" *New York Times Magazine,* 16 June 1935.

Fiedler, Cheryl. "The Lindbergh Case." Parts 1–35. *Flemington, Clinton Family News,* 26 Jan. 1988–1 Nov. 1988.

Fisher, C. Lloyd. "The Case New Jersey Would Like to Forget." Parts 1–7. *Liberty* 13 (1 Aug. 1936): p. 17; (8 Aug.): p. 31; (15 Aug.): p. 15; (22 Aug.): p. 41; (29 Aug.): p. 50; (5 Sept.): p. 16; (12 Sept.): p. 13.

Fisher, Jim. "How Can Such a Guilty Kidnapper Be So Innocent?" *Chief of Police,* Nov./Dec. 1988, p. 99.

Golden, Daniel. "Did Jury Err During the 'Trial of the Century'?" *Boston Globe,* 22 Feb. 1987.

Goldfarb, Ronald. "He Had to Be Guilty." *New York Times Book Review,* 17 June 1985: p. 28.

Gussow, Mel. "Was Hauptmann Guilty in the Lindbergh Case?" *New York Times,* 29 May 1992.

Guttman, Leslie. "Attorney Battles History's Verdict." *San Francisco Chronicle,* 29 Mar. 1992.

———. "Attorney Keeps Lindbergh Case Boiling." *San Francisco Chronicle,* 2 May 1992.

———. "He's Certain Hauptmann Was Innocent." *Milwaukee Journal,* 2 May 1992.

Haag, Lucien C. "The Lindbergh Case Revisited: A Review of the Criminalistic Evidence." *Journal of Forensic Sciences* 28 (1983): p. 1044.

Hart, Jeffrey. "An American Tragedy." *National Review* 40 (1985): p. 52.

Hauptmann, Bruno Richard. "Hauptmann's Own Story." *New York Daily Mirror,* 3–10 Dec. 1935.

———. "Why Did You Kill Me?" *Liberty* 13 (2 May 1936): p. 50. Reprinted in: *America: An Illustrated Dairy of its Most Exciting Years.* New York: Stonehouse Press, 1972.

Hoffman, Harold G., and Alan Hynd. "Things I Forgot," *Liberty* 15 (2 July 1938): p. 31; (9 July): p. 19.

———. "What Was Wrong with the Lindbergh Case: The Crime, The Case, The Challenge." *Liberty* 15 (29 Jan. 1938): p. 41; (5 Feb.): p. 38; (12 Feb.): p. 51; (19 Feb.): p. 30; (26 Feb.): p. 19; (5 Mar.): p. 47; (12 Mar.): p. 49; (19 Mar.): p. 51; (26 Mar.): p. 55; (2 Apr.): p. 44; (9 Apr.): p. 30; (16 Apr.): p. 42; (23 Apr.): p. 55; (30 Apr.): p. 37.

Horan, James J. "The Investigation of the Lindbergh Kidnapping Case." *Journal of Forensic Sciences* 28 (1983): p. 1040.

Hudson, Erastus, M. "A Scientific Verdict in the Lindbergh-Hauptmann Riddle." *Liberty* 14 (3 Apr. 1937): p. 34.

Hynd, Alan. "Everyone Wanted to Get Into the Act." *True Magazine*, Mar. 1949, p. 77. Reprinted in: Alan Hynd. *Violence in the Night*. New York: Fawcett, 1955; and Alan Hynd. *A Treasury of True* (New York: A. S. Barnes, 1956).

——. "The Real Story Behind the Lindbergh Capture." Parts 1–3. *True Detective Mysteries* 19 (Jan. 1932): p. 19; (Feb.): p. 41; (Mar.): p. 57.

——. "Untold Facts in the Lindbergh Kidnapping," Parts 1–7. *True Detective Mysteries* 19 (Nov. 1932): p. 27; (Dec.): p. 46; 20 (Jan. 1933): p. 19; (Feb.): p. 41; (Mar.): p. 56; (Apr.): p. 60; (May): p. 24.

Katzenbach, John. "Revisionism Revised." *New York Times Book Review*, 11 Oct. 1987.

Keenan, John F. "The Lindbergh Kidnapping Revisited." *Michigan Law Review* 108 (1986): p. 821.

Keith, Stanley P. "Bruno's Nails Built the Kidnap Ladder." King Features Syndicate, 1935.

——. "Identification of the Lindbergh Ladder Nails." *Iron Age* 144 (1935): p. 41.

Knight, Richard A. "Trial by Fury." *Forum*, Jan. 1936, p. 21.

Koehler, Arthur. "Techniques Used in Tracing the Lindbergh Kidnapping Ladder." *Journal of Criminal Law and Criminology* 27 (Mar.–Apr. 1937): p. U. 27.

——. "Who Made That Ladder?" *Saturday Evening Post*, 20 Apr. 1935.

——. "Wood Expert." *South Dakota Bar Journal* 3 (1935): pp. 835–41.

Logan, John. "Hauptmann," *Playbill* 92 (June 1992): p. 23.

Mack, Ed. "FBI Memos Stir Doubt on Hauptmann." *Hunterdon County Democrat*, 5 Feb. 1981.

——. "Hauptmann Juror Curious about New 'Evidence.'" *Hunterdon County Democrat*, 18 Mar. 1982.

MacKaye, Milton. "For the Defense." *New Yorker*, 12 Jan. 1935, p. 51.

Maeder, Jay. "The Resurrection of Richard Hauptmann: Continuing the Arguments in the Case That Won't Go Away." *New York Daily News Magazine*, 3 Apr. 1988.

Matteson, Leigh. "I Could Have Broken the Lindbergh Case Two Years Ago." *Today*, 27 Oct. 1934.

McDonald, Lee. "Hauptmann Widow, 92, Seeks Reprieve in Lindbergh Case." *Courier-News* (Bridgewater, N.J.), 5 Oct. 1991.

McLean, Evalyn Walsh, and Alan Hynd. "Why I Am Still Investigating the Lindbergh Case." Parts 1–10. *Liberty* 15 (23 July 1938): p. 17; (30 July): p. 25; (6 Aug.): p. 31; (13 Aug.): p. 47; (20 Aug.): p. 9; (27 Aug.): p. 51; (3 Sept.): p. 14; (10 Sept.): p. 39; (17 Sept.): p. 50; (24 Sept.): p. 51.

Mefford, Arthur L. "Did Hauptmann Work Alone?" *Real Detective*, Aug. 1935, p. 16.

Milwaukee Sentinel, 7 Apr. 1935.

Mitchell, Charles H., and Fenton Mallory. "Did Hauptmann Die in the Chair?" *Daring Detective,* June 1936, p. 31.

Moseley, Seth H. "The Night the Lindbergh Baby Disappeared," *Yankee Magazine,* Mar. 1982, p. 82.

Negri, Gloria. "New Hampshire Writers Say Lindbergh Responsible in Kidnapping." *Boston Globe,* 17 Mar. 1993.

Newman, Jeffrey. "Charles Lindbergh Planned His Baby Son's Kidnapping—He Didn't Want the Child Because It Was Malformed." *National Enquirer,* 12 Oct. 1976, p. 71.

Newsweek Magazine, 29 Sept. 1934.

New York Daily News, 4 Feb. 1935.

New York Times, 11, 12 June 1932; 22–24, 28 Sept., 22 Dec. 1934; 18, 20 Jan., 6 Feb., 25 Mar., 7 Apr. 1935; 29 Feb., 4 Mar. 1936.

Oursler, Fulton. "Jafsie in Panama Discusses New Evidence." *Liberty* 13 (28 Mar. 1936): p. 37.

Palenick, Skip. "Microscope Trace Evidence—The Overlooked Clue." *The Microscope* First Quarter (1983): p. 61.

Pearson, Edmund. "Hauptmann and Circumstantial Evidence." *New Yorker,* 9 Mar. 1935, p. 40.

Perry, Tom. "Lindbergh's Legacy: New Wave of Interest in a Famous Old Case." *Courier-News* (Bridgewater, N.J.) 21 Oct. 1993.

Phillips, Barbara D. "TV Reopens the Lindbergh Case." *Wall Street Journal,* 9 Sept. 1996.

Prescott, Peter S. "Cobbling Up a Conviction." *Newsweek,* 24 June 1985.

Resinger, D. Michael, et. al. "Exorcism of Ignorance as a Proxy for Rational Knowledge: The Lessons of Handwriting Identification 'Expertise.'" *University of Pennsylvania Law Review* 137 (1989): p. 731.

Robbins, Albert H. "The Hauptmann Trial in the Light of English Criminal Procedure" *American Bar Association Journal* 21 (1935): p. 97.

Russell, Francis. "The Case That Will Not Close." *New York Review of Books,* 5 Nov. 1987.

Sanders, Paul H. "Scientific and Procedural Aspects of the Hauptmann Trial." *American Bar Association Journal* 21 (1935): p. 62.

Scaduto, Anthony. "Bruno Hauptmann Was Innocent." *New York Magazine,* 22 Nov. 1976, p. 16.

———. "The Lindbergh Case: Is History's Verdict Wrong?" *Crime Beat,* Apr. 1993, p. 46.

———. "Scapegoat: The Real Story of the Lindbergh Kidnapping." Parts 1–6. *New York Post,* 21–26 Feb. 1977.

Seglem, Lee. "Judge Rejects Effort by Hauptmann Widow to Clear Her Husband."
Gannett News Service, 24 Sept. 1987.

Seidman, Louis M. "The Trial and Execution of Bruno Hauptmann: Still Another
Case That Will Not Die." *Georgetown Law Journal* 66 (1977): pp. 1–48.

Sellers, Clark. "The Handwriting Evidence Against Hauptmann." *Journal of Police Science* 27 (1937): p. 68.

Smith, Patterson. "The Literature of Ransom Kidnapping in America." *AB Bookmans Weekly*, 23 Apr. 1990, p. 1717.

———. "Puzzles of True Crime Literature: The Lindbergh Case." *AB Bookmans Weekly*, 25 Apr. 1983, p. 2005.

Smits, Jeanette. "How Much Did Hauptmann Tell His Wife?" *True Detective Mysteries*, Nov. 1935, p. 34.

———. "What Anna Hauptmann Believes Now!" *Philadelphia Record*, 18 Feb. 1940.

Starrs, James E. "The Prosecution of Bruno Richard Hauptmann: An Imitation of Falconry." *Journal of Forensic Sciences* 28 (1983): p. 1083.

Stetler, Carrie, and Bill Gannon. "Hauptmann's Wife Dies a True Believer." *Star-Ledger*, 19 Oct. 1994.

St. Johns, Adela Rogers. "I Covered the Lindbergh Kidnapping." *Modern Maturity*, Apr.–May 1982, p. 60.

Tanay, Emanuel. "The Lindbergh Kidnapping—A Psychiatric View." *Journal of Forensic Sciences* 26 (1981): p. 1076.

Taylor, Becky. "Hauptmann Placed at Kidnap Scene." *Sunday Times Advertiser* (Trenton, N.J.), 14 Nov. 1976.

Thompson, Craig. "Did They Really Solve the Lindbergh Case?" *Saturday Evening Post*, 8 Mar. 1952.

Treblicock, Bob. "Who Killed The Lindbergh Baby?" *Yankee Magazine*, Feb. 1994, p. 47.

Vitez, Michael. "Hauptmann Widow Turns to Florio to Clear Her Husband." *Philadelphia Inquirer*, 13 June 1990.

———. "Why Anna Hauptmann Won't Forget." *Philadelphia Inquirer*, 13 Dec. 1987.

———. "Widow of the Century." *Philadelphia Inquirer*, 19 Jan. 1992.

Walsh, Harry W., and E. Collins. "Hunt for the Kidnappers: Inside Story of the Lindbergh Case." *Jersey Journal*, 15–19, 21–23 Nov. 1932.

Ward, Geoffrey C. "Cols. Lindbergh and Mustard." *American Heritage* 45 (1994): p. 12.

———. "The Most Durable Assassination Theory: Oswald Did It Alone." *New York Times Book Review*, 21 Nov. 1993.

Wedemer, Lou. "Fifty Unanswered Questions in the Hauptmann Case: A Searching Survey of the Doubts and 'Sinister Suggestion' That Still Shadow the Famous Crime." *Liberty* 36 (4 Jan. 1936): p. 39.

Weeks, Albert. "Kidnapping of Lindbergh Baby Continues to Fascinate." *New York Tribune,* 31 May 1982.

Werner, D. G., and Avery Hale. "What Hauptmann Revealed Just Before He Died." *True Detectives Mysteries,* Oct. 1936, p. 26.

White Plains Daily Reporter, 13 June 1932.

Wilson, P. W. "The Lindbergh Case." *North American Review,* Jan. 1934, p. 14.

Wilstein, Steve. "Lindbergh Case to Be Reopened." Associated Press, 20 Nov. 1986.

Yagoda, Ben. "Legacy of a Kidnapping." *New Jersey Monthly,* Aug. 1981, p. 29.

Zito, Tom. "Did the Evidence Fit the Crime?" *Life Magazine,* Mar. 1982, p. 40.

Index

123–24; questioned, 119, 159; and request samples, 119; and trial testimony, 119–20

Hard Copy (TV show), 57

Haring, J. Vreeland, 41–42, 119

Hauck, Anthony, 33, 36–37

Hauptmann (play), 59

Hauptmann, Anna: and concocted alibis, 128–32; death of, 47, 59; lawsuits by, 46, 51–55; and Nazi connection, 77, 83; pleas to governor, 54–55, 59; TV appearances of, 58

Hauptmann, Bruno Richard: alibis of, 129–32; and anti-German bias, 138–39; arrested, 25; background of, 25–26; beaten, 139–140; and car, 25; criminal record of, 26, 153–54; dies without confession, 140; ether possession of, 155–57; execution of, 38; and "Fisch story," 26–27, 29; and Henkel affair, 154; and money in Victrola, 144–49; robs Fredericksen, 132–33; and use of courts, 139; wealth of, 135–36, 144–50; and writing tic, 157–61

Hauptmann, Manfred, 59

Hearst Corporation, 39, 51

Henkel, Gerta, 80–83, 154

Hicks, Robert W., 36

Hiss, Alger, 124

Hochmuth, Amandus, 119, 137

Hoffman, Gov. Harold G., 31–37, 40, 42, 52–53, 57, 67, 76–78, 90, 93, 95, 101, 120, 126, 157, 160–61

Hoffman papers, 45, 52

Home Box Office (HBO), 47, 59

Hoover, J. Edgar, 23, 35, 73, 77, 153

Hopkins, Anthony, 54

Horn, William F., 35, 81, 83, 135–36

Huber, Roy A., 123

Huddleson, Dr. James H., 158–59

Huddleson, Dr. John T., 158

Hudson, Dr. Erastus Mead, 6, 32–33, 45, 101–3

Hynd, Alan, 40, 56–57, 64, 72, 103–4, 157

inside job theories, 100–115

Internal Revenue Service (IRS), 152–53

Irey, Elmer, 15–16

Jafsie Tells All! (Condon), 41

Jennings, George, 87

Johnson, Elmer, 113

Johnson, Henry "Red," 105–8

Jones, Arthur, 94–95

Jones, Wayne, 46

Journal of Forensic Sciences 120

Kallok, Father Michael J., 76–84

Kampairien, Emily, 112

Keaten, Arthur T., 25, 104–5, 112, 151

Keith, Stanley R., 151–52

Kelly, Frank A., 5–6, 35, 101–3

Kennedy, John F.: assassination of, 57, 61–62, 72–73

Kennedy, Ludovic, 41, 52, 59, 75, 120–24, 126, 128

Kerwin, Kenneth, 42–43, 45, 52

Kerwin, Manser, 43

Kerwin, Mildred, 43

Kidnap (Waller), 42

Kiss, Louis, 80

Kloppenburg, Hans, 82–83

Koehler, Arthur, 23–24, 28, 36–37, 125

Kubler, Louis, 102

Kugler, Mildred, 63

Kunstler, William M., 137

Lacey, Judge Frederick B., 52, 138

ladder: crudeness of, 5, 64; distance from window, 104; and fabricated evidence, 126; fingerprints on, 6, 101, 127; impressions of in mud, 4; measurements of, 5; nails in, 127, 152–53; notebook sketch of, 125; rail sixteen of, 36; tied to Hauptmann, 125

Jim Fisher, a law school graduate, former FBI agent, and 1997 Edgar nominee for his book, *Fall Guys: False Confessions and the Politics of Murder,* has been investigating the Lindbergh crime since 1984. This is his second book on the subject.